The Illustrated Portrait of
THE BORDER COUNTRY

Overleaf: Eildon Hills

NIGEL TRANTER

The Illustrated Portrait of
THE BORDER COUNTRY

© *Nigel Tranter 1972 and 1987*
First published in Great Britain 1972
Reprinted 1973
Reprinted 1978
New edition 1987

Robert Hale Limited
Clerkenwell House
Clerkenwell Green
London EC1R OHT

British Library Cataloguing in Publication Data
Tranter, Nigel
   The illustrated portrait of the Border
   country.—2nd ed.
   1. Borders (Scotland)—Description and
   travel
   I. Title   II. Tranter, Nigel. Portrait
   of the Border country
   914.13'704858   DA880.B72

ISBN 0 7090 3147 5

Printed in Great Britain by
St Edmundsbury Press Limited, Bury St Edmunds, Suffolk
Bound by WBC Bookbinders Limited

Contents

Illustrations

Whittingham Vale and Cheviots from above Thropton
Mire Loch
Melrose Abbey

Between pages 128 and 129
Chipchase Castle, Wark
Westerkirk in the Esk Valley
Lanercost Abbey
St. Andrew's Church, Corbridge
Coquet Valley near Alwinton
Warkworth Castle
Haaf-netting on the River Nith Estuary
Jedburgh Abbey
River Ettrick near Ettrickbridgend

Map   *pages 16–17*

Picture Credits
Carlisle Public Libraries: 12; J. D. Mackay: 1, 2, 10, 18; A. D. S.
Macpherson: 9, 16; Geoffrey N. Wright: 3–8, 11, 13, 14–16.

Preface

Fourteen years may not seem a very lengthy period in the ages-old story of the Borderland, yet that interval, between the first issue of this work and the present edition, has seen many and major alterations and developments in our fast-changing times and conditions, and some of these are inevitably reflected even in this fair and so self-contained countryside. They are, needless to say, not always for the better; nevertheless, it is probably true to say that the Borders are less affected by change than are most parts of this kingdom, partly because of the nature of the territory, in the main hilly and pastoral, partly in the independent and individual character of the people, and partly on account of the very pressures of its history. The Borderland is still very much the Borderland—for which, praises be!

It has been salutory, however, to traverse much of it all once more, with a deliberate eye to note general changes and developments, explained here in the preface, as well as more particular items inserted in the body of the text. Some are fairly obvious, to even cursory observation, others have to be sought for. The land itself is, of course, enduring, unchanging in essence. Yet men have been busy in the interim, inevitably, and since we do live in these times of rapid change, there are signs to be seen. In the main the Borderland is an agricultural and pastoral entity, and here there is much evidence of changing priorities: in breeds of cattle, for instance, in the fields and on the rough grazings of the hill-slopes. Gone are the piebald Ayrshire milk-cows, replaced on a much lesser scale by Canadian Holsteins, for milk-production is less important today, as a result of European requirements. Beef-production however concerns the farmers more, and the old breeds of Aberdeen-Angus, Friesian and Hereford have been largely superseded by Charollais, Simental and Limousin, no doubt for valid economic reasons. Then there is the changing emphasis on the crops grown. Barley, especially, takes up an ever-increasing acreage, wheat somewhat less so and oats are now little seen. The new crops of oil-seed rape are highly evident to all, with their vivid yellow patterning of the landscape. Interestingly enough this crop affects the country's honey-production. Fodder-peas are now not uncommon, whilst turnips are much less prevalent. Another notable development on the agricultural scene is the fact that, owing to mechanization, far fewer men are employed on the farms, with the result that the long rows of workers' cottages are no longer so necessary, and many are disposed of for private housing. This is especially noticeable in the great Merse farm-towns of Berwickshire, some almost little villages in themselves, and so much a feature of that scene. Sadly, this has also resulted in the closure of many small country schools.

Then forestry has been greatly extended, altering the prospect on many a Border hillside, especially of course in the vast Keilder area of Northumberland. This in its turn has produced not only new and often quite exciting forest-walks and centres, and riding trails, but chipboard manufacturing plants, such as the Hexham Industrial Estate. The modern straightening of main roads and the by-passing of towns is a very evident feature, with bridge-widenings and service facilities and improved sign-posting. As well as these general modernizings of the countryside, sundry new features must strike the traveller, indicative of increased leisure, mobility and the widening of interests of the public. Caravan-parks have sprung up, leisure, sports and garden centres, even fish-farms.

The towns have changed less, although modern housing tends to spread them somewhat. There are undoubted improvements in the standards of living conditions, neatness, spaciousness and gardens and parks. Shopping arcades, pedestrian precincts and the like are often attractive, even though everywhere the big chain-stores tend to supersede the small local shops. Carparks, although so necessary, scarcely add to the scenic amenity.

Industries too are subject to the changing needs of our time. Although the Border textile production is still of major importance, much of it is now beamed on the export market. Most of all this is applicable to other parts of the country, admittedly, in a greater or lesser degree; but here, set against the essentially unchanging scene, it is the more noticeable.

Less than attractive on that scene are the power-lines which stride across the hillsides and valleys on their huge pylons from the great new nuclear power-station at Torness on the Berwickshire border, source of so many questions and heart-searching as well as electricity! But with all the present-day changes, the basic character and fascination and *difference* of the Borderland remains, its abbeys and priories and castles enduringly challenging as they are picturesque – and for this writer, a joy in the number of tower-houses and fortalices, formerly ruined but now restored as family houses once again – its antiquities better preserved and appreciated, its rivers clear-running and all but pollution-free, its magnificent seaboard unchangeable, its hills everlasting, its folk sturdily independent as always.

Long may it all remain so.

1

Beginning at Berwick

WHAT, and where, then, are the Borders, for a start? This is oddly difficult to answer, considering the so definite and particular character of the region, with every Borderer knowing very certainly that he *is* a Borderer—but not so sure of who else legitimately may be. It would be simple and convenient to say that the Borders were that portion of England and Scotland flanking the actual Border-line for so many miles on either side—say 15 or 20 miles. But that would arouse furious contradiction therein, and be quite inaccurate. There are, in fact no generalities apt to this entrancing and in some ways infuriating area. Berwick-upon-Tweed is most indubitably a Border town; and 20 miles north of it Cockburnspath, on the verge of Lothian, might just conceivably claim Border status—indeed, I have heard that claimed for Dunbar, 12 miles further and deep in East Lothian. Yet Eyemouth, only 9 miles north of Berwick, and a fishing place like Dunbar, does not shout aloud that it is in Borderland. And on the south and English side, Alnwick and even Morpeth lay proud claim to Border status, whereas, at the other end of the line, with Carlisle undeniably an anchor-town thereof, no such deep preoccupation with the Border exists. It was my good fortune to live for a year or so in the Penrith/Greystoke area and the Eden valley, without hearing the term Borders mentioned more than once or twice. A semi-circle with a radius 15 miles or so south of Carlisle would include all sorts of places such as Silloth, Cockermouth, Penrith and Alston which would never claim to be in the Borders—however much they might claim to belong to Lakeland. And so on. And Galloway, that fine and detached ancient province of Scotland, comprising the Stewartry of Kirkcudbright and the county of Wigtown, while facing across Solway to England is certainly not considered to belong to the Borders. But Peebles, for instance, a town not much more than 20 miles from Edinburgh but farther from the nearest point on the Borderline, very much considers

Berwick-on-Tweed

itself as belonging; though Biggar, only a few miles to the west, would scarcely claim it. It is all very difficult and confusing, with the map little or no help.

I fear that you will just have to take it from me, as far as this volume is concerned, as to what is Borders and what is not; the fact that you will probably disagree heartily is all part of the essential joy and fascination of it all. Not for nothing has this country been called, for centuries, The Debatable Land.

We can start, at least, amicably at Berwick-upon-Tweed—although amicability and non-controversiality are scarcely innate characteristics of that resounding burgh—or borough! Even on this spelling we may well be at issue. But at least we can all agree that Berwick is in the Borders.

Here is a town which demands a book for itself, a community so famous, ancient, blood-stained and fought-over, yet splendid, as to defy any brief delineation. Situated at the mouth of the River Tweed, it is the most contradictory municipality in the British Isles, with practically everything about it crazily conflicting with the obvious. It sits snugly on the north side of Tweed—which nobody ever claims as anything but a most Scottish river; yet it is in England. It is the obvious county town of its own county of Berwickshire; yet it is in the county of Northumberland. It is one of the most Scots-looking towns in the land; yet its main walled defences are all facing north, built to keep out the Scots. It was the original greatest seaport of Scotland, and even in Cromwell's time considered to be one of the finest ports on the east coast; yet in fact it is a most dangerous and inconvenient harbour, as any shipmaster will tell you. Although in England, and administered by a mayor and aldermen, instead of provost and bailies, it was until recently the headquarters of the King's Own Scottish Borderers—even though the local territorial regiment was the Northumberland Fusiliers. The majority of its inhabitants are of Scots extraction, with Scots names, yet live under English law; although Scots law applies to the River Tweed salmon fisheries—and not only so, but applies to 50 square miles of open sea at the mouth of the river, which under the Tweed Act is declared to be an essential part of the river and the Scottish polity, in the interests of the salmon-fishing proprietors. In the streets you will see English and Scottish banks side-by-side. I could go on and on—but must forbear. Although, even to the most biased English reader, it must occur that Berwick probably *ought* to be in Scotland, this is not so, as it happens, to all Berwickers. The old and gleefully repeated story about Berwick still being at war with Russia, because it was a separate entity—Scotland, England and Berwick-on-Tweed—when the Crimean War was declared, but incorporated legalistically in England before peace was finalized—now grows rather threadbare; but it nevertheless well illustrates an attitude of mind prevalent in this ancient town. It is in fact Border independence of spirit taken to its logical conclusion. To hell with the rest of you, we're Berwickers!

How did this extraordinary state of affairs come about? Berwick was long one of the original four royal burghs of Scotland; indeed the figure four, interlaced in a sort of Greek-key pattern, long decorated the walling of the attractive Berwick Town Hall, although not all even of its councillors understood its significance. It was in 1482 that King James III of Scotland, a cultured but weak monarch, found himself at loggerheads with most of his nobility —on whom, since the Scots king had no standing army, he relied upon for military levies. Edward IV of England, of a very different character, perceived his opportunity. James had quarrelled with his brother, the Duke of Albany, who had fled to England. Edward now encouraged Albany to seek to wrest the Scots crown from his unpopular brother, and lent him an army, under his own brother, Richard Duke of Gloucester (later Richard III), a fairly comprehensive scoundrel. Neither Edward nor Richard, needless to say, had the least interest in Albany's ambitions. But they were interested in that most important strategic key-point and seaport, Berwick-on-Tweed—at that time, strangely enough, carrying on a greater trade than almost any port other than London on the east coast. Having invaded Scotland allegedly on Albany's behalf, and got as far as Haddington, in East Lothian, Richard Crookback allowed Albany to be overthrown—but demanded the English price before withdrawing his large army from Scottish soil. That price was the cession of Berwick to England, a piece of blackmail unequalled in our island story. Weakened by internecine strife the Scots king and parliament could not get rid of the unwelcome visitors without acceding. And despite many, many attempts to right the wrong since, Berwick has remained on the wrong side of the Border.

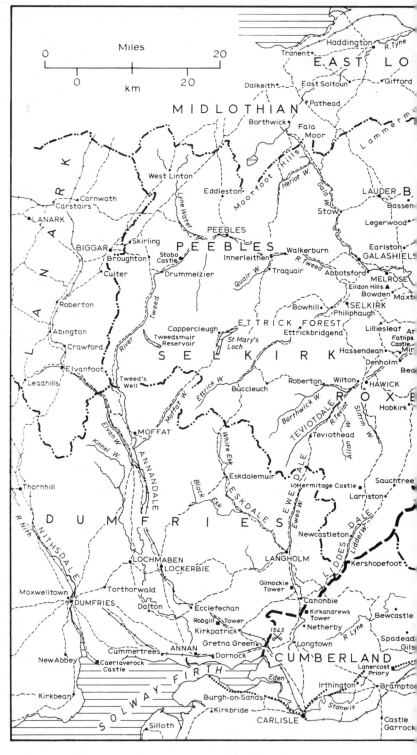

Based upon the Ordnance Survey map with the permission of the controller of H
Majesty's Stationery Office. Crown Copyright Reserved

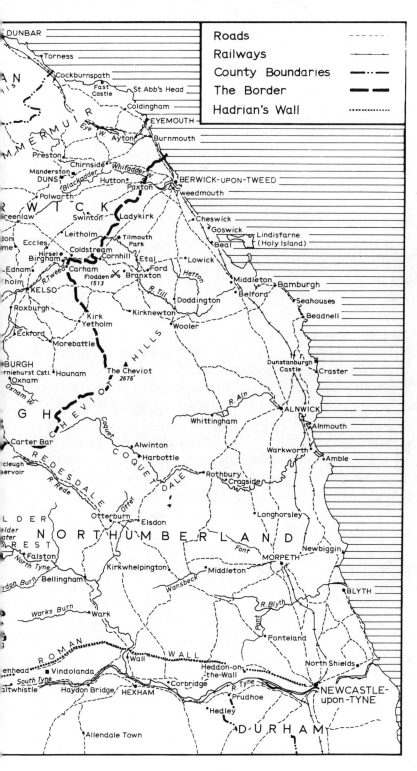

DUNBAR

Torness

Cockburnspath

Fast Castle

St.Abb's Head

Coldingham

EYEMOUTH

Eye W. Ayton • Burnmouth

Preston

Chirnside • Whitadder

Manderston

DUNS Blackadder Hutton

Paxton

Polwarth

BERWICK-UPON-TWEED

Tweedmouth

Greenlaw

Swinton Ladykirk

Cheswick

Goswick

Lindisfarne (Holy Island)

Beal

Leitholm Tilmouth Park

Eccles Lowick

Hirsel Coldstream

Birgham Cornhill Etal Ford

Ednam Carham Branxton

R.Tweed Flodden 1513 Hetton

Middleton Bamburgh

KELSO R.Till Doddington Belford

Roxburgh Seahouses

Kirk Yetholm Kirknewton Beadnell

Eckford Wooler

Morebattle

CHEVIOT HILLS

BURGH

Jedburgh Cstl. Hounam

Oxnam The Cheviot 2676'

Oxnam W.

GH CHEVIOT

COQUET Dunstanburgh Castle

Carter Bar Craster

REDESDALE R.Aln

cleugh servoir R.Rede Coquet ALNWICK

Whittingham Alnmouth

Alwinton

Harbottle Warkworth

Amble

COQUET DALE Rothbury Cragside

Otter

LDER Longhorsley

elder ater Otterburn Elsdon

REST N O R T H U M B E R L A N D

Falston Font Newbiggin

North Tyne Kirkwhelpington Middleton MORPETH

rdon Burn Bellingham Wansbeck

BLYTH

Warks Burn Wark R.Blyth

Ponteland

R O M A N W A L L Pont

enhead Vindolanda Wall Heddon-on-the-Wall North Shields

South Tyne Corbridge R.Tyne NEWCASTLE-upon-TYNE

altwhistle Haydon Bridge HEXHAM Prudhoe

Hedley

D U R H A M

Allendale Town

THE BORDER COUNTRY

As I indicated earlier, everywhere in the Borderland the past and the present are apt to merge most dramatically. Nowhere is this more evident today than in Berwick-on-Tweed, with more extraordinary repercussions on its inhabitants. Newcastle, its county town for administrative and many essential major services, is 65 miles to the south; whereas, except for Richard Crookback and his brother, Berwick would be its own county town, with all the said services—and to the great advantage also of truncated Berwickshire for which it is the natural centre. On a regional, if not national, basis, Edinburgh itself is 10 miles nearer at hand.

All that said, Berwick remains a quite delightful and attractive town. With a population of 12,000 at the last census (13,075 in 1914) it is smaller than Hawick or Galashiels on the Scots side, and Carlisle or Morpeth on the English, but well and away larger than all the other Border towns; a place of climbing narrow grey-stone streets and wynds and huddled red roofs, all within stout and massive walls and ramparts, and set above the suddenly widening river, here expanding to the almost landlocked bay of Tweed-mouth. The first sight of it from the south, either from the train, or from the A1 road high above Spittal, is heart-catching, a mellow but proud citadel of a place, its roofs and towers and steeples soaring above the deep dip of the estuary in steep steps and terraces, to culminate in the single thrusting fang of the one-time castle where so much of bloody history was made, and all backed by the shouldering green hills and cliff-girt coastline of Berwick-shire. Here is a sight to stir even the least perceptive, so *different* from anything the traveller has yet seen or experienced on the northward journey. Most obviously and scenically, after the pleasant enough but somewhat unexciting Northumberland country-side and moors, here is the Border indeed, here is change, drama, the sense of clash. Here, in fact, is Scotland, thrusting itself upon the notice in a more than physical sense, whatever the legalists may say—and to how many returning Scots, however superficially hard-headed, has that scene brought a lump to the throat and a mistiness to the eye. During the war years, how often I watched homing servicemen rise from their train-seats, to peer forward at approaching Berwick-on-Tweed, and blink—that is, when I was clear-eyed enough to observe them.

It is one of those significant little unkindnesses of topography

and scene that the undeniably English part of this isolated municipality—for Berwick is an unusually isolated town as far as neighbours go—the present suburbs, but formerly independent
communities, of Spittal and Tweedmouth, on the south side of
the river, are so dull and humdrum of appearance, so spectacularly
setting off Berwick itself, by comparison. Because this southern
side has more of flat land, more space for expansion, it is here that
the housing schemes, the industrial development and the main
dock installations have grown up, leaving the climbing medieval
town within its walls almost untouched. Which, of course, is as it
should be. The approach from the north is nothing like so dramatic.

Its three bridges contribute much to the character of Berwick,
spanning the river at varying levels, all necessary major and eye-
catching viaducts, and representing each a stage in the town's
development. The oldest is the least seen and used, since it is
lowly-placed at the waterside and not on lofty piers spanning the
trough of the valley. It is the most characterful nevertheless, the
best designed and most handsome. This is the James VI bridge, of
1603, of fine warm ashlar, hump-backed towards the north side,
and no less than 1,164 feet in length, crossing the swirling tide-
driven waters from the narrow streets of the old town on fifteen
graceful but sturdy arches, each with a little bay at either side above
the piers, as refuge for foot-travellers—for the cobbled carriage-
way was built only 17 feet wide, and was not intended to be hurried over. The erection of this bridge was a highly significant
occasion.

There had been a timber bridge here from very early times,
often swept away by floods, often demolished by raiders or defenders, and always replaced, a vital tactical entity in the centuries
of Border warfare. Then, in 1603, Scotland's extraordinary
monarch James VI, lovely Mary Queen of Scots' uncouth but
shrewd son, succeeded to the throne of Elizabeth of England as
nearest male heir. And in that day all was abruptly changed, and
James, the Wisest Fool in Christendom, began to rule over an
allegedly United Kingdom—with all borders seemingly suddenly
devalued. He wasted no time in setting out for London—after all,
he had been waiting impatiently for Elizabeth to die for years—
having no doubts as to where his best interests now lay. With a
vast train of Scots on the make, he arrived at Berwick on his way

south. And the old wooden bridge rattled and shook under him as he crossed—as, of course, it had shaken and rattled under less lofty mortals for centuries. But James Stewart was no ordinary mortal; he was Christ's Vice-Regent upon earth, in his own declared estimation, and a person not only inviolable but invaluable. Not to put too fine a point on it, however, shrewd and cunning as he might be, he was an arrant physical coward, terrified of cold steel, loud noises and running water. Perhaps he had reason. Just before he was born, his mother had seen her secretary—and some said, more than that—stabbed to death before her eyes, in her own chamber at Holyroodhouse; and from his birth until he reached man's estate, James had seldom been out of the hands of violent nobles—one of whom, to his face, had declared, "Better bairns weep than grown men!" At any rate, crossing Berwick Bridge, James suddenly was seized with utter fright. Always afraid for his life, from plot or accident, he conceived that the bridge was about to collapse under him and hurl his royal and semi-divine person into the cruel waters. Desperately he flung himself off his horse, down on to the shoogly planking, clinging to anything and anybody he thought might support him, calling on Almighty God to save him. His Grace of the newly United Kingdom had to be half-carried, bawling, to the farther shore, where he promptly sank down on his knees to kiss the ground—not because it was the soil of his new and profitable kingdom so much as because it represented *terra firma*. He declared there and then that the very first charge on his fine new English exchequer would be the provision of a good, solid stone brig here, to join his two realms. And there it still stands, solid indeed, enduring, and far from shoogly. It took a long time to erect—some say from 1609 to 1634.

The highest of the bridges was the next to be built, to carry the new railway, by the famous engineer Robert Stephenson, son of the still more famous inventor of the steam locomotive. It was opened in 1850 by King James's very different and remote descendant, Queen Victoria, and called the Royal Border Bridge. Worthy of its name, it is a magnificent and spectacular structure carried 184 feet above the wrinkled waters on no fewer than twenty-five tall, slender arches, and stretched across the abyss for 2,100 feet. The third viaduct, the new Tweed Bridge to carry the high-level modern roadway, adhered to the royal connection, being opened in 1928 by the then Prince of Wales, later Edward VIII. I wonder, on that day, whether he thought about his predecessor's, Edward I's, links with Berwick? This bridge is sited between the other two, both in position and height, broad but graceful, on only three great arches; and over it the ceaseless traffic of the busy A1 is necessarily funnelled, convenient in 1928 but now a headache indeed for Berwick. But, at the cost of civil engineering today, a fourth to add to the Berwick, Royal Border and Tweed Bridges seems unlikely. A number of years ago, Miss Wendy Wood, the veteran and irrepressible Scots nationalist, removed the 'ENGLAND' sign from the roadside at Lamberton Toll, 3 miles to the north, at the present Border-line, and placed it plumb in the centre of this bridge, half-way across the river. It did not stay there long, admittedly—but was dramatic indication that this old story is not finished yet, by any means.

How old is the story of clash and dispute about Berwick-on-Tweed? As far back as 800 B.C. there was salmon-fishing here; and 1,600 years later, in A.D. 833, there were disputes over the salmon-trade. This trade, still vitally important to the town, is even yet a parallel issue for dispute, with that of the national and county boundaries. It is not merely a question of poaching—that no doubt will always be there, so long as men remain full-blooded men; it is a matter of laws and legalities again, of feudal rights, landlordism and essential independence. But more of that hereafter. The main clash has always been national and political, and seems to have started early—and was not confined to England versus Scotland. For instance, prior to any reported English ambitions, Berwick was described by one chronicler as "capital of that part of Scotland called Lothian"—a pronouncement which Edinburgh would take hard indeed! King John of England may not have been the first to covet Berwick to the extent of annexation, but his is the first detailed account, when he stormed and took town and castle in 1216. So there was a castle here then. Only a few years later, we read of Fleming immigrants, energetic and welcome traders from Flanders, having at Berwick their own headquarters and trading colony, known as The Red Hall, which they held direct of the King of Scots on condition that they would always defend it against the King of England. It is significant that it was at Berwick that this trading colony was established.

Here is no place even briefly to sketch the history of Berwick, its town, port and castle—for that would be as much as to attempt the history of Scotland. But certain highlights might be touched on. Here, the long and desperate Wars of Independence, which threw up Wallace and Bruce and hammered Scotland into the nation it is, could be said to have started. For here it was that Edward I of England, came in 1291, by invitation, to choose out one of fourteen competitors to be the King of Scots; came as an "honest broker", a neutral neighbour, not any sort of overlord, yet took the opportunity to declare himself Lord Paramount of Scotland therefore, and chose deliberately the weak John Baliol, more than half an Englishman, to be his puppet-king. This declaration Scotland could not allow, and so for the next thirty-seven years, until Bruce at last gained the Treaty of Edinburgh in 1328, the bloodiest wars in our island history were fought, with Berwick in the battered centre of it all. It is worth mentioning perhaps that during the eighteen-months-long debate on this competition for the Crown, the English Parliament actually met in Berwick.

It was not long after the grievous choice was made in Berwick Castle, that the first fruits had to be paid; for by 1295, with even Baliol forced to repudiate Edward's arrogant claims to be master, the said Edward started on his notorious Hammering of the Scots by coming north again to take and sack Berwick-on-Tweed. He did this in cold blood, deliberately, as a gesture, a warning to the rest of Scotland as to what to expect if continued resistance was made to his claims. The gesture makes grim reading. The town, then, remember, the largest and richest in Scotland, did not capitulate. In those days it was defended only by a ditch and earthen rampart, and this fell quickly, with Edward himself one of the first across. The town then went up in smoke. Even the Flemish merchants, not forgetting their charter, fought to the last, thirty of them being burned to death in their blazing Red Hall. The fighting over, the people of Berwick were put to the sword and flames in fiercest barbarism, to the number of 17,000 men, women and children—recollect that today's total population is under 12,000—so that for two days the steep city streets ran with blood like rivers, and the Tweed was stained redder than in any spate. The bodies were not permitted to be buried; the churches were defiled and used as stables. This done on Good Friday. The castle itself held out a little longer under Sir William Douglas, father of Bruce's great friend-to-be, the Good Sir James; but surrendered on terms —which terms Edward promptly broke. Northern England was to suffer the Black Douglas's terrible vengeance for that deed for many a year thereafter. So Berwick-on-Tweed, the Alexandria of the North as it was called, became a stinking, blackened desert, as lesson to Scotland from Edward Longshanks, the First Knight of Christendom—for so he had been lauded. It never again fully recovered its stature.

The remains of this castle still stand on the heights to the north of the town, just behind the railway station, scanty now, because the station is in fact built on the site of its great hall, and much was cleared ruthlessly away to create the railroad, in true Victorian philistine fashion. But enough remains to emphasize the strength of its position, perched on the cliff-edge high above the river. Best seen from below, it lies outside the town walls. From it the prospect is fair and far-flung indeed, to all but the north; but what sights this citadel has witnessed, near and far, hardly bear contemplation. Grim scenes within it, also. Here for four shameful years, from 1306 to 1310, Isobel, Countess of Buchan, sister of the Earl of Fife, was suspended in a wicker-and-iron cage on the outside wall of the castle, night and day, winter and summer, exposed to the elements, to all eyes, and the mockery of the English soldiery, by Edward's express command—all because she had, in the absence of her brother, fulfilled the MacDuff family's privilege and duty of placing the Scots crown on Bruce's head at his coronation. How she survived is a mystery; but then, so did Bruce's own sister, Mary, hung up in exactly similar circumstances outside Roxburgh Castle, near Kelso, her crime—that she was the hero's sister.

Here, then, was enacted so much of savagery and harsh rule that the stones themselves ought to cry out—including that most humiliating scene, possibly, of all Scots history, when, the year after the massacre, 1296, with Scotland prostrate, Edward required every earl, baron, laird, cleric, sheriff, magistrate and substantial landed-proprietor in the northern kingdom, to come and swear fealty to him, personally, on bended knee, as only ruler and Lord Paramount of Scotland, on pain not only of forfeiture of lands, possessions and offices, but of death. This was the notorious

Ragman Roll—from which the term rigmarole derives, meaning a lengthy screed of but little real significance. Not all came to take that humbling oath and sign the roll—only three out of twelve of the bishops, for instance; but enough to drag Scotland's name in the mire for long. Even Robert Bruce himself, Earl of Carrick, then a young man of 22 and not yet a hero, bent the knee. But not William Wallace, or his elder brother, who was the actual Laird of Elderslie.

Edward I's walls, which he built thereafter to replace the earthen ramparts which had so notably failed to keep him out, are still quite a prominent feature of the town; though not so extensive as the magnificent Elizabethan walls which reinforced and extended them three centuries later. Together they make the finest walled city in the United Kingdom, and with their ports, or gates, give an added character to Berwick unfailing as an attraction—as well as providing a most splendid circular walk, along their summits, with unusual vistas. Not to be confused with the true gates therein, such as Scots Gate—facing north, naturally—and the Shore Gate and the Cow Port, are the thoroughfares known as Castle-gate, Mary-gate, Sand-gate, etc. These, of course, should properly be spelt gait, and refer to the streets themselves, where one 'gaed'. Berwick goes in for romantic and distinctive street-names—Ravensdown, Woolmarket, Hidehill, Palace Green—where still stands the handsome Governor's House—and Wallace Green. The latter is sometimes stated to commemorate Wallace's siege of the town in 1297 after Edward's departure; since this was unsuccessful, the Patriot having no siege engines, it is more likely to refer to the spot where part of his quartered body was sent by Edward to be exposed after his terrible butchery in London in 1305.

Another feature of Berwick, of major importance, which inevitably makes its own impact on resident and visitor alike, is its waterfront, so much more picturesuqe than many a port—almost Dutch in appearance—although, to be sure, Berwick is not much of a port today. Here is no dingy dock-and-warehouse area, but, at least on the Berwick side of the river a pleasing huddle of old riverside quays and mellow buildings, squeezed between the walls and the estuary, extending seawards of the James VI Bridge, with a Georgian Custom House on the Quay Wall, and a small and unobtrusive shipyard. Berwick has been building small ships for centuries. That in which the famous Grace Darling, daughter of the Longstone lighthouse-keeper, put out with her father in the storm to rescue survivors of the steamship *Forfarshire* in 1838, was built here.

Eastwards of the quays and the walls, the great Queen Elizabeth's Pier and breakwater stretches far out and round, to end in a red-and-white lighthouse and partially to enclose the wide tidal basin of Tweedmouth, a stalwart and notable structure which frequently has to withstand the battering of tremendous seas. It is an exhilarating place for a walk, in wild weather or calm, whether the walker is gasping for breath and dodging the spray and spume from vast rollers smashing themselves into foam on the farther side of the sea-wall; or watching placidly the salmon-netters at their fascinating trade at the Crabwater batt or fishing-stance, part-way out.

This salmon-fishing, here and at a large number of other old-established batts in the mouth of the river and some way up its course, is big business in Berwick, and always has been—and with fresh salmon fetching the price it does today, is not likely to languish. This is one of the most famous salmon rivers in the world, and the Berwick Salmon Fisheries Company employs some 250 men, netting the estuary where the great fish must funnel in to gain their spawning-grounds up-river, day in, day out during the six-months season, 16th February to 13th September. Teams of five or six men, with a high-nosed salmon-coble—a type of boat which has not changed during the centuries—and a long U-shaped drag-net, make up together an elaborate and carefully-calculated obstacle-course for the fish, with a minimum annual target of 5,000—although this is more often than not much exceeded. And the Berwick Company is not alone in the trade. Five thousand were actually caught in one amazing day, in 1959. The enormous figure of 142,930 fish, 14,247 salmon, 76,422 grilse (immature salmon) and 58,261 sea-trout, were netted in one notable year, 1842. It may seem a wonder that any fish get past this barrage of nets, to grace the famous, aristocratic and expensive angling beats up-river—but they do. Indeed, the fishery companies at the estuary obtain their licences to fish from these very up-river proprietors, corporately entitled the Tweed Commissioners, under the Tweed Act, as amended 1857, every riparian landlord of fishings to the value of £30 per year and over becoming a commissioner and controlling all taking of salmon. It is a wonderful system—for those, as it were, at the right end of the nets. Not so good for the coastal fishermen, who have been forbidden to driftnet for salmon in the open sea over an area of 50 square miles, or 10 miles up and down the coast and 5 miles out to sea. Since the international limit for territorial waters is only 3 miles, it follows that there is a belt 2 miles wide and 10 long where foreign vessels may fish freely, off the Tweed, and our own fishermen may not— a manifest anomaly, which has been the cause of all sorts of ructions along this iron-bound and dangerous coast, involving particularly the men of Eyemouth and Burnmouth on the Scots side, and Seahouses on the English. Incidentally it gave me the background drama for a topical novel called *Kettle of Fish*, over which at one time I myself was in danger of falling foul of the law, through thus publicly seeming to take sides while a prosecution was *sub judice*. So clash and dispute are far from gone, even yet, in this Border area—especially with salmon-poaching by more normal methods, and as private enterprise, a highly lucrative and well-established local activity by no means unanimously frowned upon by the local community. Always it has been that way. We read that, in 1895, a royal commission, no less, was appointed to enquire into fishing conditions at Berwick. Even the steam-boat in which the said commissioners, royal and Tweed, made their investigations had to be covered with thick wire-netting to protect all concerned from volleys of missiles thrown by people who lined the pier, this, it adds sadly, "with the sympathy of most of the people of the town". All very stirring. Berwick, undoubtedly, would not be the same place without its salmon. As footnote, we might add that, as far back as 1725, it is reported: "The Largeness and Cheapness of this Fish make it much coveted by Housekeepers, who have large Families and so often cater that it is said that the Servants, when they are to be hired, do usually indent with the Masters to feed them with Salmon only some Days of the Week that they may not be cloyed with too often eating them. . . ." Sadly both sea and river fishing have declined somewhat these last few years with a consequent drop in the number of men employed in the estuary netting.

Berwick-on-Tweed now has its industries better diversified, and is a forward-looking place too. But even today it is bedevilled by the problems of its dichotomy and situation. It has looked rather longingly at the corporate efforts of the Scots Border burghs to improve their industrial development, while itself being very much a far-away tail-end and allegedly neglected corner of Northumberland. The Regional Planning Committee for South-east Scotland foresaw this situation many years ago, and advised that, for planning and development purposes, Berwick should be incorporated in that area, pointing out that Berwickshire, in Scotland, was as essential for Berwick town, as the other way round. Today Berwick plays an increasing part in the Eastern Borders Development Association, Scots-aligned as that body is. And with regional reform very much on all present-day government programmes, who knows what the future may hold? It is amusing to note that, when Berwick's magistrates could get scant satisfaction over their coat-of-arms from the English College of Heralds, they turned promptly to Scotland's Lord Lyon King of Arms, who happily gave them the required—and correct—armorial bearings and device, as a Royal Burgh of Scotland. So there are advantages as well as inconveniences, perhaps, in thus straddling the fence.

Little has been said about Tweedmouth and Spittal. Yet they are very much entities of their own, and were indeed independent communities until the mid-nineteenth century, socially and administratively. They are both of ancient origin. Tweedmouth's parish church, although rebuilt in 1783, is on the site of one erected as far back as 1143; and even this Norman stone building was probably replacing an Anglian wooden church. Prior to the Reformation it was dedicated to St. Boisel, or Boswell—after whom St. Boswells in Roxburghshire is named. He was an Anglian missionary, who became Prior of Melrose, dying in 661. And it is interesting to note that, though he died so long ago, the date of his death is thought to have been 18th July—and this is commemorated in the timing of the well-known Tweedmouth Feast, which begins on that day if the 18th is a Sunday, or on the Sunday next following. So the probability is that the original Tweedmouth church went back to the seventh century—which would make it one of the oldest foundations in the land.

The name Spittal, of course, is a corruption of Hospital and refers to a lazar-house situated there in pre-Reformation days. These lazar-houses were scattered about the country, and took their name from the Biblical Lazarus, who was thought to be a leper. They were at first usually leper hospitals, and sometimes under the care of members of the military and hospitaller Order of St. Lazarus of Jerusalem—an ancient chivalric order still functioning, and to which the author has the honour to belong. But other orders, and non-orders, were apt to use the term lazar-house, and not only in connection with leprosy; so that they became merely general hospitals and shelters for the poor, handicapped and needy —the ancient Church taking the part of the Welfare State, a function which is often forgotten today. As a result, when the Reformation put down the monasteries, abbeys and therefore these hospices and lazar-houses, the country was over-run with their former inmates, the lame, the halt and the blind—to the great offence of their more comfortable and prosperous fellow-citizens, who preferred to have them kept well out of sight. The rhyme of that period: "Hark, hark, the dogs do bark; the beggars are coming to town!" exemplifies the attitude. Laws and penalties against gaberlunzies, sturdy beggars, and the like thereupon issued in a flood from organized and respectable society on both sides of the Border—an aspect of the Reformation we tend to overlook. The Spittal lazar-house was dedicated to St. Bartholomew.

Spittal has a feast also—just as Berwick has a fair. But all three are rather different in character. The Tweedmouth Feast started as a religious festival, and still has certain religious characteristics, though with its sports, Salmon Queen and so on, this is less apparent than formerly. Spittal Feast was a social occasion, at first, with a commercial background, and the salmon season linked. And Berwick Fair was instituted by royal charter, of trading significance, by James VI and I—though possibly it replaced a charter of Edward I.

It is good that these two lesser communities should cling to their own identities, even though now all part of the municipality of Berwick-on-Tweed. At least, there has never been any doubt about *their* nationality—although, who knows, they might find themselves incorporated in Scotland, with Berwick, even yet! Stranger things have happened at the mouth of the Tweed.

2

The Border-Line

FROM Berwick-on-Tweed, it is perhaps apt and advisable to trace the actual line of the Border across the country. For it is by no means always obvious or straightforward, or even reasonable; and it enshrines within it much of significance and drama. It runs for some 60 miles, in a generally south-westerly direction, to reach the Solway by the Sark Water at Gretna—some 60 miles as the crow flies, and a high-flying crow, but nearer 110 as the Border-line twists and turns and climbs. The reasons for many of these abrupt and capricious deviations, which can ignore all natural features and seemingly evident courses, are often hard to fathom—but no doubt were explainable once by the ambitions and positions of properties of influential magnates, the apprehensions of wardens, the intrigues of courtiers—or by uneasy compromise or sheer accident. The name of the quite large section known as The Debateable Land speaks for itself; and in fact, over long periods of history, few if any did know just where the actual line ran in these empty Cheviot wastes—for, of course, the Border is even now not marked on the ground save for the odd cairn of stones, however definitive it seems on the map.

Basically, it is convenient to say that the dividing line between the two kingdoms is the Tweed, the Cheviot watershed and the Solway—with variations. It has varied during the centuries, but seldom by much—at least not since around the death of Malcolm Canmore, in 1093. Prior to that, there were great alterations and fluctuations, especially in the South-west but also in Lothian. The ancient Celtic kingdom of Strathclyde stretched as far south as Lancashire, and indeed came to be called Cumbria; and Lothian, though an early Pictish kingdom, became dominated by the Angles, and was not finally incorporated in Alba, or Scotland, until the Battle of Carham was fought, in 1018. It is a rather odd coincidence that it is at Carham, on the Tweed, that the Border-line now makes its great bend southwards, away from the river.

It was William Rufus, William the Conqueror's son, who finally seized Cumberland, which as part of the Kingdom of Strathclyde had belonged to Scotland, and rebuilt the great fortress of Carlisle to hold it. So the Scots gained Lothian and lost Cumberland all about the same period; and after that the Border-line never departed greatly from the present course—save in the vexed matter of Berwick-on-Tweed.

An attempt was made in the reign of Alexander II (1214–1249) to fix and establish the Border equitably and for good. Commissioners on both sides were appointed to perambulate the Marches, as they were called. These failed to come to terms, unfortunately, and the Border remained undefined. But between 1246 and 1249 another attempt was made, with twelve Scots and twelve English knights, under the Sheriffs of Berwick and Northumberland respectively, really determined to make a definitive line. Their findings were enshrined in the Laws of the Marches, of 1249; and subsequent legislation of the two kingdoms accepted this. The Treaty of Northampton (more properly of Edinburgh, where it was finalized and signed, in 1328) which marked Bruce's eventual triumph and the end of the thirty years' Wars of Independence, seemed to settle the matter once and for all. There were, however, minor adjustments and changes thereafter for a long time—and the process may not yet be ended.

Although tracing the Border-line on a large-scale map is obviously the satisfactory exercise for those interested, some brief delineation here may be attempted—to be skipped by those not greatly concerned. It is generally assumed that everything north of the Tweed is in Scotland; but because not only Berwick but what is called Berwick Bounds was included in the blackmail transaction of 1482, in fact the Border strikes due north of Tweed almost 5 miles west of Berwick, for 2 miles, to near Mordington— Mordington, where incidentally, Robert the Bruce's devoted and able secretary and chaplain, Bernard de Linton, was vicar, later to become Abbot of Arbroath, Chancellor of Scotland, and compiler of the magnificent Declaration of Independence of 1320, famed the world over. From Mordington the line swings north-eastwards, by Lamberton Toll on A1, to the sea just north of Marshall Meadows Bay, a strangely arbitrary line without any obvious reason behind it. There is an interesting coincidence that

Hadrian's Wall

Lamberton was the name of another of Bruce's greatest friends and supporters, William, Bishop of St. Andrews and Primate of Scotland, excommunicated by the Pope for sustaining the hero-king—and William indeed first recommended Bernard de Linton to Bruce. So these two places, so close together on the Border, contributed much indeed to Scotland's fight for independence. No doubt these two stalwarts birled in their graves when the shame of 1482 brought their respective localities almost on to English soil.

It is near Gainslaw, then, that the centre of Tweed now actually becomes the Border-line, opposite West Ord on the English side. Thence the boundary continues along the main channel of the great river for about 19 miles, arbitrarily leaving this island in Scotland and that in England. The Till comes in from the south about half-way along this stretch, near Tillmouth Park, a major tributary with its own fame, the river which played such a notable part in the fateful Battle of Flodden. Oddly enough, although the Till's course is entirely in England, it ranks as a Scottish river in law, as respects salmon-fishing—much to the offence of at least some of those who reside on it. This is in theory, to avoid legal differences and difficulties, and to keep fishing conditions the same on Till as on Tweed—and salmon-fishing is, of course, bedevilled with much legal regulation, the salmon always having been a strangely controversial fish. Let it soothe the ruffled feelings of good Till folk that the reverse situation applies at the other end of the Border-line, where the Solway is assumed to be an *English* water, for fishing purposes, and its tributaries, though in Scotland, have to observe English regulations.

Till has an unenviable reputation for its swift-rising spates and deep pools. The ominous rhyme is well known:

> Says Tweed to Till, "What gars ye rin sae still?"
> Says Till to Tweed, "Though you rin with speed,
> And I rin slaw, Whaur ye droon ae man, I droon twa!"

Just a little past Coldstream, the Border-line takes a strange little loop inland, on the south side, leaving the river for almost half a mile, and enclosing in Scotland a sliver of land of what should be England, below the weir of Lees. This odd little foray may be due to a slight change in the course of the river, perhaps because of the weir—although more romantic reasons have been put forward. The 'ENGLAND' and 'NORTHUMBERLAND' road-signs dotting the B6350 which threads it, are amusing.

Another 6 miles, and the March makes its abrupt swing, not only to the south but to the south-*east* again, at Carham, over the low ground of Wark Common, to make a large and unaccountable re-entrant near Nottylees, half a mile deep. Hadden, or Halldean (where the name of Haldane also derives) is here. It was the site of frequent meetings of the Scots and English commissioners, to adjust boundaries and adjudicate in disputes relevant to the East March. Haddonrig, a low ridge here, was the scene of a battle between Scots and English in 1540. On this occasion, the Scots won.

Thereafter, the line rises in an irregular series of leaps and bounds generally south-eastwards, climbing the Cheviot foothills, but crossing the deep Bowmont valley at Shotton before ascending into the high hills by Yetholm Mains. It then strings the summits of Eccles Cairn, White Law, Black Hag and the Schil, to Auchope Cairn at 2,382 feet, above the impressive gut of Hen Hole, a typical Cheviot beef-tub where the Border reivers of either nationality were wont to assemble their lifted cattle, secret and secure, from a wide area on either side of the March, until they had a large enough herd to escort in strength homewards.

Auchope Cairn, an outlier of Cheviot itself, is at the very head of the College valley, 17 very rough miles from Tweed. At this point the Border-line suddenly takes a 300-degree bend west by south, to follow another long string of summits, from Score Head and King's Seat, by typical Border heights like Windy Gyle, Beefshaw Hill, Lamb Hill, Brownhart Law and Hungry Law, to the watershed at the head of Redesdale. Here is the well-known Carter Bar, on the A68 highway coming up from Tynedale and the south, by Catcleugh Reservoir, for Jedburgh and the north. Here took place the famous Redeswyre Raid, or Fray, in 1575, sometimes described as the last Border battle, now the highlight of the annual Jedburgh Common Riding celebrations. This was another recognized point for settling disputes by the Wardens of the Marches, this time the Middle March. And here, as usual, assembled for the Wardens' Court in July, Sir John Forster, for England, and Sir John Carmichael, of Fenton Tower in East

Lothian, for Scotland, with their trains. Why a non-Borderer should have been chosen as Warden on the Scots side is not clear; and it is known that he was not popular; but he was a friend and neighbour of 9-years-old James VI's Regent, the Earl of Morton. At any rate, after all going smoothly for a while, a dispute arose when Carmichael asked Forster to hand over a well-known Northumbrian going by the odd name of Farnstein, who had been making a particular nuisance of himself to the Scots. Forster, for some reason, refused—although this was what Wardens' Courts were all about. Insults followed; and then, without warning, a shower of arrows from the Redesdale and Tynedale men. Scots fell, and a general *mêlée* ensued, amidst extreme confusion—for it must be realized that these annual courts were in the nature of social occasions, with enmities being put aside temporarily, booths set up, pedlars selling things, and general jollity. The Scots, taken entirely by surprise, were getting much the worst of it, when a diversion changed all. It so happened that the Jedburgh Provost and contingent, although nearest to the scene of the meeting, were sadly late in arriving for the court. Battle was well in progress before they turned up. But galloping up the quite steep grassy slopes and shouting, "Jethart's here! Jethart's here!" they so disconcerted the Englishmen at a vital moment that they turned a slaughter into a victory, almost by accident. The tide turned, Sir John Heron, Keeper of Tynedale, was slain, along with scores of others, the English Warden and many other Northumbrian notables taken prisoner, and marched off to the Regent Morton at Dalkeith, and no doubt vengeance wreaked on the unfortunate English non-combatants—if any Borderers were ever non-combatants. This business provoked the most fearful outburst from Queen Elizabeth—it was twenty-eight years before James succeeded her—who on occasion could fly into a passion and fury to rival her late sire, Henry VIII. Morton was moved to return the captured Warden Forster, with a placatory gift of some falcons—delivered to the Queen by Carmichael himself. This drew from the Borderers the comment that he had made a poor bargain—yielding up live hawks for dead herons!

At all events, Jedburgh's representatives found themselves the heroes of the incident, and have been gleefully living on the fame of it ever since, with "Jethart's here!" their continuing slogan—

and a convenient overlooking of the fact that it all happened only because they were late for their appointment. Each year, at the Redeswyre Rideout in July, the affair is commemorated, and an oration is pronounced by some innocent invitee, standing on the Redeswyre Stone up there on the breezy upland, with horsemen and bairns milling around. If a personal anecdote may be permitted, I recollect that I was the inadequate who performed this task one year—1953, I think. After my halting tribute, one Englishman brought up and introduced to me by the Provost of Jedburgh confided in me that he reckoned the entire proceedings a classic example of juvenile xenophobia—if I knew what that meant! He added that it was all really only the Scots giving themselves a loud cheer —for as far as he could see, he was the only Englishman present— and that it was therefore an entirely one-sided celebration. Anyway, history was bunk. This rankled rather, for there was just a little bit of truth in it. And gradually the notion grew on me that there were the seeds of a novel somewhere in this. And perhaps more than just a novel.

It occurred to me that, if the English Borderers would send up their horsed contingents and municipal representatives to meet with the Jedburgh and other Scots burghs' standard-bearers and riders at this annual exercise, the whole thing would much increase in significance as well as drama. So I started a one-man campaign, dragging in my minister and doctor merely to make it look respectable, and we made a pilgrimage round the English Border communities of the East and Middle Marches, asking their leaders if they would attend the next Redeswyre celebration, either horse- or car-borne, provided they were invited by the Jedburgh Provost. I met with no joy, until I reached Morpeth, where Mayor Alfred Appleby welcomed me and my proposition with both kind hands—he was a bookseller, of course, and so perhaps more receptive towards the strange notions of authors than others might be; also he was a man of often great vision and enthusiasm. Anyway, the next year, an official Morpeth delegation attended the celebrations; and thereafter a mounted corps of Northumbrians were welcome guests at the Jedburgh Common Riding and the Redeswyre Stone, for better or for worse. Using this good material, and hotting it up just a little in the interests of the reading public, I produced the novel *The Night Riders*—so reimbursing myself for the Northumberland run-around. When that novel was launched in suitable style at the Spread Eagle Hotel at Jedburgh, there was to be viewed the inspiring sight of the mayor and town clerk of Morpeth, the chairman of the Hexham Rural District Council, and the provosts of Jedburgh, Hawick and other Scots burghs, even the ex-Lord Provost of Edinburgh, toasting each other in good Scotch whisky paid for by my London publishers. Stand the Borders where they did?

From the Carter Bar the Border-line continues south-westwards along the hill-tops for a further 11 miles, by Carter Fell, the Keilder Stone, and Peel Fell, to the head of the North Tyne valley at Deadwater of the ill-omened name—where incidentally I once launched another Border novel, entitled *Balefire*, and where I toasted it in some of the same Deadwater, being that unsociable outcast a teetotaller, while my guests did rather better. This is a bleak spot, where the headwaters of Tyne flowing to the North Sea, and those of the Liddel, flowing to the Atlantic, rise within a quarter mile of each other amongst the sheep-dotted but otherwise empty hills, and the great new Keilder Forest spreads far and wide down into Northumberland. Getting my unfortunate guests to this outlandish spot was, I admit, something of a Border epic in itself.

Before there was any Border, the Romans came this way, thrusting *their* roads straight across the country, against the grain of the land with superb engineering and an equally superb disregard for natural difficulties or expense—not, as we do, following the valleys and lines of least resistance. Of course, they had no labour problems. The Wheelcauseway, strangely named, a mighty engineering feat, still strides across these hills and moors and mosses, straight as a die, crossing the Hexham–Hawick road near Deadwater, a humbling reminder to those who will see and heed.

On from Deadwater the line crosses the remote Larriston Fells, high above Liddesdale to the south, still on a most erratic course until it strikes the headwaters of the Kershope Burn at the Cumberland border. We here are nearing the true Debateable Land where, whatever boundary-makers and cartographers might say, the Border-line was never accepted as in any way a practical proposition or inconvenience in the old days. Down the Kershope Burn to the Liddel Water it runs, and so to that river's junction with Esk.

But reaching the low, green and alluvial levels which could neither be defended nor kept inviolate, it thereafter tended to wander, now here, now there. This had its advantages for the tougher inhabitants—and only the tougher ones survived in The Debateable Land. When it was uncertain which law, English or Scots, should apply to quite a wide area of land, no law at all was apt to apply—and the weakest went to the wall. The Armstrongs ruled here, and they were anything but weak, perhaps the toughest and boldest of all the Border clans, as strong on one side of the disregarded line as the other. In the fifteenth and early sixteenth centuries they held the West March, and much else, in thrall. More of them later.

At Esk, then, instead of remaining with that river, the boundary finally agreed between the two kingdoms in 1552, strikes off westwards over higher ground to the River Sark, and an earthwork now known as the Scots Dyke was thrown up to delimit it. Thereafter the line follows the rather insignificant Sark down through the Solway Moss to salt water at Gretna, about 4 miles north-east of the Esk's estuary. The reason for this diversion is not clear, for the Esk itself, running wide and deep, would seem to be the obvious line. But the level banks thereof would certainly prove difficult of defence; and it may be that the Scots commissioners preferred to yield a little bit of country, and to base their line on higher and more defensible ground, so as to leave the undefendable parts to England!

This then was, and is, the Border-line—110 miles of it, a long and narrow belt of country where conditions applied which were to be found nowhere else in the British Isles. It was not only a case of confusion, and of difficulty in enforcing laws; for here special and distinct laws were involved—if not always enforceable. The term Border Law was no mere figure of speech indicating chaos—like Jethart Justice, where a man was hanged first, for security's sake, and tried afterwards. The Border Laws, accepted by both kingdoms, contained many provisions which made them unique and which sound very strange today—but which evidently were formed to meet conditions prevailing. For instance, a wanted fugitive on one side could reach sanctuary by crossing the Border and ringing the bell of any church, whereafter he could not be arrested and brought back for trial. Again, the possessor of goods stolen and carried across to the other side, could claim them back, but had to be prepared to assert his right by duel or personal combat on the March itself. Proof by witnesses and trial by jury were not accepted as sufficiently effective; personal combat, by self or representative, was necessary. No man, even though he possessed lands in either realm, or both, could be impeached elsewhere but on the March itself. The 'hot trod' custom is well known—whereby any aggrieved person whose cattle had been lifted, could cross the Border without hindrance, up to six days after the stealing, to try to recover his property—but he must bear a burning peat at his lance-tip as intimation of his business and right. No persons residing on different sides of the Border might marry save with the permission of the relevant Wardens. And so on. More of this hereafter.

It will be seen that such laws and customs laid an enormous responsibility upon the six Wardens of the Marches of the two countries—other than their duty of repelling invasion and keeping approximate peace. That these had to be powerful men in their own right, goes without saying. Often the office was more or less hereditary in certain families, such as the Maxwells, Douglases, Kerrs and Homes, on the Scots side; and the Forsters, Fenwicks and Dacres on the English. Disputes between the Wardens themselves were not infrequent—and all too apt to be settled by the old-fashioned and unarguable methods of armed force and cold steel. But there was a procedure laid down to do so by more peaceful means, with six jurors on either side, appointed by the Wardens concerned, forming a sort of court of appeal.

These Marches, then, were clearly defined, however uncertain at times the Border-line itself might be—the east, the middle and the west. The east ran from the North Sea to Auchope Cairn on Cheviot; the middle from there to the head of the Kershope Burn in the Larriston fells; the west hence to the Solway coast. Since these divisions applied on both sides of the line, it will be convenient to look at the Borderland hereafter partitioned laterally into these age-old components.

3

The Scots East March—the Merse

So far as Scotland is concerned, the East March and the Merse are more or less synonymous terms. Merse and March are of the same derivation, of course. But the name of Merse has long been given to that great and wide champaign—for it is that rather than any low-lying plain—which lies between the Lammermuir Hills, which rim Lothian, and the Tweed. This comprises most of Berwickshire, and a segment of East Roxburghshire also, and forms a fairly distinctive as well as highly attractive area up to some 250 square miles in extent, the richest and most fertile part of all the Borderland, bar none. Indeed it forms the largest plain, if that word can be used, in all Scotland, and contains some of the finest agricultural land in the two kingdoms, with some of the biggest and most prosperous farms. Just because of this, and of its position —as well as the quality of the folk who lived on it—the same land is probably the most blood-soaked in all these islands, acre for acre.

Let us be clear what we mean by the term, the Merse. At various times the area so called has altered. In modern territorial terminology it refers to the largest and most southerly of the three divisions of Berwickshire, comprising about 130,000 acres. Sometimes it has meant the whole of that county, Lammermuir and Lauderdale included. Again, at one time, it was held to cover all the lower-lying ground between the Lammermuirs and the Cheviots, extending as far west as lower Teviotdale, with Roxburgh town and castle actually its capital. Few would think of that as in the Merse, today; but in ancient writings, when the March was referred to, without adding Middle or West, this is what was meant. Moreover March gave its name to a great earldom; and though the early Earls of March were also Earls of Dunbar, the two titles were distinct, as were the territories—and it is noteworthy that the principal castle of the former was at Earlston—why it got that name—formerly the Ercildoune of Thomas the Rhymer fame, in

Lauderdale. However, for our purposes, it is convenient to think of the Merse as being the great oblong of lower land—although some of its green ridges rise to 500 feet—lying between the southern slopes of the Lammermuir Hills and the River Tweed, bounded on the east by the sea and on the west by a curving line from Kelso through the Smailholm ridge to Gordon and Greenlaw.

To all intents and purposes, then, this *is* the East March of Scotland—although it does miss out that very area where the East March disputes were traditionally settled—or attempts were made thereat—*south* of Tweed at the Redden Burn (Riding-burn, referring to march-riding) near Hadden. Also, to be fair, it includes in the Merse that coastal area north of Berwick, including Burnmouth, Eyemouth, Coldingham, St. Abbs and Fast Castle, which is a world unto itself, and anything but typical Merse-land. Yet, the fact remains that this fringe area was always under the ownership and domination of the great Merse families, mainly Dunbars, Homes and Logans, even in the pre-Reformation days of Coldinghame Priory, and therefore cannot really be considered as a separate entity.

All that said, and looking at the Merse as a whole, certain features stand out as so very different from the rest of the Borderland. The sheer fertility of the place strikes one forcibly, the vastness of its broad acres, the rolling loveliness of its green demesnes, the utterly misleading atmosphere of settled peace so appallingly at odds with its turbulent history. It is a land by itself, cut off from the rest by encircling hill ranges, a fair and wide land of far-flung vistas and great skies, verdant and unspoiled by industrial unsightliness. Strangely enough, for so large a segment of the southern Scottish scene, it is comparatively little known or observed by either visitors or by the remainder of the Scots population. This presumably is because both the major north–south roads skirt it by fairly deep valley-bottoms which hide the Merse itself from travellers' view. The railway-line likewise. The A1 from Berwick clings to the edge of the coastal cliffs, as does the train, with the Lamberton and Ayton Hill ridges blocking the prospect to the west, and then from Ayton runs up the Eye valley for 10 miles—by which time it is deep in the Lammermuir Hills and the Merse behind it. While the A68 from Carter Bar, although offering an

Polwarth Church

utterly splendid panorama from the summit that does include a distant sight of the Merse plain, thereafter plunges down into the vale of the Jedwater, and proceeds onwards well to the west, with high ground between. This is a pity, in a way—though it does tend to keep this storied and delightful terrain unspoiled and inviolate. Nevertheless, it should be infinitely better known and appreciated than it is. To use a deplorable modernism, its tourist potential is as yet unexploited.

For, of course, there is scarcely a yard of this fair land that does not shout aloud—or sometimes whisper—of story, battle, daring, feud, legend and romance. Here are the names which sing the songs of balladry—Ladykirk, Bassendean, Kimmerghame, Polwarth-on-the-Green, Billie, Bunkle and Blanerne, the Hirsel, Blackadder and Whitadder, Edrom and the rest. This is the land where ancient families cling to their ancestral acres—largely, no doubt, because the soil *is* so rich—and great estates abound, the land of the Homes in especial, though the Swintons and the Scotts are not backward. It is a country of large farming properties, with large farm-touns. Nowhere in Scotland is the farm-toun so developed as hereabouts, almost to the exclusion of normal small villages, each great establishment having its own tight hamlet of cot-houses, often with its own smiddy and mill, formerly even schools, trig and neat and independent, some as large as small villages in other parts. There are true villages, of course—but not as many as a county of this size might be expected to support, Chirnsides and Paxton, Hutton and Swinton, Ladykirk and Birgham and Eccles, Stichill, Ednam and Preston, and so on. But a great proportion of the rural population lives in the farm-touns—though less than once, for depopulation is sadly at work here, mechanized farming and modern conditions playing their part. The total population of the county is only 18,270, although the acreage is 300,000. And that is a steady decrease. The Merse had only the two burghs —Coldstream, on the Tweed, with well under 2,000 inhabitants, for all its resounding fame; and Duns, the county town, isolated away up on the rising foothills of Lammermuir, not much bigger. Kelso can hardly be called a Merse town. There is something far wrong when land such as this ceases to hold its folk—but that is not a subject for discussion here.

In any survey it is only decent to start with the county town—

although this little burgh, terraced on the south-facing lap of the hills and looking out over the Merse most fair, hardly aspired to that honour. Main roads and the railway pass it by. Berwick was, and is, the obvious focal point of the county; but Duns must do its best with the problem landed in its modest arms. It is only in comparatively recent times that it has had this status thrust upon it; Greenlaw was the county town before that—an even smaller place. The fact that Duns does not aspire to be a bustling metropolis, however, in no way condemns it; quite the reverse. For a pleasanter, doucer little town would be hard to find, even though it wears its large Berwickshire High School, Whitchester Hospital and local authority buildings, a little self-consciously. And at Festival Week, when the Duns Reiver rides, and "Duns Dings A'!" resounds, no one will name Duns sleepy. It was a great occasion for the town when, in 1956, the Queen herself found her way through the Merse to attend one of the march-riding ceremonies. Duns dinged—or beat—all, that day, and cocked a snook at all the other Border common-riding burghs.

"Duns Dings A'!" is the burgh's motto, and how it got it makes a typical Border story. In 1377, the Earl of Northumberland, English Warden of the East March, rode into the Merse to avenge the slaughter of a Northumbrian party by the Earl of Dunbar and March—normal procedure. He got as far as Duns, burning and slaying, and camped outside the burgh, no doubt intending to deal with it in salutary fashion on the morrow. But during the night, the Duns folk sallied out, with the contrivances they used to frighten deer and marauding cattle from their unfenced crops. These were a kind of rattle, made of dried skins stretched on a framework, to form a sound-box, with stones inside, which when shaken made a loud and booming noise. With these the burghers crept upon the English horse-lines, and then created such a frightening uproar that the horses all stampeded off through the sleeping camp, causing utter chaos. Not only the horses panicked. Assuming that they were being attacked by a Scots army, Northumberland's troops took to their heels; and, lacking their horses and apparently all disciplined command, were set upon by the locals. Though most fled, and escaped, in the confusion, many were killed; and the Bloody Burn commemorates the occasion till this day. All these common- and march-riding celebrations have some such historical incident behind them—and Duns at least can take rather more legitimate pride in theirs than can Jedburgh!

Possibly a still more laudable source of pride for Duns is that it is the birthplace of one of the foremost scholars and philosophers of early international distinction—John Duns, commonly known as Duns Scotus, born here in 1275, son of a local small laird, Duns of Grueldykes. He was trained for the Church, and became a Franciscan friar; went to lecture in theology and philosophy at Merton College, Oxford; and then moved to Paris, where he became known as Doctor Subtilis, the Subtle Doctor—presumably a compliment, because sometimes it was changed to the Angelic Doctor! He was then sent by his order to Cologne to found a university there, in 1308, but died soon after, and is buried in the great Cathedral of Cologne. So he was only about 33 when he died, and had made a most notable mark on religious thinking by an early age, being in opposition to the theories of St. Thomas Aquinas to such effect that theological thinkers were split into two camps, the Thomists and the Scotists. His doctrine of the Immaculate Conception of the Virgin seems to have been one of the causes of rupture. As late as 1639 his collected works were published at Leyden in twelve volumes—not bad for Duns in Lammermuir. He does not seem to have concerned himself much with his homeland, however, once he got to foreign parts—like not a few other ex-patriate Scots—for though this was the dire period of the Wars of Independence, his name never once comes up in that context, even in the many appeals to and negotiations with the Pope and Vatican.

Duns has innumerable other claims to fame, of course, down its stirring history, however quiet it may be today. The present town stands a good half-mile to the south of the original burgh, burned by the English under Bowes, Governor of Berwick in 1544, again next year during Hertford's invasion, and a third time in 1558 when the Earl Percy of Northumberland, and Bowes again, destroyed what was left so thoroughly that not a trace remains now save the name of some fields, the Bruntons, or Burnt Town, where a cairn marks the site.

In that same drastic sixteenth century—when Scotland was so wide open to terrorist invasion after the great *débâcle* of Flodden—

took place here an event which linked Duns with a colourful and well-known character in Scots history, the gallant, handsome and swaggering Sieur de la Bastie. It was in 1517, during the long minority of James V, that the Regent Albany appointed the celebrated French knight to be Warden of the East March—positively asking for trouble. But then, Albany was himself little better than a Frenchman, having lived his life more or less in exile there and married to a French wife. This was the beginning of that period of maximum French influence in Scotland, which ended with Mary Queen of Scots. Anyway, the Homes of the Merse looked upon the East March Wardenship as their personal possession—indeed, the Lord Home, head of the clan, had just been expelled from the position, possibly for very good reason. So de la Bastie—or Batty, as the Scots called him—whose ideas of indiscriminate justice could scarcely be expected to appeal to the Homes, had to be taught a lesson. An ambush was arranged, near Fogo, 4 miles south of Duns, as he rode from Kelso through the Merse for Dunbar. But, exceptionally well-mounted, the Frenchman managed to escape this. The Homes pursued him, in full cry, chasing him through the streets of the town; but knowing the lie of the land better than did he, they managed to head him into a swampy area near the Stoneymuir, still known as Batty's Bog, where his horse floundered and the unfortunate Warden was caught, abused and slain. Home of Wedderburn himself, chief of that important branch of the family, cut off the reputedly beautiful head—he was often called de la Beautie on account of his looks—and hanging it from his saddle-bow by its long, plaited tresses, rode with it back to Duns, where he hung it on the mercat cross, as warning to regents, kings and all others who might think to interfere with the Homes in the Merse.

This mercat cross, a fine example, used to stand in the market square, but it was removed in 1816 to make room for the sham Gothic extravagance of the town hall which now rises in the centre thereof in ornate and ridiculous splendour. The cross was eventually re-erected in the public park, near the war memorial. This park is a quite astonishingly large and fine one, for a community of this size, and was gifted to the town in 1891 by Mr. Andrew Smith of Whitchester.

As indicated, the Homes did, and still do, cut a wide swathe in the Merse. Indeed, the names of Home and Merse have been practically synonymous since the thirteenth century, when William, a grandson of the third of the semi-royal Cospatrick Earls of March and Dunbar, wed his kinswoman Ada, of the same line, heiress of the lands of Home in the mid-Merse, and took the name of Home from the lands. Perhaps this is as good a point as any to deal with that inevitable and evergreen question—Home or Hume? The answer is quite simple, despite the reams that have been written about it. The local pronunciation of the word home is 'hyim'—and 'hume' is as near as 'foreigners' are likely to get. People have consequently been spelling it wrongly for centuries. The famous philosopher David Hume—incidentally a son of Home of Ninewells, a branch of Wedderburn—deliberately elected to change the spelling himself, despairing of ever convincing his London friends of the correct pronunciation otherwise. Though there were many examples of the Hume mis-spelling before his day, notably one of 1553 referring in a contract to ". . . the noble and mighty Lord Hume". But Home is correct as to spelling.

The Homes, then, prospered and proliferated mightily—while, strangely enough, their more lofty kinsmen of the main March and Dunbar line—who, when surnames became advisable, adopted that of Dunbar—declined. The earls, in fact grew just too powerful for any Scots monarch to tolerate as subjects, especially as they tended to make their own arrangements, even treaties, with the English kings—for they were descended from a grandson of King Duncan, slain by MacBeth, and also from a granddaughter of William the Conqueror. In the fifteenth century they were brought low by a combination of royal policy and murky Douglas ambition—and the great house of Douglas grew the greater on their ruin, until in due course, it had to be brought down in turn. But the Homes did not aspire so high, being content to restrict their ambitions and domination to the Merse and thereabouts. But here they made themselves masters, with a remarkable application and single-mindedness. Here, of all places, they managed to cling, in the most vulnerable, accessible and fought-over lands in Scotland, the prize for the reiver, the ravager and the rogue, as well as the invading army; and not only to cling, but to expand and consolidate, through all the tides of war, feuding and mosstrooping.

And here they are still, in a big way, and playing no inconsiderable part at that.

There was an odd thing about the Homes—their status-level. Like the Grand Army of Mexico, there were always more generals than privates. They were all lairds. In this they were different from the true clans, Highland and Lowland, where the chiefly element was upheld by a great substructure of clansmen, in peace as in war. There must have been some lower orders amongst the Homes, of course; but seldom indeed do we hear of them. The resounding list of Home lairdships in this Merse of Berwickshire, great and not so great, is impressive indeed and reads like a gazetteer of the county. We see the Homes of Wedderburn, of Polwarth, of Marchmont, of Manderston, of Blackadder, of Simprin, of Kames, of Broomhouse, of Ninewells, of Whiteriggs, of Cowden-knowes, of Bassendean, of Bunkle, or Bonkyl, of Preston, of Edrom, of Hutton, of Paxton, of Fastcastle, of Linthill and of Eyemouth. No doubt there were many others.

Home Castle itself, the principal and original bailiwick, is now represented by a rather ugly sham-battlemented erection, a false ruin, on top of the authentic craggy mount outcropping from the fertile plain, 3 miles south of Greenlaw in the western throat of the Merse, and at 600 feet a major landmark from near and far. The site, therefore, is magnificent, and it is sad indeed that this outsize folly is all that remains of the once proud seat and strong-hold of the Lords Home, scene of so much excitement in the past. The old castle was involved in sieges and affrays innumerable, and before the general use of artillery was considered to be well-nigh impregnable. Tradition says that here Queen Mary of Gueldres was lodging when her husband, the young James II, was killed by the bursting of a cannon at the siege of Roxburgh, 8 miles away, in 1460. The protector Somerset captured Home for the English in 1547, after a stiff resistance by the Lady Home, whose husband had died just previously at the Battle of Pinkie. Again, in 1569, it surrendered to Sussex and his army which included a thousand horse and five great cannon. What a century for trouble the sixteenth was.

Memories of a third and more lastingly significant siege, by Cromwell and his Ironsides, in 1650, are enlivened by the verses of 'Willie Wastle' and by the letter which the Earl of Home's captain sent to the English attackers: "Right Honourable, I have received a trumpeter of yours, as he tells me, without a pass, to surrender Home Castle to the Lord General Cromwell. Please you, I never saw your General. As for Home Castle, it stands upon a rock. Given at Home Castle this day before 7 o'clock. So resteth, without prejudice to my native country, your most humble servant, T. COCKBURN." Sad to say, despite this spirited epistle, Home Castle was forced to capitulate by Cromwell's cannon.

Just why Home Castle eventually passed to the Homes of Polwarth, in lieu of the main stem, which continued to flourish, I have not discovered. But it did, and in the eighteenth century the then ruinous stronghold was built up, out of its own fallen masonry into the present rather unsightly affair, by the third Earl of Marchmont—the Homes of Polwarth having climbed the brae to their own earldom.

The present head of the whole clan, of course, lives about 9 miles to the east, at Coldstream, and was until a few years ago, the fourteenth Earl of Home. Sir Alex Douglas-Home, now Lord Home of the Hirsel, known to all and admired even by his political enemies, has brought lustre on the name—though many regretted his ·stepping down from his ancient earldom in the interests of politics. He is thirty-fourth in descent from the William and Ada of the thirteenth century. It is interesting to note that he is Sir Alexander Cospatrick Douglas-Home, keeping alive the name of the line of King Duncan's grandson, who was known as Comes Patrick, the 'comes' referring allegedly to Count or Earl of Northumbria, which the family had gained by marriage with the conqueror's granddaughter. The eighth descendant of William and Ada was created Lord Home, in 1473; and in 1605, the sixth of that line was made first Earl of Home. The Hirsel, near Coldstream, has been their seat for many generations now, a fine house with an old nucleus, in a most attractive estate wherein is a large artificial lake. Hirsel means, strangely enough, a flock of sheep—which is the last thing that anyone might call the Homes. But that seems to have been the name for a very long time, although in early days it seems to have been spelt Herissille—although spelling in those days mattered little admittedly. We read that when Cospàtrick, Earl of Dunbar and March, founded the Cistercian nunnery at Coldingham, his Countess, Derder or Dierdre, granted to the new foundation the church of Hirsel. The sheep metaphor may have been more apt for a religious institution than for a fortified house of the Homes. In the grounds, some time ago, stone coffins and a great number of bones were dug up, indicating that the place is one of very early settlement. Although there is a tradition that many of these may belong to a host of members of the Scots nobility who fell at the fatal field of Flodden, for it is said that the prioress of the Cistercian Priory, founded here by another of the Cospatrick earls, ordered that the bodies of as many as possible of these 'Flowers of the Forest' be brought here in carts and given burial on consecrated ground.

Coldstream, the Merse's other burgh, is very different in siting and character from Duns. Best known, no doubt, because it gave its name to the second oldest of Foot Guards; the Coldstreamers, contrary to the generally accepted notion, were *not* raised here. The regiment had been in existence for ten years, as part of the Commonwealth army, when in December 1659 their first commander, General Monk, came to establish his headquarters at Coldstream. He had formed the unit out of Fenwick's and Heselrige's Regiments, earlier, in 1650, to fight against the Presbyterians of Scotland, and the men were mainly Borderers. Typically so, they seem to have cared little for which side they fought on, King's or Commonwealth's, Scots or English—but loved their colonel and followed his changes of allegiance cheerfully. By the Coldstream period, after ten years in Scotland, Monk was fighting *against* the Commonwealth forces, Cromwell having died. A month after coming to the town, he crossed Tweed into England in a swift advance on Newcastle, which surrendered before him. Confusion reigned amongst the Commonwealth leaders. Soon Monk marched his stalwart troops right to London, and restored King Charles II with little trouble. It is recounted how, on the arrival of the King, Monk reviewed his men, ordered them to lay their arms on the ground and consider themselves disbanded; and then immediately commanded them to pick them up again and consider themselves recruited anew as soldiers of the Crown. The regiment's title thereafter was the lofty one of My Lord General's Regiment of Foot Guards, later just the Second Foot Guards. The Coldstream appellation was merely, at first, a sort of nickname which stuck to them, from the place from which they had started their triumphal march. The former headquarters—of General Monk rather than of the regiment itself—is in the pleasing, quiet market square, south of the main street.

The River Tweed dominates—or better, enfolds—Coldstream; and its history is mainly connected therewith. For here was the first major and reliable ford upstream of Berwick Bridge; and there was no other bridge, of course. Consequently this was, as it were, the staging-point for invasions innumerable, in both directions, small-scale and large. I cannot imagine that Coldstream took up a very positive attitude in this vexed matter, one way or another. 'A plague on both your houses' was probably the prevailing sentiment. It would not be until well after the Union, and there was no more danger of invasions, that the Home chiefs could consider it a practical proposition to take up their main residence at the Hirsel.

Sooner or later, almost every monarch of Scotland, and most of England, with their great ones, arrived at Coldstream. Here crossed Edward I in 1296, before his sack of Berwick. Here Bruce and the Black Douglas wore a trail on their incursions to bring Edward II to a peace conference. Here James IV led the flower of Scotland to Flodden, and did not lead them back. Here the great Montrose waded, first to cross the swollen river, in 1640, to encourage his Covenanted men. And so on.

Today, Coldstream is a long, narrow, clean little town lying between the green river banks and the woodlands, where the clump of anglers' waders sounds loud, and hostilities were kept within the former town council's chambers until the alleged reform of local government, recently imposed. The old bridge toll-house here used to vie with those of Gretna and Berwick as mecca for runaway elopers intent on making irregular marriages under the Scots law system of wedding by simple declaration before witnesses. Until 1856 such folk could be married at a moment's notice, and by anyone; but thereafter the three weeks residential qualification was imposed, and the traffic happily subsided—although, not altogether. It is odd that the pull of Gretna Green still draws clients, when nobody any longer thinks of Coldstream as the start of a new life. Yet one place is as good—or as bad—as another. Odder still, indeed almost unbelievable, is the fact that amongst the characters who have elected to get married in this undignified and hole-in-corner way are no fewer than three Lords Chancellor of England, the Lords Eldon, Broughton and Erskine.

The bridge here enabled Robert Burns to make his first incursion into England. He had been staying with the Ainslies at Duns —where at church on Sunday, 6th May 1787 he had made a verse about his host's daughter, Rachel, not being able to find the preacher's text in her Bible; the next day he came here, to set foot on 'foreign' soil. His diary records the event. "Coldstream—went over into England. Cornhill—glorious river Tweed, clear, majestic. Fine Bridge."

Of the villages of the Merse, Chirnside, more or less central, is probably the largest, climbing for nearly a mile one of the many low ridges that rise like whalebacks out of the green sea, this one near the junction of Whitadder and Blackadder—the 'adder', by the way, does not refer to snakes but is merely a corruption of water. The old parish church retains a Norman doorway. Industry in a modest way came to Chirnside, in the shape of a woollen factory, and paper and saw mills—but not so as to spoil the amenity. The Ninewells estate of the Homes is just to the south, home of Davie the Philosopher, and also of his nephew, Davie, the eminent criminal jurist, the Baron Hume. Ninewells is often given as the birthplace of the philosopher; but in fact he was born in the Tron Kirk at Edinburgh, an intriguing start for a sceptic of no mean order. Perhaps he felt that he had to live down this unusual nativity. He was, of course, something of an oddity— could anyone be otherwise who set out to write, in multiple volumes, *A Treatise on Human Nature?* His own philosophy does not seem always to have stood him in good stead, for when, in 1745, he sought the position of Professor of Moral Philosophy at Edinburgh, and was turned down on account of his scepticism and heterodoxy, he was so upset that he contemplated abandoning the academic life and joining the army. His appearance can hardly have helped. The following is a description by Lord Charlmont: "The powers of physiognomy were baffled by his countenance; neither could the most skilful in that science pretend to discover the smallest trace of the faculties of his mind, in the unmeaning features of his visage. His face was broad and fat, his mouth wide, and without any other expression than that of imbecility. His eyes vacant and spiritless; and the corpulence of his whole person was far better fitted to communicate the idea of a turtle-eating alderman than a refined philosopher."

Yet this character produced innumerable essays and lengthy volumes of a scope indicated by such titles as *Inquiry into the Principles of Morals, Essays Moral and Political, A History of England, The Natural History of Religion,* and so on. And, despite his looks, on his death-bed, at the age of 65 he was still conducting a highly intimate correspondence with two particularly celebrated and affectionate French ladies, the Marquise de Barbantane and the Comtesse de Boufflers. He had always had a partiality to French women—and apparently it was reciprocated. He was said to hate the English—even though he chose to write an enormous *History of England*—a Merse Home to the end.

Chirnside produced other problem children of the Kirk. In 1674, the wife of the parish minister, the Reverend Henry Erskine, died and was buried in the kirkyard, still with a valuable ring on her finger. The beadle was a man of practical mind, and presumably felt this to be a sorry waste. He filled in the earth on top of the coffin only lightly, therefore, and after dark returned to dig up the body. Opening the coffin he sought to pull off the ring—but it would not come. So he drew his clasp-knife and began to saw off the finger—whereupon the deceased sat up and yelled, jumped out of coffin and grave and ran to hammer on the door of the manse, demanding to be let in for she was "fair clammed wi' the cauld"! This lady in due course became the mother of the Reverends Ralph and Ebenezer Erskine, founders of the Original Secession Church. What happened to the beadle is not detailed.

Before we leave this very lively family one other Home story—of a very different nature. About 4 miles south-west of Duns, on the western edge of the Merse, is Polwarth-on-the-Green, once a lovely village, and now all but deserted, though still lovely, with a handsome whitewashed church dating from 1703. On what was the notably non-level village green are two ancient thorn trees, round which it was the centuries-old custom to dance at each wedding—a custom celebrated in song, one by Allan Ramsay being famous. The story revolves round the aforementioned church, which was in fact rebuilt in present form by Patrick Home, first Earl of Marchmont, although it had dated from A.D. 900. It was here that the said Patrick of Polwarth, before being ennobled, a fervent Covenanter, lay hidden in the vaults below the church for several weeks in the winter of 1685, while the government forces hunted for him; and his 12-year-old daughter Grizel, later the famed Lady Grizel Baillie, each night came secretly through the benighted graveyard to keep him supplied with food and drink, a tale of courage which has caught the imagination of many generations.

Seven miles east of Polwarth, in the midst of the Merse and on the Leet Water which finally joins Tweed at Coldstream, lies the village of Swinton, this one far from deserted, and quite large, with green, mercat cross with several sundials, and an old church having a bell called Mary dated 1499. In the church is the recumbent effigy of Sir Alan de Swinton of that ilk, believed to date from 1200. The Swintons claim to have the oldest charters and records of any family in Scotland—and they are still domiciled at Swinton House. Edulf de Swinton supported Malcolm Canmore (1058–1093) and got a charter of the lands confirming him in the entire parish of Swinton—so they were there before that time. Another early representative, Ernulf, was knighted by David I about 1140—the first recorded knighting in Scotland. Sir John Swinton played a valiant part at the rather farcical Battle of Otterburn in 1388 and was later to die at the tragic field of Homildon Hill. His son, another Sir John, slew English Henry V's brother, the Duke of Clarence, at the Battle of Beaugé in 1421, with the Scots aiding the French—as per the Auld Alliance—against the English. Of a different calibre was Alexander Swinton, Lord Mersington, known as the Fanatic Judge, who personally led a riotous attack on the Chapel Royal at Holyrood in 1688. And so on. A recent Swinton became Lord Lyon King of Arms. They make a remarkable family, by any standards.

I could go on and on about the Merse, its families and its sheer character. But must not. Let me end with a highly modern development which yet has something of the old, challenging, hard-riding Merse tradition about it—Charterhall Motor Racing Track, famed as one of the finest in the country, and for its links with the late Jim Clark, son of a Merse farmer, was created here in Fogo parish on the site of a former aerodrome, five miles from anywhere. Yet thousands flocked here from near and far, to national and international events. Sadly, it has now been closed and is only used once a year for a Jim Clark memorial rally. A Roman camp lies at Chesters, nearby, approached by a causeway through a bog. I feel sure that the Romans would have appreciated that motor-racing track.

4

The Scots East March—Coldinghamshire and the Berwick Coast

I HAVE said that the coastal area north of Berwick Bounds is scarcely typical of the Merse. Although inevitably part of the East March, it is hardly true Border country either. In fact, it is something of a world unto itself, very much concerned with its own affairs, which tend to relate to the sea rather than the normal Borderline preoccupations. Fishing, shipping, smuggling, even wrecking, used to be its main interests—and, of course, religion. The wrecking is now happily replaced by coastguard and life-saving activities. For it is a fierce and dangerous seaboard, however picturesque, and there are no fewer than five coastguard and lifeboat establishments in the 20 miles between Berwick and Cockburnspath.

This stretch of country, really the clenched fist of south-eastern Scotland shaken in the face of the North Sea, used to have its own name—or most of it did. Coldinghamshire. It was never a shire or county of its own, in the accepted sense, but it was a semi-independent ecclesiastical jurisdiction under the princely Priory of Coldingham—which naturally was more or less a Home private monopoly. Cut off from Lothian and the Merse by the Lammermuir Hills and the valley of the Eye Water, it is a rugged place of high, whin-grown heathery moors, hidden communities and tremendous cliffs, covering an area perhaps 12 miles long by half that in width, a country of short, sharp watercourses, of lonely farms cowering behind wind-sculptured trees, of sheep pasture and wide whaup-haunted heaths, of skyscapes and winds and the smell of the sea. But rather more populous than might appear at first sight. It is an entity whose divisions you will never see on any map. Yet it is a distinct and distinctive place, proud of its name and title for centuries before many a more modern shire was set up—undoub-

tedly, 95 per cent of the people of Scotland have never set foot or wheel in it, and even fewer have come from England.

This is strange, for it is no remote backwater. It lies only an hour's run from Edinburgh, and one of the major and busiest highways of the two kingdoms borders it, A1; as does the main east coast rail-route to London. But these are in the valley of the Eye, and rising ground to the east hides all this intriguing land in the same way as that to the west hides the Merse.

There are roads in Coldinghamshire; indeed one quite main highway, A1107, threads it, climbing over moors, diving deep into narrow valleys leaving A1 at Cockburnspath Tower on the north and joining it again at Burnmouth 15 miles to the south. But surprisingly few choose to take this road—to their loss in all but mere time. Side roads are few; and the savage and daunting coastline itself is roadless entirely. Yet it is this coastline, undoubtedly, which dominates all. In Coldinghamshire, one is never unaware of its presence. Indeed one can usually hear it, from quite a long way inland, the thunder of great seas on an ironbound seaboard; and the taste of salt spray permeates the air for miles.

How did this territory come to be under at least nominal ecclesiastical rule and sway? It is an old story. Edgar the Peaceable, one of the succession of sons of Malcolm Canmore and Queen Margaret the alleged saint, reluctantly fought his brother Edmund and his uncle Donald Bane, for the Crown of Scotland, under the banner of St. Cuthbert and with the help of England's William Rufus. In return for heavenly and terrestrial aid, in victory he gave all this curious territory, an eighth of Berwickshire, to the monks of Durham as votive offering, with many rentals and privileges, and built the magnificent church and priory of St. Mary at Coldingham, deep in a valley in the centre of the area and not far from the picturesque village of St. Abbs, under mighty St. Abbs Head. This was already holy country, for St. Abba, or Ebba, a daughter of King Ethelfrid, had established a monastery here centuries before, and ruled it as abbess until her death in 683, a double monastery and nunnery living under her single government—most unusual. Here came St. Cuthbert himself to visit the redoubtable lady in 661. And here, even though its reputation had become, perhaps inevitably in the circumstances, somewhat tarnished, so that St. Adamnan prophesied its doom by fire for its sins, in 870 came the

St. Abb's Head

Danes, to ravish and burn; but not before the nuns at least had cut
off their noses and lips, to preserve their honour—or so tradition
avers. So it was a suitable place for St. Cuthbert's monks of
Durham—especially as with it went the parishes of Eyemouth,
Ayton, Lamberton and Aldcambus, parts of Mordington, Foul-
den, Chirnside, Bonkyl and Cockburnspath. Unfortunately or
otherwise, as the percipient reader will have noticed, certain of
these names have a Home-ish ring to them; and whatever King
Edgar and his successors might say, the Prince-bishop of Durham
had the greatest of difficulty in consolidating his rule, as in garner-
ing the rents and wealth thereof. The Scots in general and the
Homes in particular thought otherwise, down the years. And, to
cut a long story short, they succeeded eventually in making
Coldingham Priory and its shire practically their own private preserve. King James IV—who did not like Henry VIII, his brother-in-
law, nor the English nation, for that matter—managed to get the
Pope to transfer the superiority of Coldingham from Durham to
Dunfermline Abbey. Which, strangely enough, did not entirely
please the Homes either. St. Adamnan's prophesy was adequately
fulfilled. Even the Reformation did not wholly end this process.
Hardly a serene history, despite its sainted origins. But then, there
is not a lot about Coldinghamshire, even today, to give any
impression of gentle calm. When easterly gales blow, and the
spume-clouds drift inland from the riven, tortured cliffs, and even
the seabirds seek shelter in the secret deans, it is not hard to sense
the drama and violence that is endemic in the place.

   Coldingham itself is a delightful village, however, almost a
little town by Scots standards (once it was a burgh of barony,
under the Earls of Home) snugly tucked away in the confluent
deep valleys of two streams—indeed so well concealed that from
even a quarter of a mile away no one would know that there was
a community there at all. It clusters, of course, round the ancient
priory—or what remains thereof, for only the choir still stands,
and even this has been shorn of much of its beauty, the Reformers'
zeal having, as so often, dinged doun almost all that was lovely
and attractive in the interests of improved religion pure and un-
defiled. The usefulness of good worked stone and building material
for erecting lairds' houses on the former church lands must not be
overlooked either.

There was a vast amount more than the mere church buildings here, of course; for it was a very large and proud establishment. That was part of the trouble and offence. It is written that "so arrayed was the office of Prior of Coldingham in the trappings of worldly glory that, unlike any other ecclesiastic in the kingdom, he maintained a retinue of seventy functionaries who bore titles, sustained appointments and shared a curious division of labour, fitting the magnificence of a princely court". Such behaviour not unnaturally drew covetous eyes and grasping steel-mailed fists, like a magnet, especially with the Homes so close around. How many times the place was seized and pillaged and burned, before the Reformation finally disposed of it, is not to be known. Tradition has it that when the priory was eventually destroyed, its great bell was taken, presumably as the spoils of war, to Lincoln, where it is still said to toll its sonorous note.

The existing cruciform building, truncated, defaced, its roof altered and flattened, is semi-Norman without and First Pointed within, and is now used as the parish kirk. Still some magnificent stone-carved work remains.

St. Abbs, renowned as a holiday village, lies over a mile to the north-east, with its harbour and lifeboat station, and one of the few stretches of sand on this rock-bound coast. A picturesque place, it nestles under the mighty 310-foot promontory of St. Abbs Head, one of the most impressive headlands of all the east coast seaboard. It is, however, less outstanding here than it would be elsewhere, just because of the challenging competition of so much around it. The cliff itself is separated from the mainland by a deep gully that was spanned by a bridge, and is crowned by a light-house visible 21 nautical miles away. Numerous caves pierce the cliffs, inaccessible from the land—and if, as claimed, they were much used by smugglers, then theirs must have been a hazardous occupation indeed, for any approach from sea is bedevilled by an endless and angry series of jagged rocks and spouting reefs, over which the seas snarl and boil on even the calmest day. Small wonder that this is a favourite haunt of the artist and those who love exciting scenery, the photographer and the bird-watcher—for these cliffs are alive with screaming, circling sea-birds. The archaeologist, too, for within a mile or so of the top of St. Abbs Head there are no fewer than seven large earth-work sites of camps, indicative of the fact that this area must have been highly populous in prehistoric days. They cluster round the rather bleak Coldingham Loch, said to be abundant with perch. When the visitor is quite exhausted with all that this glorious but savage coast has to show him, he can always go sea-bathing on the St. Abbs sands, like St. Cuthbert. It is said that when he visited the Abbess Ebba here, he used to immerse himself in the water for the best part of the night—but not for the sport of it. He came here for prayer and vigil, immersing himself until the water reached his arms and neck, it is alleged, whilst the seals came and nestled to his side. I wonder whether the good Cuthbert had that vouched for by witnesses? The seals must have been distracting, to say the least of it. No doubt there were plenty of them about then, as now. They breed in their thousands on the Farne Islands, 25 miles to the south, and haunt all this coastline near the mouth of the Tweed, where the salmon congregate to enter the river, playing great havoc with the fish. Their annual culling, to keep them down to manageable numbers, now stopped, formerly produced equally annual protests from animal-lovers. St. Abb's Head is now a nature reserve managed by the National Trust for Scotland.

The Princess Ebba chose this dramatic spot for her nunnery-monastery because she was wrecked here, and set up the establishment in gratitude for her delivery. There have been a lot of wrecks since, induced and otherwise. Indeed some of the most dramatic shipwreck photographs ever taken have come from hereabouts. And the reef-girt shore is littered with the battered remains of proud ships. It still happens, despite all the modern applicances and navigational aids.

Probably this is why Fast Castle was sited where it was, some 5 miles farther north along this awesome coast, where the wreckers plied their ghastly trade. There seems to be no other reason why anyone should seek to build a castle in such a spot, part-way down a beetling cliff hundreds of feet high, not on any shelf but precariously surmounting the fang of a semi-detached stack, only reachable from a dizzy gangway after a hair-raising descent of the cliff-face. "Imagination can scarce form a scene more striking, yet more appalling, than this rugged and ruinous stronghold, situated on an abrupt and inaccessible precipice, overhanging the raging ocean and tenanted of yore by men stormy and gloomy as the tempests they looked down upon." So wrote Sir Walter Scott about Fast Castle, prototype of his Wolf's Crag in *The Bride of Lammermuir*; and for once we can forget about artists' licence, novelists' exaggeration, and early nineteenth-century romanticism. For this is one of the most extraordinarily-placed castles in all castle-haunted Scotland, perched dizzily between sea and sky, soaring 150 feet above the waves and reefs, quite unscaleable from below and giddy-making enough of access from above to turn all but the most level of heads. The nearest road runs miles away. Whoever built a castle here was undoubtedly of a strange and stormy mind—and a bad conscience. King Jamie VI said as much, as he sailed by in a ship below. "The man who built it must have been a knave at heart!" that curious but percipient monarch is reported to have said. And he ought to have known. How many masons died at the building of it, is not recorded.

Despite Fast's customary linking with the notorious Logan of Restalrig—who may not have been quite so black as it suited some folk to paint him—this wild eagle's nest of a place was in fact a Home stronghold. Just who built it is lost in the mists of antiquity; but it was in existence in the fourteenth century, and was sometimes in English hands. Presumably it was built by, or with the consent of, one of the Cospatrick Earls of Dunbar and March, since they owned and dominated all the area at the time. We read that, on a dark night in 1410, Patrick, fourth son of the tenth Earl, managed to recapture the place from an English garrison, taking prisoner one Thomas Holden, the governor. A few years later, in 1419, we hear of Alexander Home of Wedderburn and the Prior of Coldingham (who would almost certainly be another Home) waylaying one James Colstoun and relieving him of 2,000 merks, the property of the King of England, and taking the money in bags to Fast Castle. Sir Patrick Home, fourth son of the first Lord Home—eighth in descent from the Earl's younger son who married Ada Home—was designated as of Fast Castle in 1488. He was high in the favour and counsels of James IV, as was his nephew, the second Lord, and acted as ambassador on sundry occasions. He was not always so respectable, however, for in 1463 he is said to have turned out the prior and brethren of Coldingham and occupied the place himself, with all its great lordship, without better title than a sharp sword. The Crown was not strong enough to do anything about this, in Home country. The Pope's own outraged emissary wrote: "Sir Patrick Home and John Home have ben aboutward to distresse every mandatary that takith uppon him to do . . . anything against them. I dar noght tharfore take uppon me for fere of deth to seke thair persons." Home of Fast Castle was duly excommunicated, but kept Coldingham Priory thereafter for fifteen years.

His reign at Fast was fairly typical. A famous Border murder, that of Sir Robert Ker of Caverton, Warden of the Middle March in 1500, had its echo here. The murderers—Northumbrians including the Bastard Heron from Ford Castle, and seven others—were caught and confined in Fast's grim vaults until they were dead—whether of starvation or by more violent means is not reported.

Oddly enough, three years later, it was used for a very different sort of purpose, almost unbelievable as it is. For it was considered a suitable halt and resting-place for the 14-year-old Princess Margaret Tudor, sister of Henry VIII, on her bridal journey north to wed King James. Her great train of 1,000 Scots and 500 English notables were lodged at the priory, 5 miles away; but the bride was brought to spend the night at this grim wreckers' and robbers' nest on the soaring cliff-face. What she thought of her new country if this was the first Scots house she slept in, it would be interesting to know. The only comment we have is that "there was good cheer, so that every man was content". Nothing is said as to the cheer and content of the queen-to-be and her ladies.

Sir Patrick's successor's story is equally eventful. Cuthbert, a younger son, had gone overseas on a jaunt through Christendom with King James's illegitimate favourite son, Alexander Stewart, 16-year-old Archbishop of St. Andrews, and somehow got himself captured by the Turks. "The lord of Fast Castell . . . passing into Turkie came to the emperor of Turkie at the citie of Caire, who reteined him in seruice and gaue him good intertainment so that he remained with him till he heard that the liuing of Fast Castell was fallen to him by lawfull succession; notwithstanding that when he departed out of Scotland there were eight seuerall persons before him to succeed one after other, which in the meane time were all deceased." Obviously there was a high mortality rate amongst Homes. Cuthbert had to pay a large ransom for the privilege of getting away from the Grand Turk despite the "good interteinment"—namely forty-seven sacks of Lammermuir wool, each weighing 640 pounds, to be exchanged for gold. The new laird however was little longer-lived than the rest of his line, for he died on Flodden Field with his King and Archbishop Alex three years later.

His successor at Fast was the third Lord Home himself, all the rest of the family seeming to have been wiped out—Home was one of the few survivors of Flodden. His loyalties seem to have been equivocal, to say the least of it. He was one of the nobles who invited the Duke of Albany to come from France to be Regent for the infant James V, but doesn't seem to have been long in falling out with Albany, for the English Warden, Lord Dacre, is soon writing to his Privy Council: ". . . the Lord Home will never obey the Duke without King Henry his consent, if he regards his promises. He vituals Fast Castle, meaning to do the Duke all the annoyance he can, and take refuge in England if compelled." Actually, he tried to capture the Queen Mother—the same Princess Margaret Tudor—with her children, and to bring her to Fast Castle, to use them as pawns in his game. But this attempt failed, Home was outlawed, Albany himself took the castle—and the Homes recapturing it, pulled it down rather than have it in other hands again. Lord Home was in due course executed.

The castle was rebuilt—which shows that in spite of all the inconveniences of its situation and access, it was considered highly valuable. I could go on and on about its murky adventures. But it eventually fell to an heiress, Elizabeth Home, who married Sir Robert Logan of Restalrig, near Edinburgh; and their grandson was the notorious character who so enlivened James VI's reign. There was an interesting sequel, for when this Logan died, the then Lord Home married his widow, who had been the Lady Margaret Seton, sister of one of the famed Maries of Mary Queen of Scots—and incidentally an English spy in the pay of Elizabeth. Lord Grey wrote to Somerset in 1548, that he had been sent news of the French fleet, come to aid the Scots against the English invaders, by the Lady of Fast Castle. And twenty years later, Fast was still a nest of treason, for here came secretly Elizabeth's special envoy, Sir Nicholas Throckmorton, to meet the Queen of Scots's two-faced Secretary, Maitland of Lethington—who incidentally had married another of the Queen's Maries, Mary Fleming. Also present was Sir James Melville and the said fifth Lord Home. The Queen herself was at this time imprisoned by her lords in Lochleven Castle; and these negotiations with her enemy were typical of the unsavoury politics of the period, Elizabeth paying handsome pensions to not a few Scots leaders. Throckmorton in his despatch describes Fast as "fitter to lodge prisoners than folks at lybertye, as yt is very little so yt is very strong".

I will spare the reader more of the wild doings which emanated from this savage stronghold during the desperate Logan of Restalrig's reign here, doings which brought his name constantly before the King and Privy Council, kept the East March in a ferment, and caused "his wife for to weep". It is one long catalogue of assault, theft, murder, rebellion, and "treasounable conspyring, consulting, traffiquing and devising" with the King's enemies. Because of the immunity offered to him by this extraordinary stronghold on the cliff, Logan could cock a snook at all. I will end this account of the bloodstained fortalice above the spray, by referring to a different type of incident. In 1594 Logan made a curious compact with no less an individual than the famous and respectable John Napier, Laird of Merchiston and inventor of logarithms, to search for treasure believed to be hidden somewhere in Fast Castle's difficult walls. An unusual partnership this, between the fierce and lawless freebooter and the studious mathematician and pillar of society, to hunt by means of the latter's strange arts, no doubt, for ill-gotten gold from the past ". . . to do his utter and exact diligens to serche and sik out, and be al craft and ingyne that he dow, to tempt, trye and find out the sam". However, despite all the diligence, craft and ingenuity, even the sacrificing of a jet-black cockerel, the gold seems never to have been discovered. It is interesting that recently there has been another quite ambitious treasure-hunt, using odd divining methods likewise. The instigator has published a book on the subject, plus the accompanying curse. There has been no success so far— and as the principal has suddenly died, Fast may be left severely alone again. It is perhaps significant that the name Fast is derived from *faux* or false.

Eyemouth, about the same distance south of Coldingham as

Eyemouth Harbour

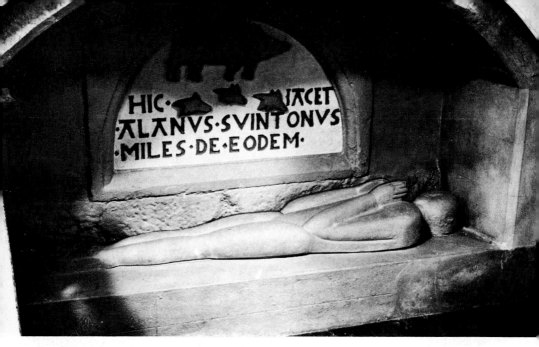

Effigy of Sir Alan de Swinton, Swinton Parish Church

Celtic cross-shaft in Rothbury church
now used as the base of the font

View of Lindisfarne Priory through the west doorway

Cragside, near Rothbury—Norman Shaw's house for the first Lord
Armstrong

Smailholm Tower

Whittingham Vale and Cheviots from above Thropton

Mire Loch looking south from St Abb's Head

Melrose Abbey

Fast is to the north, where the Eye Water finds its way to the sea through a dip in the mighty cliff wall, is by far the largest centre of the district, and its only burgh, a sturdy little fishing town. Its harbour, recently enlarged and improved at great cost—though not entirely to the satisfaction of all—dominates the town, but is itself rather curiously dominated by the squat bulk of an uncompromising mansion called Gunsgreen House, whose Home laird must surely have had some very notable reason for placing it just there. A concern for matters not unconnected with the Customs and Excise is the accepted explanation—and indeed Eyemouth was famous as a smuggling centre, with many of its older houses still able to show deep hiding-holes for use in 'the trade'. Wreckers stories abound. As a dependency of Coldingham Priory, Eyemouth served as a port of far more than mere local worth, and was important as early as the reign of Alexander II. Curiously enough, for reasons which escape me, the great general who became Duke of Marlborough, and ancestor of Sir Winston Churchill, took his first title from here, as Lord Churchill of Eyemouth in the peerage of Scotland, in 1682. And here, in 1787, came Robert Burns, recounting in his *Border Tour*: "Come up a bold shore from Berwick, and over a wild country to Eyemouth —sup and sleep at Mr. Grieve's . . . made a Royal Arch mason of St. Abbs Lodge."

In recent times, Eyemouth has been much involved in the Tweed salmon drift-net controversy, naturally—for its fishermen have been amongst the prime sufferers in the ban on drift-netting for salmon in the open sea, imposed at the behest of the Tweed Commissioners as aforementioned. How galling for these sturdy fishermen to be told that the wild and dangerous seas outside their harbour walls are, for legal, parliamentary and landed-proprietorial interests, part of the River Tweed, and not to be fished for salmon. What with foreign fishermen able to defy the ban because of the 3-mile limit, fishery-protection cruisers, the Tweed Commissioners' bailiff's launch (which once was Hitler's) and local fishermen and their boats necessarily amongst the toughest on the east coast, this area does not have to look back into history for its excitements.

With its narrow climbing streets, curious twisted alleys, closely-packed houses and air of wary watchfulness, Eyemouth is a strange place to come to at the end of long country roads through wild territory, with an atmosphere all its own. It is, in fact, the largest community and burgh in Berwickshire, even though it numbers not much more than 2,000 of population. Remember that number when you consider the disaster which struck this area in October 1881, when one of the terrible storms to which this seaboard is frequently exposed hit the fishing-fleet practically without warning, tearing out masts, capsizing even these sturdy craft, smashing others on to the wicked rocks. Of the thirty Eyemouth vessels involved, only about half a dozen got safely home. One hundred and ninety-one men were drowned, 129 from Eyemouth itself, leaving 107 widows and 351 children under 15 years of age. For weeks thereafter families searched the cruel coast for bodies of the missing men.

Eyemouth became a burgh of barony under Sir George Home of Wedderburn in 1597, with the privileges of a free port. It was made a Police Burgh in 1882, with its own provost and bailies. Although off the direct invasion route from Berwick to Lothian, it suffered its share of aggression. The English Protector Somerset erected a fort on the headland to the north of the town, guarding its use as a supply-depot for his huge invasion forces in 1547; he had no fewer than thirty transports and thirty ships of war. This was the invasion which culminated in the fatal Battle of Pinkie. This fort was destroyed, and later rebuilt by Mary of Guise; and again by Cromwell.

Perhaps one of the most interesting items in Eyemouth's story, however, concerns of all folk a lawyer. Somehow Eyemouth hardly seems a likely terrain for such. But George Sprott was obviously a rather special lawyer. He distinguished himself in Scots legal annals by getting himself hanged in place of his client —an unusual outcome of litigation. He was notary for the aforementioned Logan of Restalrig, whom King Jamie VI accused of being involved in the murky Gowrie Conspiracy, one of the nastiest pieces of royal skulduggery. Whether he was or not is hardly to the point—he was certainly capable of it. And though Logan eventually died in his bed, poor George Sprott was executed in Edinburgh in 1608, eight years after the event, with James safely in London for five years. The King obviously had a long memory.

Usually spoken of in the same breath as Eyemouth is Burn-mouth, an astonishingly placed fishing-village set at the foot of a deep cleft of the cliffs 2 miles nearer Berwick. The A1 highway passes along the top of the cliffs, where there is an inn and some modern housing. As does the railway. But hidden down in the steep ravine is this romantic-looking village, clinging like one of its own limpets to a toehold between sea and precipice, with its long, curving and so necessary breakwater. It is a tiny place; but, unlikely as it may seem, two treaties between England and Scotland were actually signed here, one in 1384 and another in 1497. It is, of course, the first true village north of the Border at Berwick Bounds.

After Eyemouth, Ayton is the largest community on the verge of Coldinghamshire, population 600—and the best-known, for before it was by-passed it lay athwart the A1 with the unending traffic pounding through. It is an attractive place, sloping down to the Eye Water with its rather good, single-arch bridge, an interesting old inn now a hotel, and the fine modern church beside its ancient ivy-grown pre-Reformation predecessor. Incidentally, the lodge-house at the church-gate was formerly a toll-house for payment of road-dues. All crouches below the dominating regard of a great redstone castle, modern Scottish Baronial but highly impressive, and on the site of an ancient fortalice of the Norman de Vescis, demolished by Surrey in 1498.

Ayton, which should really be Eye-toun, was another favoured place for the holding of official parleys between Scots and English representatives arranging truces, and the like. A famous seven-year truce was concluded here in the reigns of James IV and Henry VII, largely by the influence of the Spanish ambassador to Henry's Court, Pedro de Ayala, who seems greatly to have impressed both kings.

I have said little or nothing about the central portion of the great lozenge that is Coldinghamshire—for the good reason that there is but little to say. It consists almost entirely of high rolling moorland, many thousands of acres of it—Coldingham Moor or Common amounting to over 5,000. The strange thing about this is that, although its height averages between 500 and 700 feet above the sea, the waves themselves are often closer than that horizontally, so sheer and sudden is the drop. The aforementioned

Coldingham Loch, for instance, though at over 400 feet, has its shore within 300 yards of tide's edge. Down through the centre of this windy upland, south by east, runs the Ale Water, the principal tributary of the Eye, carving for itself in places a deep, secret and picturesque valley. It is composed of three feeder burns, which join at Threeburn Grange, above Press Castle, one of the former granges or monkish farms of the Priory. Strangely enough, Thomas the Rhymer wrote one of his prophesies about this place. So far as I know, this has not been fulfilled nor has anyone concocted even a far-fetched fulfilment for it—unlike most. It runs:

> At Threeburn Grange on an after day
> There shall be a lang and bloody fray;
> Where a three-thumbed wight by the reins shall hald
> Three kings' horses, baith stout and bauld,
> And the Three Burns three days will rin
> Wi' the blude o' the slain that fa' therein.

How long do we have to wait for that three-thumbed wight? And it must get ever more difficult to assemble three kings, especially on horseback.

Where Ale and Eye join, stands the fine old seventeenth-century laird's house of Linthill, formerly another Home stronghold. We commenced our review of Coldinghamshire with that violence-prone family; so we will end it. One night in 1752, the widow of Patrick Home of Linthill was set upon by a confidential servant named Norman Ross, and barbarously murdered. Her assailant's end was even more barbarous than that of his mistress, for he earned the distinction of being the last man in Scotland to be mutilated before execution and hanged in chains afterwards.

5

The English East March—Northumberland

IF IT is difficult to set limits to the Borderland on the Scots side, it is just as much so, if not more, on the English. Some places have a distinct Border atmosphere; and others, sometimes considerably closer to the actual Line, have not. There is no difficulty in de-limiting the East March laterally, of course, on both sides, since it runs from the sea to the Hanging Stone on Cheviot, near Auchope Cairn. But how far *down* does the East March reach from Berwick and Cheviot?

No clear line can be drawn. And the fact that the Borderline slants so drastically south-westwards further complicates matters, since it means that actual latitudes on the map have no relevance. Newcastle is in fact further north than Carlisle and parts of Scot-land; but nobody would include Newcastle in the Borders. Yet Morpeth is only 15 miles north of Newcastle, and many of its folk consider themselves Borderers. It is 48 miles south of Berwick—almost as far away as Edinburgh; though not so far from Carter Bar. And Ashington, and other coastal places much nearer the Line have no 'feel' of the Border at all; indeed, as on the Scots side, the seaboard seems to be somewhat unsympathetic to the Border tradition. We are probably well advised, therefore, to confine our attentions to places and areas which have the right atmosphere, irrespective of distances in miles—a rather eclectic procedure, but practical. Anyway, the Borders are a strange and eclectic country.

On the English side, geography and topography are against us, on the East March. There is just no comparison in aspect, character and scene—or in richness of land—between the two sides. Here is no mere Scots bias. On the coastal plain, the area south of Berwick all the way to Alnwick, nearly 30 miles, lacks drama or much in the way of beauty or character, save in small patches. The long,

shelving, sandy coast itself, by Cheswick and Goswick to Beal, has its attractions of course—endless empty beaches, smooth and featureless after the rocky stretch near Scremerston, scored only by the spidery stakes of fixed salmon-nets and backed by dunes; but it is hardly exciting. Holy Island, or Lindisfarne provides off-shore variety and character for the great tidal bay of Fenham Flats; and is, needless to say, a magnetic and highly famous place and a great asset to Northumberland. But its atmosphere is not that of the Borderland, towards which indeed it seems to turn its back. The magnificent pile of Bamburgh Castle, on its soaring rock, enlivens the stretch of flattish coast to the south, by Seahouses and Beadnell, until the superficially similar but lesser pile of Dunstan-burgh takes over that duty. Thereafter is a rather more diversified seaboard, but still flat. Craster is picturesque and Alnmouth a joy. But here we are south of Alnwick.

Inland, it is the same story. The A1 highway, and the country it traverses, from Berwick, by Scremerston and Middleton to Bel-ford, is fairly straight and dull; and if it improves somewhat, scenically, thereafter, with some undulations and woodlands, it remains essentially unexciting all the way to Morpeth—which, of course, is probably all to the advantage of a major highway. But it all savours little of the essence of the Borderland. One has to go much further west and up into the moorlands of Ancroft, Bar-moor, Duddo and Lowick, to get a different atmosphere; and even here it lacks challenge geographically and in the sense of history. It is not until the great Till valley is reached, strangely cut off from the rest and opening northwards towards the Merse of Scotland that the English Borderland really begins to come alive, with names like Ford and Etal, Branxton and Flodden, Dodding-ton and Wooler, singing their ancient songs amid scenes that rouse. And here the mighty Cheviots draw close, and thereafter it is the hillfoot villages which take up the tale of reiving and raiding, foray and fight—Kirknewton and Akeld, Powburn and Glanton, Whittington and Rothbury.

Then the empty heather and the curlew-haunted hills.

All this is a vast area, perhaps some 500 square miles. It is strange, but a fact, that most of the English East March was, by and large, less involved in all the wild and romantic upheavals which constitute the Border story than was any other part, on

Twizel Bridge

either side. Why this should be is not easy to fathom; but it is not of the northern and eastern parts of this March that the ballads sing or the tales proliferate. Probably these lands were too readily defensible from Berwick-on-Tweed, where the English monarchs took care always to maintain an independent governor and powerful garrison, irrespective of the East March Warden and his local levies. Indeed these two not infrequently clashed in their interests and loyalties, the latter so often being the Percy Earls of Northumberland or their nominees, who were by no means always on good terms with London and the ruling house. Even the main tides of invasion and foray tended to pass this area by—again because of Berwick's fortress guarding the crossing of Tweed, and with the next feasible crossing of the great river at Coldstream some 15 miles up, and which opened on to the central valley of the Till, by-passing the rest. It was by this route, therefore, or still further west by Carter Bar or Deadwater in the Middle March, that the Scots always invaded—even though thereafter they might have occasion to trend south-eastwards towards the rich pickings of Alnwick and Morpeth areas.

For present purposes, then, only a few localities may be touched upon, a few incidents recalled.

Basically, the vital point of the English East March, if Berwick is excepted, is Tillmouth. Here, just east of the Coldstream fords, is the entrance to the wide valley which leads directly and invitingly into the heart of Northumberland, a gift to all with hostile intent. And here, too, was another vital hinge, Twizel Bridge, "greate and strong and of one bow". The Till itself constitutes a major barrier, for it is deeper if less wide than Tweed, and a hazard to cross, with few bridges in its lower course. As its name implies there was a ford at Ford, some 5 miles up, where there is now a bridge; but this was by no means always passable and was guarded by its own strong castle; and there was no other crossing for a long way. So Twizel bridge was the effective link with Berwick and all the eastern and seaboard lands south of Tweed. Any invading army had only to take and hold it, to form an enormously strong salient, and to ensure that their left flank at least was secure. To aggressors and defenders alike, Tillmouth and Twizel were all-important, and they played a significant part in history. Yet, strangely enough, little appears to have been written about them, or their importance recognized, by historians and authors of books dealing with Northumberland and the Border area.

Twizel is, of course, renowned in a sad way, for the part it played in Surrey's strategy before the Battle of Flodden, when Scotland's splendid army was outflanked on the hills of Flodden and Branxton Edge, 4 miles to the south, the English commander having made his dramatic secret march down the east side of Till, to cross at Twizel behind the Scots—something which the chivalrous-to-a-fault King James IV doesn't appear even to have considered. Just why this most elementary precaution, of strongly holding the bridge, was omitted we shall probably never know; it remains one of the mysteries of history. The veteran Earl of Angus, Bell-the-Cat, is said to have remonstrated with the King that he ought to swoop down from their strong positions on the high ground and attack Surrey while he was crossing the bridge; and the Lord Borthwick, Master of Artillery, actually fell on his knees imploring James to allow him to open fire on the columns at the crossing. James's refusal, on the score that this would be to take an unfair advantage of the enemy, and that they would fight it out on equal terms on a plain field, was utter chivalric folly admittedly; but the fact remains that nobody seems to have thought of leaving the bridge held and garrisoned, Angus, Borthwick, or any other of the host of Scots notables.

Legend has its own answer to this grievous omission, of course. Heaven itself was involved, to punish James for a broken vow. All know how the young King, although a pawn in the hands of ambitious nobles, felt himself to be partially responsible for the death of his father, James III, at Sauchieburn, twenty-five years before, and thereupon vowed to wear an iron chain round his loins for the rest of his life, as penance and reminder. This itself is no legend, for every few years thereafter the Lord Treasurer's Accounts debit an amount for "ane link for the King's chain", indicative of increasing royal girth. All his days James wore this sore reminder. And then, on this strangely romantic invasion of England in 1513, done at the behest of the Queen of France, who sent him her glove and besought him to "move a yard into England and break a lance for my sake"—how well she knew her James—in order to take some of Henry VIII's armed pressure off the Scots' French allies—then, James, tarrying at Ford Castle here, and dallying with the beautious Lady Heron, put off his chain at last. The story goes that she coaxed him to it, with her beautiful body, something no other woman had been able to do—although it must have been an uncomfortable appendage for love-making. At any rate, James Stewart is said not to have been wearing his chain in the days that preceded Flodden; and superstitious, shattered and appalled Scotland thereafter, in the greatest and most terrible defeat in its history, did not have far to look for the cause, or the reasons for such contributory factors as the failure to hold Twizel Bridge.

The names of Tillmouth and Twizel are commonly almost interchangeable, and seem to have been used indiscriminately for long. This is hardly to be wondered at, although they are by no means identical. Tillmouth is the greater, and should include the lesser. It is, of course, the area where Till joins Tweed, and was a lordship of the Riddell family, still strong in the neighbourhood, from very early times. Strangely enough it was not in those days considered to be part of Northumberland at all, but situated in Norhamshire, another ecclesiastical jurisdiction like Coldinghamshire, but this time part of the Bishopric and County Palatine of Durham. The term Norham and Islandshires is still extant as a part of Northumberland—the islands referred to being Holy Island and the Farnes, which also belonged to the See of Durham. Tillmouth was held of the Prince-Bishop thereof for the token rent of half-a-knight's fee; and in the thirteenth century the holder was Jordan Riddell. The last of this stem, Sir William Riddell, died in 1325, leaving only daughters, one of whom carried Tillmouth to Sir Alan de Clavering her husband. The Claverings held the lands for many generations.

It has come to be assumed that Twizel is on the east bank of Till, and Tillmouth on the west, which is not quite accurate since both were in Tillmouth lordship. Admittedly there is a Twizel Mill half a mile further upstream on that side, and right down at Tweedside is Twizelhaugh, the green flat where the Scots army encamped after crossing the Tweed fords eighteen days before Flodden; moreover the present great demesne of Tillmouth Park, now a hotel, lies on the west bank. But the lords of Tillmouth seem to have lived at *Twizel* Castle. There is now a somewhat sham ruin on the site, a little way below the bridge, called that; but a map of

1513 shows *Tillmouth* Castle marked there, on the east side. All very confusing. The puzzle is somewhat resolved, however, by a royal survey of 1561 which declares that at Twizel there is "one towre, or pile, which is of auncyent time decayed and castdowne, and there remayneth one parte or quarter thereof, and a barnkin about it". It goes on to add: "In the same towne is a little towre or pile, much in decay, and a little barnkin about ye same ... Robertus Clauerynge, armiger, tenet vill. de Tilnemouth."

Obviously, then, there have been *two* castles here; though one of them would be probably no more than what is usually called a bastel-house in the Borderland, for the protection of villagers and tenants. So we have the lordship and a village, now disappeared but still so described in 1825, dependent on the manor-place, and the lord's castle named Twizel, with the bridge. How the latter came to be transferred from the east to the west side makes quite an interesting story, and of much more than merely local importance.

The clues to this are given in another Border Survey of 1542; the English seem even then to have been much more bureaucratically minded than the Scots, and always making surveys. This says: "At Twysle ... there is standing the walls of an old fortresse or castell, rased and caste downe by the Kinge of Scotts in a warre xl yeres and more since." Obviously this was not the affair that ended in Flodden, which was only twenty-nine years before 1542. It was in fact a campaign of seventeen years earlier, which has been largely overlooked in history-books, overshadowed by the dramatic disaster of 1513. A young man, Perkin Warbeck by name, arrived in Scotland in 1494, naming himself the Duke of York and true heir to the English throne. He alleged that he was one of the two famous Princes in the Tower, sons of Edward IV, who had been imprisoned and then reputedly murdered by their ambitious and ruthless uncle, Richard Crookback, Richard III— the same who engineered Berwick's transfer to England by blackmail. Scotland's dashing and highly popular James IV, whether he believed the story or not—and it was supported by the Duchess of Burgundy, sister of the late Edward IV and therefore aunt of the princes—took up Perkin and used him as a weapon to strike at Henry VII, who had twice endeavoured to have James poisoned. With Perkin magnificently clad and escorted as Duke of York,

James crossed Tweed at this same point, calling on all loyal Englishmen to rise in favour of their rightful Plantagenet king and throw out the usurping Tudor Henry. Unfortunately or otherwise, the cautious English did no such thing, and James and his protégé found themselves looked upon as invaders, not deliverers. There was no real warfare, however, for James insisted that it was not a hostile expedition; and Henry ignored the whole affair with masterly inactivity. The Scots kicking their heels, with nothing to do, faced the choice of marching on the long road towards London through a hostile country, on behalf of a very doubtful claimant to the throne; or else rather ignominiously returning whence they had come. They salved their pride by attacking, casting down and burning sundry castles and strengths—allegedly against James's orders. It must be remembered, in this connection, that these were not royal or national troops, for the Kings of Scots had no standing army but were dependent upon the unruly levies of equally unruly lords. Perkin Warbeck, imposter or none, seems to have been a young man of some principles, for he protested vigorously to James over the attacks on English houses, including Twizel, Tillmouth and Duddo, all belonging to the Claverings, declaring that he would be iron-hearted indeed not to be moved by the sufferings of his own people. James, rather sourly for that gallant individual, retorted: "You seem to worry yourself over what does not concern you, for you have called . . . the English your subjects; yet not one of them has offered to help in a war waged on your behalf."

Perkin, offended, returned to Scotland forthwith, while James stayed a few days longer besieging the strong castle of Heiton, 2 miles further up Till. Then, on hearing that an English army was at last heading north from Newcastle, and recognizing that he was daily suffering major desertions of his bored and plundering levies, he ingloriously "with his hool power retourned and stale away into Scotland". It is thought by some that the humiliation over this abortive and bungled affair was largely responsible for James's return seventeen years later, with the greatest and most splendid army Scotland had ever fielded, to lead all to utter catastrophe at Flodden, one of the most extraordinary and unlooked-for incidents in all Scottish-English history. So that in both these affrays Tillmouth and Twizel were prominently involved. The shattered castle of Twizel was never rebuilt. The property passed to the Blake family towards the end of the seventeenth century, and they built a new house to the west, on the site of the present park. Later, one of them built up the old ruin in the form of a folly, or mock-ruin, in typical Romantic late eighteenth-century style.

Norham Castle lies 3 miles north by east of Tillmouth, in another bend of the Tweed, opposite Ladykirk on the Scots side. Here is a delightful village, with an ancient although not very happily restored church, and a market cross. The castle is a renowned place, even in its ruins highly impressive, a massive and lofty square keep set above steep banks, with a ravine guarding one side and artificial moat the rest. It must have been a magnificent pile in its day, well supporting the lofty pride of its prince-bishops. Although started as a timber castle in 1121 by Bishop Flambard, this great stone keep, outer and inner baileys and gatehouses were completed fifty years later. But it suffered much battering and alteration down the centuries, so that the present remains represent a number of periods of building. David I captured it twice. His grandson, King William the Lion, made a treaty with King John of England here, but a few years later was besieging the place again. Edward I made it his headquarters in 1291, when he was commencing his campaign of king-making to trick Scotland into accepting him as overlord—the castle's then master, Bishop Anthony Beck, being one of Edward's favourite and toughest commanders. Here, a year later, the Scots Guardians, to their shame, swore fealty to Edward as Lord Paramount. So strong was this hold that, after Bannockburn in 1314, when Bruce carried fire and sword as far south as York, only Norham Castle, with the fortresses of Berwick and Carlisle, remained in English hands north of Richmond. It was still holding out thirteen years later, for we read that Bruce chose to make a sudden and secret assault upon it, for propaganda purposes, in 1327, on the very day that Edward II was deposed and his son, Edward III, aged 14, was crowned in his stead. Actually, on this occasion, the surprise would probably have been successful had not a Scots member of the English garrison got word of the attack, and warned the goverror. He may have been a de Soulis supporter, who was against the King of Scots. Bruce was still besieging Norham in 1328, a sick man and within a year of his death, when at last he gained the treaty of peace with England for which he had been striving in the fifteen years since Bannockburn.

Norham was sufficiently powerful to be free of all local raids and Border frays; but it was a magnet for trouble on a national scale. During the fifteenth century it was just as much involved as in the previous two, being taken and held now by the Yorkists and now by the Lancastrians in the Wars of the Roses, being unsuccessfully besieged by James IV in his Perkin Warbeck invasion and seriously damaged by him again before Flodden. It finally fell a victim to the word, rather than the sword, for the Reformation really spelt the end of its power, it passing out of the hands of the influential prince-bishops at last in 1559. Walter Scott uses Norham at the start of his *Marmion*—as well he might.

An equal distance on the other side of Tillmouth, facing across Tweed to Scotland, is the sister castle of Wark—not to be confused with the Wark Castle of the Lordship of Tynedale, near Hexham. Wark, of course, is the same word as work, meaning structure or building, and there are many so named, especially with the prefix of New. This one seems always to have been a royal, or state, castle. But sadly little remains of a formerly great stronghold, only grassy mounds and foundations on its green motte-hill above the river. But considering the number of times it was assaulted, bombarded, battered and burned, this is hardly surprising. It had not Norham's advantage of belonging to Holy Church—even though the Scots were not altogether inhibited from laying violent hands on ecclesiastical property when occasion warranted; but it probably did help, a little. At any rate, Wark was taken no fewer than seven times by the Scots in four centuries of Border warfare—and attacked without actually falling many more times. It was here, Froissart tells us, took place the famous incident which led to the institution of the Order of the Garter, in 1348, with its notable motto of *Honi soit qui mal y pense*, which has companioned the royal arms of England, and thereafter of the United Kingdom, ever since. The story goes that Edward III was here with his Court, two years after Crécy. Just what he was doing on the Border, when all his preoccupations at this period tended to be with France, is not specified. But it may be that it had to do with the murky business involving his younger son, Lionel, Duke of Ulster, who was intriguing with certain

Border lords, especially the influential Henry Percy and Ralph Neville, to get *him* made King of Scots instead of Edward Baliol whom they were supposed to be supporting in that effort—while Bruce's young son, David II, was held prisoner in England. It could well be that Edward would frown strongly on such un-official adventure on his son's part. At any rate something had brought the King, with his Queen Philippa, all the way to Tweed. And, dancing in the Great Hall at Wark one night, one of the Queen's ladies, the Countess of Salisbury, had the misfortune to drop her garter on the floor—no doubt to her considerable embar-rassment. Worse still, the King not only noticed it, but stooped to pick it up, and to hold it aloft. But not, it transpired, to snigger or make a joke of it. Presumably others of the company were doing just that, for the royal reproof was swift and stern. "Evil be to him who evil thinks!" he declared. And the accusation has echoed down the centuries—even though it does seem rather a massive hammer with which to crack so small a nut. It is not surprising that he said it in French, for this was still the language of the Court. What is surprising is that a great Order of Chivalry should arise out of this unimportant and far from characteristically chival-ric incident—something that has always puzzled me. As the *raison d'être* for the institution of England's first actual Order of Knight-hood, something of tremendous significance and royal and national pride, in those days, it just does not seem to ring true, somehow. I am sure that there is more in this than meets the eye.

Wark had the distinction of falling one time—on this occasion from Scots back into English hands—owing to a preoccupation with sanitation, a highly unusual concern in those days. It was in 1419, and it so happened that a flue from the castle's 'disposal system' had been constructed to carry the effluent down to the river-bank. It must have been a large one, suitable for a royal castle; and known, no doubt, to one of the former staff. For up this unprepossessing sewer crawled a band of dedicated Northum-brians one night, to get inside the castle, where they were able to surprise and slay the entire Scots garrison. Obviously there is a moral here, somewhere.

It is between the villages of Cornhill and Wark that the Border-line takes its strange little diversion southwards, away from Tweed for almost half a mile. And here were fought two national-scale battles, both called 'of Carham', this being Carham parish, and one at least of major significance. The first, fought in 833 between invading Danes and English defenders, was notable amongst the many such affrays in that there fell no fewer than eleven bishops. If this seems scarcely credible, it must be remembered that in the early Church bishops were not the diocesan potentates they became under the Romish polity, and there would be more of them on the ground; but still, there seems to have been no doubt about the Church Militant in the ninth century. The second Battle of Carham took place in 1018, and in fact decided that the Border-line should be drawn here, along Tweed, rather than far to the north along Forth. For this was the contest which finally included Lothian in Scotland, fought between Malcolm II and the Earl of Northumbria and the Angles. The Angles at this period were dominating all the area between Tees and Forth; and Malcolm collected the greatest army Scotland had ever seen and led them south from Perthshire. It is related that a comet had appeared in the sky, and shone for thirty nights beforehand—which seems to have unnerved the Angles rather than the Scots, for some reason. At any rate, they lost the battle. At the time it was considered one of the greatest disasters ever to befall the English.

It may be interesting here to note that King Malcolm, the victor, when he died sixteen years later, left only two daughters, Bethoc and Donada. Bethoc married Crinan, Hereditary Abbot of Dunkeld in the old Celtic Church; Donada married Finlay, Mormaor of Moray and produced MacBeth. Bethoc had two sons, Duncan succeeding his grandfather as Duncan the First, later slain by MacBeth who became king instead; and the second son, Maldred, ruler of the Strathclyde sub-kingdom of Cumbria, married the heiress of the same Earl of Northumbria who lost the Battle of Carham. It was *their* son, Cospatrick, Earl of Northumbria, who was driven out of Northumberland by the Normans, came back to Scotland, was created Earl of Dunbar and March and founded that august, semi-royal line—and therefore the Home family. Maldred had another son, illegitimate, who stayed put, accepted Norman rule and founded the Neville line of Raby here, of whom we have just been reading. That is the

Borderland. When you read about mixed loyalties therein, recollect this sort of thing.

All this part of the English East March seems to centre round Flodden. The site of the great battle—not truly at Flodden at all, but at Branxton—is only from 4 to 8 miles from all these places mentioned. Here is no place to enter into any description or discussion of that famous occasion, which can be read about in books innumerable. But what may perhaps be apt for mention is that here may be seen annually the only true expression of the Border march-riding spirit on English soil. But not by the English. For to the Field of Flodden, each year, as part of the Coldstream Common Riding celebrations, comes a cavalcade of riders and a flock of folk on foot and in cars, to pay homage to the 'brave of both nations'. It is a notable occasion, by the simple granite cross under Branxton Edge, moving, significant. Yet perhaps the most significant thing about it is the fact that though both nations are commemorated, only one nation is represented. For this is a Scots affair; and though efforts have been made to involve the local Northumbrians in the ceremonial, this never seems to come to anything. I myself had the privilege, one year, of making the oration at this ride-out; and it was most evident that though there was a large crowd and much cheerful excitement, practically all of it emanated from across the Tweed.

Here is a problem which intrigues me. Border history being what it is, necessarily a two-way business, why is it that this extraordinary, colourful and vital common- or march-riding tradition, enshrining that history, is confined to the Scots side? Or almost entirely so. Every single Scots burgh within 20 miles or so of the Borderline has its march-riding festival, the most important week in its year. Yet the corresponding English communities, originally equally involved in what it is all about, do no such thing. I know that certain towns have an occasional ceremony of perambulating the bounds—Berwick and Morpeth do this, for instance; but it is a brief, minor and intermittent municipal function. Nothing to be compared with the whole-hearted and extended Scots excitements. Strange, when the Northumbrian and Cumbrian towns are just made for this sort of activity. Romantic Alnwick within its castellated walls; smiling douce Rothbury in its fair valley; battle-scarred Hexham on its proud hill; Haltwhistle, which was claimed to be part of Scotland once; Wooler, Bellingham, Belford and the rest. And Carlisle, needless to say. Why not? The raids and forays and ongoings which the Scots celebrate so lustily, were perpetrated against these very places—which were by no means backward in returning the compliment, in those old days. Why not today? Such affairs are most admirable instigators of local patriotism, civic pride and community consciousness—all so much needed in these days of mass-media and centralized control, when all concerned in local government are desperately aware of the need for communal individuality and identity—assets to the towns concerned. It is Hexham's Priory flag which is carried with such aplomb by the Cornet at the Hawick Common Riding—or a replacement of that venerable banner. Why doesn't Hexham play up? I make Hexham folk forcibly try to take that banner back, in my novel *Cheviot Chase*—and in fact, after publication thereof, some young people did make a gesture at the next Hawick festival. But it was a very minor and individual gesture only. Could not the *town* do something? Could it not rise to the challenge? The people—is it sacrilege to suggest it?—are really very much alike. They look alike, sound similar, and have so much in common. They are basically of the same racial stock in the main, separated only by a few miles of green Cheviots or sheep-dotted moors. And the English side is a horse-riding, fox-hunting country with no lack of the necessary riding talent. And I imagine they have just about as long memories as their Scots counterparts. So what is wrong?

Perhaps the fact that burghs, or rather boroughs, are so scarce on the English side is partially responsible. This is a strange thing, presumably rooted in the long-standing polities and attitudes of the countries concerned. Many communities in Northumberland and Cumberland are larger than their Scots opposite numbers; yet they are not boroughs, self-governing municipalities, with their own mayors, town councils and organized municipal identities. Hexham, Alnwick, Rothbury, Wooler, Haltwhistle and others, are governed merely by rural district councils under the local authorities. Whereas the Scots towns were all burghs—even little Lauder, on the edge of the Merse, with 640 of population, is a royal burgh, and maintains its own fine annual common-riding. There is a significance in this, I feel—and England is the loser. I shall deal with the common-riding phenomena more fully under the Middle March, where it reaches its finest flowering. It is sincerely to be hoped that the recent comprehensive 'reform' of local government in Scotland, which does away with town and county councils, does not not in any way harm these excellent activities.

No account dealing however sketchily and selectively with the English East March could omit mention of Alnwick. This is one of the most picturesque and dramatic little towns in the two kingdoms, dominated by its great castle—just as its story has been dominated by the doings of the House of Percy, lords thereof. Nevertheless, it has very much its own authentic challenge and character. Although nowadays it has spread some way outside its containing walls, it is still very essentially a walled town. Traffic, indeed, is left in no doubts about the matter, as it queues from the busy A1, although now the main highway itself by-passes the town centre. The narrow defensive gates still represent a hazard, as they were meant to do. Most of the walls and gates, with evocative names like Pottergate, Bondgate Within and Without, Narrow Gate and so on—though again, these should be spelt 'gait', meaning street, to distinguish them from the true gates, or ports—most of the defences date from the mid-fifteenth century, when the second Percy Earl of Northumberland fortified the place as protection against the Scots. The massive Hotspur Tower, with its narrow tunnel of roadway, spanning the route from the south, its bulk known to all travellers even if its story is not, was built in 1450—although the famous Hotspur himself, Henry Percy, father of the builder, fell at the Battle of Shrewsbury in 1403. This fiery customer, whom Shakespeare brings into *Henry IV*—against which monarch he was fighting at Shrewsbury—was the son of the third Percy of Alnwick first Earl of Northumberland of that line. But he never became earl himself, managing to get killed before his father—who fell at Bramham Moor. (Incidentally, his son, who succeeded his grandfather as second Earl was killed at the battle of St. Albans in 1455; and four of *his* sons were slain in the Wars of the Roses.) The Percys were as turbulent a lot as their opposite numbers on the Scots side, the Douglases, and true Borderers in that they were just as likely to fall fighting against their own monarchs as for them.

Although Otterburn itself is in the Middle March, not the East, this is probably as apt a moment as any to make some reference to that extraordinary conflict, renowned as the source of more than one ballad, and perhaps better known in England as Chevy Chase. Alnwick was much involved in this rather mysterious affair, on which no two accounts ever seem to agree. Indeed so contradictory and unlikely are many of the alleged details of the chroniclers, perpetuated and improved upon by the balladists, that many folk have come to the conclusion that the entire proceedings were no more than a romantic fiction. But this is not so. There was a Battle of Otterburn, and Alnwick, like Newcastle, suffered. In fact the walls we see today probably owed their building largely to the business.

It makes a tangled skein to unravel. In 1388 Robert II of Scotland, Bruce's grandson, was nearing the end of his amiable but rather feekless reign. He was no warrior, despite his grandfather—and unfortunately or otherwise, there were a great many more rousing and king-sized characters in his warlike realm than himself—including four of his own sons, who were in fact quite out of control. These, the Earls of Fife, Buchan and Strathearn, and the Lord of Brechin, despairing of stirring their lethargic and unmilitary sire into suitable action against the Auld Enemy, with or without his permission concocted a major expedition into England, in company with that puissant warrior, James, second Earl of Douglas—who was married to their sister Isobel. He was the grand-nephew of the famous Black Douglas, the Good Sir James, Bruce's friend, and, 34 at the time, Scotland's most renowned soldier. Just what his objective was in agreeing to the wild young princes' suggestion, we do not know. But, by what transpired, almost certainly it was not unconnected with the Douglas feud with the Percys, already by then well established. These two were hereditary Wardens of their respective Marches.

At any rate, in the autumn of 1388, with the harvest safely in, a most ambitious if unofficial invasion took place. The start of the Scots ballad gives a totally wrong impression:

> It fell about the Lammas tide, when muir-men win their hay;
> The doughty Douglas bound him to ride into England to drive
> a prey.

This seems to imply no more than a Border raid, a reiving. But when we read that the force consisted of no less than 3,000 cavalry, largely knights, lairds and esquires, young bloods generally, and 40,000 foot, we get a different picture. I have no doubt that these figures are an exaggeration; but from the many great nobles involved, all able to field large numbers of men-at-arms, it is probable that it was indeed a very large army. It made a two-pronged entry into England, half the force, under three of the King's sons, assailing Cumberland and Westmorland, via Carlisle; and the force we are concerned with, under Douglas, his brother the Earl of Moray, and that royal ruffian the Earl of Buchan—none other than the notorious Wolf of Badenoch—marched directly south, by-passing Berwick, spreading fire and terror throughout Northumberland, to fall upon Alnwick, not find Hotspur there, and proceed on to Newcastle, where it seemed that Henry Percy was installed for the time being.

Just what happened at Newcastle is not clear. Presumably Hotspur was not in a position to do full battle at this stage. There was some sort of indecisive skirmish before the city, in which the Scots had the best of it—for at least Douglas was able to capture the Percys' precious pennon. Evidently Hotspur retired behind the city walls; and Douglas thereafter gleefully promenaded below —out of bowshot, presumably—parading the flag and declaring that he would carry it back to Scotland and plant it in some shameful spot on his castle of Dalkeith, for all to behold. "That thou shalt not!" the furious Percy shouted back—but had to defer action for the moment. At any rate, the Scots, well laden with booty and prisoners, satisfied seemingly with their expedition to date, without siege-engines to assault the fortified city itself, retired northwards, and in due course camped for the night at Otterburn, in Redesdale, 16 miles from the Border at Carter Bar.

It was bright moonlight, and the Scots could have continued their retiral and reached home soil had they so desired. But the chroniclers all indicate that Douglas was deliberately waiting for Percy—some say had indeed challenged him to meet there. It was still very much the age of chivalry, however barbarous much that masqueraded under that name:

Yet I will stay at Otterbourne, where you shall welcome be;
And if you come not at three days end, a fause lord I'll ca' thee!

Thither will I come, proud Percy said, by the might of Our Ladye!
There will I bide thee, said the Douglas, my troth I plight to thee.

This all makes rather a nonsense of what is alleged to have followed, for the ballads at least all agree that the Douglas was taken
by surprise, indeed was fast asleep, with most of his army, and was
only roused by a page bringing the word that the English were
upon them. Moreover the Earl had taken off, or much loosened
his armour, and had to be harnessed up again in haste. This is
important, for whatever else may be poetic licence, this fact was
borne out by events.

They had camped in the marshy bottom-land of the Rede—
deliberately no doubt, so that the ground would be too soft for
cavalry charging, an elementary precaution. The battle that followed, therefore, took place on foot, contrary to normal chivalric
and knightly preference.

The Scots and English versions of the battle vary greatly—not
unusual. English sources make Percy's force about 9,000 strong—
pretty good at a few hours' rustling up—and they came up first
against the Scots horse and baggage lines, losing precious time and
surprise in fighting these humble folk, while Douglas, on foot, led
his knights round in the shadows and scrubland of the higher
ground, to fall on the Percy unexpectedly in flank. The English
say that Percy, discovering that his lordly opponents were on foot,
gallantly ordered his own people to dismount, to fight on equal
terms. But if in fact the contest was fought in the soft bottom-
land, this would be necessary anyway.

So they fought it out, there in the moonlight, many thousands
of men. We cannot be certain that Douglas and Percy in fact came
face to face—even though this was presumably the object of the
exercise. The romantic balladists say that the two heroes had what
amounted to a Homeric duel, swipe for swipe, the Englishman
eventually having the best of it and felling Douglas to the ground
—and then weeping tears over his fallen rival. But the chroniclers,
who are more to be believed since they were at least writing alleged
history rather than frank entertainment, have it that the two
leaders did not actually meet, though Douglas fell when trying to
get at Hotspur. There is much interesting detail which I cannot go
into here; but the latter interpretation seems to be verified in that

always this has been known in Scotland as the occasion when "a dead man won the battle". Scots tradition has it that the Douglas was struck down, from behind, through a gap in his improperly laced-up armour; and falling, urged his companions to carry on as though he was still alive, shouting his slogan of "A Douglas! A Douglas!" so dreaded in those days. None were to know that he had fallen. Which they did, and in due course the Scots did win, believing their renowned earl was still leading. This, of course, would have been impossible had Douglas and Percy been fighting it out, known to each other, and with the English leadership witnesses of Douglas's death.

A subsidiary Scots tradition, little known save in the Aberlady area of East Lothian, where I live, is that Douglas was in fact struck down by Bickerton of Luffness, his own armour-bearer, who bore him a grudge for some reason—and who was later hounded down and slain here, at Aberlady, by other Douglases. There is a circumstantial ring about this, for only his armour-bearer, whose duty it was to harness his lord up properly, could have known that there was a gap in Douglas's armour sufficient to insert the fatal dirk. Knights in those days were highly efficiently encased in steel.

Be all that as it may, though Douglas died, the English lost the night, and both Percy and his brother, Sir Ralph, Seneschal of York, were captured. It is interesting to note that Hotspur's actual captor was Sir John Montgomery, ancestor of the Earls of Eglinton; and that, as ransom, the doughty Percy had to build for Montgomery the castle of Polnoon, near Eaglesham, Renfrewshire, which for a time was chief seat of that earldom. The chroniclers give the losses in this very strange encounter as 1,860 killed, over 1,000 wounded, and 1,040 captured, on the English side—and 100 dead and 200 missing on the Scots! Which sounds unlikely, to say the least. Considerably later, the English balladists got busy with these figures, and amended them thus: "Of four and forty thousand Scots but eighteen got away"! And of the English 9,000, only 500 survived. So much for imaginative reportage.

There was a great deal more to the Battle of Otterburn than this, of course—but not for recording here. What happened to the other prong of the Scots invasion seems never to have been adequately reported—at least not by the chroniclers. At any rate, the

King's four sons all got safely home—which, in the circumstances, was perhaps a pity. Scotland could certainly have done without three of them!

An old and tangled story? But with its own significance, revealing much of the wild yet chivalric spirit which permeated the Borderland.

Alnwick is deservedly renowned for its walls, gates, narrow streets, and the quite magnificent and well-known castle of the Percy Dukes of Northumberland. But less well known is the fact that there was an abbey here. It was founded by the Percys' predecessors, the de Vescis, in 1147, a Premonstratensian establishment; and its remains lie just within the entrance to Hulne Park. Little survives of a great religious institution, save a fourteenth-century gatehouse bearing the arms of the Percys. This is not to be confused with Hulne Priory, a somewhat lesser Carmelite religious house, whose better-preserved remains lie 3 miles up the Aln, and which was founded by another de Vesci who went on a Crusade to the Holy Land, found a Northumbrian monk at the monastery on Mount Carmel, and brought him home to found this priory beside a hill which allegedly bore a strong resemblance to Mount Carmel. Needless to say, the establishment had a strong defensive tower incorporated, as refuge for the friars from the unspeakable Scots.

6

The Scots Middle March—Tweeddale

To MOST people, probably, in Scotland at least, when the Borders are mentioned it will be the Middle March that is first thought of. For this section of the whole is the Borderland *par excellence*, the essence of it all, a world unto itself, the ballad country, the peel-tower and abbey country, the Scott country; the land of the Douglases and the Kerrs, the Scotts and Turnbulls and Elliots; the hosiery and tweed country, the rugby-playing and fox-hunting and common-riding country. It is also the most populous area. Here are the sturdy, independent burghs such as Hawick and Kelso, Selkirk and Galashiels, Jedburgh and Peebles, names that have resounded for their character and quality and individuality, for long centuries.

The Middle March runs, laterally, from The Cheviot to the Kershope Burn, a distance of some 40 very wild and twisting miles. In depth, back from that line, who can say how far it goes? Twenty miles in some places, more in others, depending on this so elusive yet highly distinctive Border atmosphere. But if we average a depth of 20 miles, that gives us 800 square miles of the Scots Middle March country—a large and notable territory by any standards. It will be convenient, for our present purposes, to divide this into three, since divided it must be, which we might term Tweeddale, Teviotdale and Ettrick and Yarrow—though a deal more than these main valleys are involved in each, needless to say. They make as apt a grouping, geographically and historically, as any.

To deal with Tweed first since already we have traced its lower course through the East March. This magnificent river is, of course, one of Scotland's greatest, coming next after Tay and Clyde in actual length—118, 106 and 97 miles respectively; but yielding place to none in character, beauty and sheer worth. It rises at 1,500 feet, at Tweed Wells, high in the lonely Tweedsmuir hills some 8 miles north of Moffat, where Peeblesshire, Dumfriesshire and

Lanarkshire join, actually nearer to the Atlantic than the North Sea coast. Oddly enough, Clyde rises less than a mile away; and not only Clyde, but the great Dumfriesshire river, Annan. So that the ancient rhyme speaks true:

> Annan, Tweed and Clyde
> Rise a' oot o' ae hillside.

At first Tweed flows northwards through the empty heather hills, for 15 miles, gaining strength from a host of hill burns coming out of many remote and attractive glens, before turning eastwards towards Peebles, Melrose, Kelso, and eventually Coldstream and Berwick, draining a watershed of no less than 1,870 square miles in the process. At its most northerly point it is almost 40 miles from the nearest stretch of the Border-line; yet it would be a brave man who declared that anywhere Tweed was less than a Border river.

The Kelso area, although definitely in the Middle March, has something of the Merse about it, a low-lying gentleness of scenery which marks it off as vastly different from the rest—and is as totally misleading as far as character and history go. This district, needless to say, had to be more than tough to survive at all as a populated area, so close to the easiest approaches from England, so lacking in natural defensive features. Situated where Tweed and Teviot join, and south-facing towards the Cheviots across a green plain, Kelso is without doubt the most attractive but atypical town of the entire Borderland. It was never a walled or defensive place, being in reality the abbey-town, relying presumably, however often it was disappointed, on the great religious house for its protection; while the castle-town, which was defensible, lay under the shadow of the mighty fortress of Roxburgh a mile up Teviot. Roxburgh Castle's proximity, however, tended to be more of a liability than an asset since it was the first major target of so many invasions, the key to the middle Border, so that Kelso became a highly convenient base for assaulters—and suffered after the fashion of communities which provide comfort, shelter and womenfolk for invading armies. Nothing remains of great Roxburgh today, no trace of its town, and only tall green banks between the two rivers, with humps of masonry, to show where was one of the mightiest royal fortresses in two kingdoms. Yet the town was one of the original four royal burghs of Scotland, a

Melrose Abbey

walled city with three churches, schools, even the Royal Mint, and so many houses that a new town had to be built to contain the overflow, as early as the twelfth century—the site of the present tiny village of Roxburgh. That such an important community should vanish, entirely without trace, is one of the mysteries of the Borderland. The castle, as often in English hands as Scots, was the scene of some of the most stirring events of Border history. Captured by Edward I, it remained in English occupation during most of the Wars of Independence, a scourge to Scotland. And here was hung, in a cage over the walling, Bruce's sister Mary, on Edward's personal command, from 1306 to 1310, partnering the better-known caging of the Countess of Buchan at Berwick, appalling savagery scarcely believable today. The Good Sir James Douglas succeeded in recapturing it three years later. But in 1332, the puppet usurper, Edward Baliol, surrendered it, along with the independence of Scotland, to Edward III, alienating castle, town and country of Roxburgh as an annexation to England. Needless to say, this shameful deed was soon overturned; but the subsequent Kings of Scots, however hard they tried, could not oust the English garrison from the castle. And here, still making the attempt in 1460, more than a century later, James II died when one of his cannon burst. A yew-tree, in Floors Castle grounds to the north, marks the spot. But at least that siege *was* successful, and his widow, Queen Mary of Gueldres, then dismantled the awkward stronghold. Typically enough, it was the English who again rebuilt it, in 1547. But in half a century or so the two kingdoms were united under James VI, and at last peace came to Roxburgh.

Nearby Kelso and its abbey did not escape throughout this long travail, the latter especially being a positive magnet for avaricious raiders, so rich it became. Not always realized is the fact that Kelso, or Calkou as it was originally called, was something of an afterthought, ecclesiastically. For this Tironensian abbey was actually founded at *Selkirk*, 22 miles up Tweed, in 1113; but removed down to Kelso thirteen years later, for undisclosed reasons—probably because of the infinitely more valuable lands there, and its Abbot Herbert, Chamberlain of Scotland, was ambitious. Certainly it grew to be a prize indeed for those prepared to risk excommunication, possessing the revenues of thirty-three parishes—one as far away as Aberdeenshire—the Priory of Lesmahagow, innumerable manors, farms and granges, the fishings of the Tweed, the fines and forfeitures of Berwick town and county, and so on. Its mitred abbots took precedence of all others, until 1430, when they were superseded by St. Andrews; and they were the first ecclesiastics on the roll of parliament, frequently filling the role of ambassador. In 1152, the Prince Henry, only son of David I, founder of the abbey, died at Roxburgh, and was buried here. And here was crowned the infant James III, after his father was killed by the cannon. A significant and typical note—on the very night after the disaster of Flodden, from which the Earl of Home was one of the very few to escape, the said earl came here, expelled the abbot and took personal possession of the abbey. In the circumstances, could cynical opportunism go further? The last Abbot of Kelso, like the last abbot of so many another establishment, was in fact one of the innumerable illegitimate sons of James V, the Gudeman o' Ballengeich—like most of the others, by different ladies, called James Stewart. Half-brothers were Abbots of Melrose, Dryburgh, Coldingham, Holyrood, St. Andrews, and others. This, of course, was in the manoeuvring for one of the biggest land-grabs in history—the Reformation in Scotland, where the old Church owned half of the best land. The Crown did rather well in the process—and the King got his bastards provided for at no cost to himself. Curiously enough, it was the abbey's fate to fall to a force of Spaniards in 1545, at Hertford's invasion, that earl having a company of such in his army. The Reformers largely demolished the handsome building, eventually; though as so often elsewhere, the nave of the chapel was used as the parish church for long—and, of all things, the clerestory area, above, ceilinged off and used as a prison, with a thatched roof. Which does not sound very secure. It was insecure in more ways than one, for in 1771 the roof gave way during divine service below—and out ran the worshippers, suddenly remembering that Thomas the Rhymer had prophesied that the kirk at Kelso would fall when at its fullest, a peculiar prediction from a man who lived three centuries before the Reformation. Today, only the west end of the great church remains; but the ruins indicate strikingly how magnificent was the original, almost certainly the finest of all the Border abbeys.

Kelso town is renowned for its highly attractive Flemish-style market square, so different from the narrow streets and wynds of the typical Border burgh—which of course tended to be huddled within strong defensive walls. There are some modern blemishes, but by and large Kelso's modest excellence of appearance remains; and happily the largest and latest addition, the handsome new high school, set amidst spacious green sward, is no blemish. This is a successor of the old grammar school, where Walter Scott was a pupil. Although he was here only for six months, it was at Kelso school that he met the brothers Ballantyne, who were to be so greatly involved in his career, as printer and publisher of most of his work.

The splendid bridge over the Tweed at Kelso, Rennie's master-piece, was opened in 1803, to replace its predecessor which had dramatically collapsed during a great flood in 1797—with half of the Borders there to watch, for cracks had appeared hours before. As is well known, Rennie used his new five-arched Kelso bridge as model for the renowned Waterloo Bridge at London, completed in 1817. And two of the iron lamps from Waterloo were brought to set up at Kelso, when that most notable London land-mark was demolished. Kelso Bridge, however, for all its fame and fine lines, was long a sore spot in the Borderland, a source of scandal indeed. For it cost £15,000, which the Government supplied—to be recovered by toll. The classical toll-house still sits rather primly at the town-end of the bridge. But no time-limit was put to the toll-gathering—and twenty-one years later, the privilege of collecting the tolls was being let at £900 a year! And thirty years on, it was fetching £1,450. Kelso's citizens, necessarily the main sufferers, rose in righteous riot—actually first on Queen Victoria's birthday, 1854, the celebrations for which provided a splendid excuse for fireworks of a more positive nature. Later disturbances even resulted in the 1st Dragoon Guards being brought to deal with the situation, and the Riot Act was read. However, the Kelso folk won the day, and the tolls were eventually abolished —although the accounts therefor, which had long been demanded, were never published. Perhaps there is a lesson here for the people of Scotland, who have had tolls for the Forth Road Bridge imposed upon them, despite widespread protest, as an antiquated anachronism in the twentieth-century main road system.

Some 6 miles west of Kelso, in knobbly foothill country near the western edge of the Merse, stands perhaps the most authentic, stirring and satisfying of all the Border peel-towers—Smailholm Tower, sometimes called Sandyknowe, from the farm and hillock on which it stands. Nothing could be more dramatic than the situation and aspect of this tall, stark hold, on its rocky ridge above a dark, lonely, reed-fringed lochan, a land-mark for miles around —indeed described as "a conspicuous mark to direct vessels to Berwick"—and that is over 30 miles away, as the crow flies. Why no film-maker has exploited the sheer romance and challenge of this place, I cannot understand. I have tried to interest many. Indeed I sought to get the makers of the popular television series, *The Borderers*, to use this site for their outdoor scenes, when they consulted me on sundry matters—for nowhere that I know of offers a more succinct and striking epitome of the entire Border ethos—but without success. Smailholm has to be seen to be *felt*, for the impact is almost physical, especially against a sunset or on a wild day of lowering cloud. It is a thick-walled fifteenth-century tower, built by the Pringles but taken over by the reiving Scotts of Harden in the early seventeenth century. Sandyknowe, the farm, was tenanted by Sir Walter Scott's grandfather, and this was his frequent resort, from earliest childhood. Indeed, it is recorded that once "the lonely infant was found, in a thunderstorm, lying in the soft grass at the foot of the old grey strength, clapping his hands at each flash and shouting 'Bonny! Bonny!' " Who knows how great an effect Smailholm had on the young and vivid imagination of the future novelist. Probably Scotland, the English-speaking world indeed, has much to thank Smailholm for. Scott introduces it into both "The Eve of St. John", almost his earliest ballad, and *Marmion*:

> These crags, that mountain tower,
> Which charmed my fancy's wakening hour . . .
> Methought grim features, seamed with scars,
> Glared through the window's rusty bars.

Today the tower houses a most excellent permanent exhibition of miniature models, in authentic costume, of Scott's and Border ballad characters by the artist Anne Carrick.

Due west of Smailholm 4 or 5 miles, at a great bend of the Tweed valley, is the highly dramatic area where the River Leader comes in from long Lauderdale. Here is crowded delight upon delight, Dryburgh, Bemersyde of the Haigs, Ercildoune and the Eildon Hills of Thomas the Rhymer, and Melrose of undying renown. Also Trimontium of the Romans. A wealth of interest and excitement, only to be touched upon here. The three peaks of the Eildons dominate all, one of the most photographed prospects of Scotland—which is saying something. This is hardly to be wondered at, for by any standards the Eildons stand out, in their dreaming isolation. This, of course, is the heart of the Scott country; and a particular vista of the Eildons and their richly wooded environs, has been singled out as Walter Scott's favourite view, the fact pleasingly substantiated by the fact that at his funeral, when the procession was contouring Bemersyde Hill, on its way from Abbotsford to Dryburgh Abbey below this point, his old horse, passing the view-point, paused of its own account, as it had been wont to do always when carrying its master. This has become a place of pilgrimage—and on this occasion, sentiment is fully justified, for the prospect is magnificent.

Both Bemersyde and the Eildons are forever linked with the name of that strange character, Thomas the Rhymer—Scott himself made sure of that. But, despite his stressing of the supernatural and the story of the seven-year journey to Elfland, and other legendary material, True Thomas was no figment of romance, or of a novelist's invention. He was, in fact, if we read between the lines, a particularly practical character—as a Border laird had to be to survive in most eras. For he was Thomas Learmonth of Ercildoune —which was the ancient name for present-day Earlston, 3 miles up the Leader—born about 1225, and believed to have died about 1307, which made him a very old man for those dangerous times of the Wars of Independence, despite his highly unusual adventures. He witnessed a charter, in the Melrose Chartulary, for Peter Haig of Bemersyde, between 1250 and 1260. One of his best-known rhymes is concerned with the Haigs:

> Tide, tide, whate'er betide,
> Haig will be Haig of Bemersyde,

a jingle which gained new currency and appreciation in 1919, when, after the First World War, the nation presented Bemersyde and its mansion and sturdy peel-tower to Earl Haig, in gratitude for military services. Things had looked doubtful for the prophecy many times since that rhyme was made, especially when one of the lairds, in the eighteenth century, sired a dozen daughters before his patient wife presented him with an heir.

Thomas made innumerable such predictions; and whether by faith, coincidence, stretch-of-imagination—or by waiting long enough—quite a large proportion appear to have come true. This sort of thing:

> When Tweed and Powsail meet at Merlin's grave,
> Scotland and England shall one monarch have.

This refers to the Tweed at Drummelzier, 10 miles above Peebles, where is one of the many reputed graves of the much-travelled Merlin. And in 1715, Pennicuik informs us that on the day in 1603 when James VI was finally crowned King of England in London, the Tweed, by an extraordinary flood, did rise so high as to reach this spot beside the Powsail Water—an event never seen before or since.

Just when Laird Thomas started on his prophesying career is not clear. But he was evidently fairly well established by 18th March 1285, precisely. For this was the occasion when he really made an impact, the night before that grievous day when the good Alexander III fell to his death over the Kinghorn cliff, to leave Scotland leaderless—the cause of all the Wars of Independence, of the struggles of Wallace and Bruce, of Bannockburn and so on. The night before, Bellenden the chronicler informs us, the Earl of March and Dunbar, whose March or Merse seat was at Earlston, Thomas's overlord,

demandit ane prophet namit Thomas Rymour, othirwise namit Ersiltoune, quhat wedder [weather] suld be on the morrow? To whom answerit this Thomas that on the morrow, afore noun, sall blow the gretest wynd that ever was hard afore in Scotland. On the morrow quhen it was neir noun, the lift [sky] apparing loune but ony din or tempest [lowering but without any noise or storm], the Erle send to this prophet and reprevit hym that he prognosticat sic wynd to be, and nae apperance thairof. This Thomas maid litel answer, but said noun is not yet gane. And incontinent ane man came to the yett [gate] schawing the King was slane. Then said the prophet, yone is the wynd that sall blaw to the gret calamity and truble of Scotland.

From then on, I imagine, Thomas never looked back.

Where, then, fits in this extraordinary tale which Thomas later told of his amatory adventures with the Queen of Elfland, which Scott made so much of?

> True Thomas lay on Huntlie bank, a ferlie he spied wi' his ee;
> And there he saw a ladye bright come riding down by the Eildon
> Tree.

Well, I have my own ideas about this. Thomas had reached the useful stage when people believed what he said—and he decided to make practical use of the faculty. This was a very unhappy period for Scotland and the Borders, with English Edward seeking to impose his will, and the Earl of March and Dunbar in a very vulnerable position, having lands on both sides of the Border. Thomas did not have to be a very acute prophet to see that there was serious trouble ahead, and that he, as vassal of the Earl, would be involved in it inevitably. Actually, the Earl *did* choose to take the English side, and great were the tides of war which washed over Lauderdale, as elsewhere. I esteem Thomas to have been a man of peace—or, at least, who cherished his own comforts and well-being. So he decided to absent himself—and seven years in Elfland with the Fairy Queen was as good a tale as any—especially as he told it. It seems entirely evident that Thomas chose Aberdeenshire as the scene of his self-appointed exile—a wise choice indeed, as it proved, for of course this was the heart of the Comyn country, which could expect to suffer least from any of King Edward's ire, and warfare generally, since the Comyns were Baliol supporters and kinsmen, prepared at least in the earlier stages to co-operate with the English, in a remote and far-away fashion. So to Buchan went Learmounth of Ercildoune—the Earl of Buchan was chief of the Comyns—and one gets the impression that he maintained himself quite nicely by the utilization of his gifts. At any rate he was very busy making prophecies, and there is hardly an old estate in that area which cannot sport one of his rhymes, for better or for worse.

Some of these are quite remarkable—although this is hardly the time to go into them. But two may indicate their scope.

> When the heron leaves the tree,
> The Laird o' Gight shall landless be.

Gight is in west Buchan. And 400 years later, when the Hon. John Byron, the poet's rascally father, married the Gordon heiress of Gight, the herons which for centuries had nested in a magnificent tree there, forsook the area and migrated to Kelly. And within a year or two, the heiress was a widow, and penniless.

Again:

If ever maiden malison did licht upon dry land,
Let nocht be found on Forvie's glebes but thristle, bent and sand.

I am not sure about the first line's significance; but there are no doubts about Forvie's glebes. Forvie, at the mouth of the Ythan, 20 miles north of Aberdeen, was a fine and fertile parish, with its own village and church. All was overblown with sand in the seventeenth century—after the fashion of the better-known Culbin tragedy in Moray—and today there is only a roofless church amongst the vast tract of sand-dunes—indeed a notable nature reserve.

True Thomas does not disappoint, right to the end, keeping up his carefully-planned mysteries to the last. Nobody knows for sure just when and where he died; he did not intend that they should:

Some said the hill and some the glen, their wondrous course had been,
But ne'er in haunts of living men again was Thomas seen.

The story went, of course, that one day towards the close of that troubled thirteenth century, Thomas was making merry with his friends in his peel-tower by the Leader, when somebody came running, in some alarm presumably, to declare that a stately hart and hind were together parading up and down Ercildoune village street in unchancy fashion. Thomas at once perceived the long-awaited sign from his Elfin Queen that his time was up. He rose from the table and followed the two deer back into the woods—and was never seen in Ercildoune again.

For long it was held that, whatever the mode of Thomas Learmonth's leaving this vale of tears, he was indeed dead in 1294 when "Thomas de Ercildoune, son and heir of Thomas Rymour de Ercildoune" conveyed his lands to the Trinitarian religious house of Soltre, or Soutra, by a charter signed 2nd November 1294—a pious donation by which ultimately and curiously Edinburgh Town Council, which eventually came to administer the

Trinity House Charity, continued for long to draw feu-duties of the Rhymer's Lands at Earlston, and their successors may still do so. What made True Thomas's son part with these hereditary acres so soon after his father's removal to another sphere? I imagine that he was acting on strict paternal instructions—and not posthumous ones.

You see, Thomas the Rhymer doesn't seem to have been dead at all—nor yet in Fairyland. Unless you can so describe Central Ayrshire. Patrick Gordon, author of *The Bruce*, published in 1615, declares that Thomas survived until 1307. And Sir James Murray, an expert on the Rhymer, believed that after transferring his estate to his son, in name at least, he sought the comfortable bosom of Mother Church, and retired to end his days at the Priory of Fail, near Ayr.

It seems to have been a highly suitable action of a prudent and far-seeing man, during the grim Wars of Independence. Blind Harry, the chronicler announces:

> Thomas Rymour at the Faile was then . . .

this at least three years after the nominal transfer of the Rhymer's Lands to Soutra. So we can make a kirk or a mill out of that. For myself, I am quite happy to accept that Thomas senior, now getting on in years, recognized that with the invading English occupying southern Scotland and bloodshed and warfare rife, if he couldn't be actually in Elfland, a good, comfortable monastery, likely to be respected by all factions, was as good a place to end his days as any he would find—especially if he had a sound financial arrangement with the management whereby the income from his lands did not altogether pass him by. Present-day landowners tend to make rather similar dispositions in the interest of death duty avoidance. The monastery had been founded in 1252, and was rather notable in that the monks "never wanted for gear so long as their neighbours' lasted!" Indeed the jingle goes:

> The friars of Fail drank berry-brown ale,
> The best that ever was tasted;
> The monks of Melrose made gude kail,
> On Fridays when they fasted.

I raise my bonnet to Thomas Learmonth, the Rhymer of Ercildoune, a man of imagination, initiative and many talents—and far-seeing in more ways than one.

Below the Eildons, where Thomas met his Queen, lies probably the most famous and lovely of all Scotland's abbeys, Melrose. It is strange indeed that it and Dryburgh—which lies at the foot of Bemersyde Hill across Tweed, where Scott lies buried—should be so close together, two great monastic establishments exactly 3 miles apart. The reason for this escapes me—especially when Kelso Abbey lies only another 8 miles eastwards and Jedburgh Abbey 7 southwards. But there it is. Melrose was there first, of course. It was founded in 1136 by David I, for the Cistercians or Black Friars, and was the successor of an ancient Celtic monastery at Old Melrose, 2 miles to the east. It suffered the usual harrying and burning by English invaders, especially in 1322, 1385 and 1545—but despite this, or perhaps because of it, much of its magnificence survives, a soaring symphony in mellow rose-red stone, with some quite wonderful tracery-work, its flying-buttresses a feature. The reason for the magnificence was the 1322 burning by Edward II, when that petulant monarch slew Bruce's friend the Abbot Peebles and many of his monks, in barbarous fashion, because the Scots scorched-earth policy had left him and his army hungry. Bruce thereupon awarded the then enormous sum of £2,000 for the rebuilding and maintenance of the abbey—even though the Scots treasury did not contain half that sum! Nevertheless the reconstruction was notably fine. It was here, of course, that Bruce's heart—as distinct from his body—was interred, under the chancel's east window. The story is that on his death bed the hero-king sent for his good companion, Sir James Douglas, and told him that when he was dead Douglas was to cut open his body, take out the heart, and carry it on a Crusade against the Infidel, in payment of a vow Bruce had made in one of his dire extremities and had been prevented from fulfilling in person. Thereafter the heart was to be buried in Melrose Abbey—the King's body being interred at Dunfermline Abbey beside that of his Queen Elizabeth de Burgh. All was duly done, but Douglas himself was slain on the said Crusade, casting his master's heart deep into the heart of the battle, as it had been its wont to go, and plunging to his death after it. The heart was recovered, however, and brought back to lie in this sequestered spot beside the Tweed. This special fondness of Bruce for Melrose is a little strange—for there is no record of him having been frequently there during his so active life; whereas

at other abbeys, such as Arbroath, Cambuskenneth, and Dunfermline, he was a constant visitor.

Another notable interment here was that of Michael Scott the
Wizard, one more thirteenth-century character who rivalled even
Thomas the Rhymer in public awe and esteem. Thought to have
been a son of the Laird of Balwearie in Fife, he seems to have
quickly exhausted the educational facilities of his own country,
went to Oxford about 1230, gained a high reputation there before
proceeding to Paris where he was sufficiently esteemed to gain the
title of Michael the Mathematician. From there he went to Padua
in Italy, specializing in judicial astrology. Then on to Spain, where
at Toledo University he became a conspicuous figure, translating
from the Arabic into Latin Aristotle's nineteen books on the
History of Animals. Then he became Astrologer Royal to the
Emperor Frederick II, betook himself to the study of medicine,
and soon gained a great reputation in that profession. He crossed
to England, where Edward I made much of him, and eventually
came home to Scotland, knighted. He was sent, with Sir Michael
Wemyss, another Fifer, to bring home to Scotland the infant Maid
of Norway, when she heired the throne after the tragic death of
Alexander III in 1286, when he must have been over 70. He died
in 1292, and left, at least in Scotland, an awesome reputation as
necromancer, magician and wizard, rather than scientist, philosopher, physician and linguist, as he was known in other countries. 'Auld Michael' was a term to frighten naughty children, for
long. He was alleged to have set down innumerable spells and
wizardries in a 'mighty book' of necromancy, which was supposed to be buried in the same grave in Melrose Abbey.

Melrose was rich in statuary—and, despite the Reformers and
their hammers, still is. One depicts the Virgin Mary with the
Infant in her arms. The Child is headless however, and the story
goes that when one demolisher of idols at the Reformation struck
at this, the head fell on his arm, permanently disabling him. This
put an end to the desecration. The individual was thereafter
known as Stumpy Thomson, and the event was even the talk of
Rome. Another carving which has survived is the extraordinary
one of a pig blowing the bagpipes. It would be interesting to know
the why and wherefore of this.

The little burgh of Melrose clusters round the abbey, all

beneath the towering Eildons, a pleasant place with an air of peace quite at odds with its story. Seen from above, the site could hardly be more attractive, and it is not strange that it has become quite a notable haven of retired colonels and ex-Empire-builders. With less than 2,000 of population it is no metropolis; but small as it is, Melrose does not fail to run its own Common Riding festival each year and support all the other Border burghs at theirs, its standard-bearer called the Melrosian. This is a comparatively modern development, something that is to be remembered about this Scots Border phenomenon—for it is a living, even growing thing, rooted in the past admittedly but burgeoning and flowering anew, in rivalry and vigour, a most heartening as well as picturesque feature of the whole Border scene. Of something of the same outgoing and vigorous nature are the Border seven-a-side rugby games held at Melrose, when this little burgh draws enthusiasts from far and near.

Almost a suburb of Melrose, to the west, is the delightful village of Darnick, red stone amongst tall trees, with its ancient tower-house, still inhabited, in a walled garden in the midst. Walter Scott coveted Darnick Tower, and sought long and hard to have its laird sell it to him. But the Heitons had been there for centuries, and would nowise give it up. So anxious was Scott to have this little castle that the wags even called him the Duke of Darnick. It makes interesting speculation to consider what might have been the result had Scott indeed gained the place, and so had not been spurred to go and build the enormous palace of Abbotsford 2 miles to the west—the vast cost of which bankrupted him and was the source of so much anxiety and care. But also the source of so many novels and other volumes. For by enormous writing labours he had reduced his insolvency from the daunting sum of £102,000, in the Ballantyne collapse alone—with more elsewhere—to something like £20,000 at the time of his death six years later. Had he settled in little Darnick would the world have been the poorer? Perhaps not, for almost certainly he would have lived longer; and the quality of his work might have been enhanced. The popular notion that authors do their best work starving, in garrets or elsewhere, is not borne out by facts.

Another Border tower also linked with Scott stands nearby, 3 miles to the north-west. Here is an example of the power of the pen, if you like. Glance at the map of the Tweed valley area and you will see the Allan Water coming in to join Tweed from the north 2 miles west of Melrose. Up this side-valley you will note the name of Glendearg, and here is a large farm with an ancient ruined castle, known as Glendearg Tower. But known so only since Walter Scott's time. He used this valley and tower in *The Monastery*, and for some reason changed the name from its original and typically Border Hillslap to the rather unsuitable Highland-sounding Glendearg. And thereafter, gradually, Glendearg it became, so that today even local people have not heard of Hillslap, and the maps know only the fictitious name. A pity, I think—and rather alarming to the writer. Hillslap is a typical, tall *L*-planned tower-house of the late sixteenth century, with a stair-turret supported on a 'squinch', an architectural device fairly uncommon, the name for which I can only imagine is derived from a 'squint arch'—for it is a little stone arch set across a re-entrant angle as a sort of bracket. Off hand, I cannot think of any others in the Borderland, although there are three in East Lothian.

An interesting question is why Hillslap's original Cairncross laird ever built his tower here, in the first place. For there are two more little castles just up the glen, a mile away—Colmslie and Langshaw. These were both Borthwick places. It is highly unusual to find such fortified strongholds in such close proximity, their lairds preferring to have considerably more elbow-room than this, by the very nature of things. Two Borthwick towers almost side-by-side are just conceivable; but why this Cairncross one? Happily, Hillslap is now restored from ruin and Langshaw could be.

This green valley of the Allan Water, remote-seeming and off-the-beaten-track today, was an important highway once, for up it ran the bridle-path which linked the Abbey of Melrose with its daughter-house of Soutra or Soltre, already mentioned in connection with True Thomas. There would be much monkish coming and going along this route, for Soutra was an important hospice, much used by pilgrims and travellers generally, prior to the Reformation. Probably, once the Church's protective power was brought down, these late sixteenth-century robber strongholds arose to exact tribute from the travellers who continued to use the old routes—something which at least the ecclesiastical Reformers had not taken into consideration, however much some of the lairdly laity had mused on the matter.

Only a mile west of the Allan Water confluence, the Tweed takes a great bend southwards, where the Gala Water comes in from the north-west. The low-lying land enclosed within this bend was that involved in as bitter and long-drawn a feud as any which has torn the Borderland in the past. This is the area which the modern planners decided was ideal for a great new development, almost a new town, to further industrial and residential potential in the east and central Borders—and which the local people, or many of them, thought otherwise. It would ruin a most lovely stretch of their Tweed valley, they said, a hallowed, storied reach, and on the very verge of Scott's Abbotsford itself. It must not be. Besides, it was low-lying, subject to flooding, and otherwise unsuitable. Led by the owners of the land in question, who refused to be bought out, they dug in their heels, using every device of non-cooperation, legal objection and public outcry to delay, dissuade and confound the forces of enlightened central government. Enquiry followed enquiry, but the development went ahead, bureaucracy winning eventually. It has proved to be less of an eyesore and white-elephant than was prophesied, although perhaps also less of a god-send to the area than its advocates asserted. Another controversy arose nearby in typical Border fashion, with a new hospital complex being planned for the Huntlyburn and Chiefswood estates, on the northern skirts of the Eildon Hills. Some folk felt strongly that this should be sited elsewhere than on such scenic territory much linked with the name and fame of Sir Walter Scott. Development in the Borderland can be a prickly business, as planners frequently find out.

The large burgh of Galashiels lies here, at the junction of Gala and Tweed—indeed, the new Tweedbank development is little more than an extension of the town, which is part of the trouble. Galashiels, or Gawly as it is called locally, is a busy, thriving place of woollen, tweed and hosiery mills, the site of the Scottish Woollen Technical College, necessarily one of the most advanced establishments of the sort in the world and a mecca for aspiring textile leaders. With a population of around 12,000 Gala is second only to Hawick in size, and great is the rivalry in consequence, in almost every sphere, with the Galashiels Braw Lad and the Hawick

Cornet in as constant though friendly competition as their respective rugby teams. A milling town, it could hardly be expected to be beautiful; but the setting is fair, amongst the green hills. And it has the distinction of having one of the finest war memorials in Scotland, the imposing clock-tower of the Municipal Buildings, by Sir Robert Lorimer, with in front the quite magnificent statue of a Border mosstrooper, in bronze, epitome of the enduring tradition, the sculptor being Thomas Clapperton.

Although it is an ancient place, and once contained a hunting seat of the Scots kings—it lay on the edge of Ettrick Forest—and featured in the dowry arrangements of James IV and Margaret Tudor, Galashiels did not become a municipal burgh until 1864, having previously been only a burgh of barony under its Scott lairds, with little more than village status. Its population rose, in fact, from 2,209 in 1831 to 15,330 in 1881—tweed manufacture, of course, being responsible. Oddly enough, the word tweed, now accepted all over the world as applying to the cloth coming from the neighbourhood of this great river, has really nothing to do with it. The word was purely the mistake of an English clerk, reading the Scots word tweels, or twills, for tweeds, and the error being perpetuated. The lairdly family of the Scotts of Gala still subsists but they no longer live in Old Gala House, part tower-house of the sixteenth and seventeenth centuries, in the suburbs of the town, which is now used as an arts centre and for community purposes.

Abbotsford lies only a mile east of Galashiels, but on the other side of Tweed, in a fine terraced situation above the river. The house itself is imposing rather than fine, in the sham-gothic and bastard-baronial style of its time. But the setting is very lovely—despite the original farm's name of Clarty Hole. Clarty is an old Scots word meaning dirty; and it is scarcely to be wondered at that the great name-changer Scott decided on an improvement, to Abbotsford—although whether any abbots ever forded here is another question. That was not the sort of thing to worry Sir Walter. Not only its name would be less lovely, once, for Scott greatly improved and planted the property, with an eye to landscaping. The house is one of the most popular places to visit in all Scotland—and deservedly so, for it is a fascinating monument to one man's dreams and aspirations, as well as being a highly interesting interior, full of treasure, for its own sake. Much remains almost exactly as Scott left it, with his desk, armchair, library and personal relics. Sir Walter left no son and heir to his lands and baronetcy; but Abbotsford passed to his granddaughter and has been transmitted, largely through the female line, to the present delightful owners, the Maxwell-Scott sisters.

Beyond Abbotsford the Tweed makes another of its major bends, due westwards again, and its valley takes on a very different character for a while. Gone is the wide smiling vale and green haughlands with their distant vistas. Instead is a deep defile, narrow by comparison, though richly wooded, with the hillsides rising close and high. By Yair and Fairnilee and Caddonfoot the river traverses this great ravine, but far from being grim or gloomy it is for many the finest stretch of a long course. It opens a little beyond Caddonfoot, but the valley remains much more close, narrow and deep than heretofore all the 6 more miles to Holylee and Walkerburn. One mile along, on the south bank, is the estate of Ashiesteil, which Scott rented before Abbotsford was built, for eight years—in which some of his finest work was done in what was probably the happiest part of his life. The mansion incorporates an ancient tower, like so many another in the Border, but little of this is evident today.

Only a little further up is Elibank—which indeed used to be Scott's favourite walk from Ashiesteil—where high on the south bank, in a commanding position, is the ruined ancient castle of the Murrays, Lords Elibank. This renowned family had the unusual distinction of having its peerage granted, in 1643, to "heirs male whatever"—which almost assures its unending succession. To this family adheres the story of Muckle-mou'ed Meg, daughter of Sir Gideon Murray, heroine of the ballad, who wed young Scott of Harden, son of the famous Auld Wat, in 1611, in inauspicious circumstances. Young Will Scott was caught raiding Sir Gideon's cattle, a normal hazard. But for once a choice of fate was offered. Hang—or wed the unwanted and large-mouthed Meg. Scott is supposed to have taken some time to make up his mind on the matter—but the match is said to have proved to be a happy one.

At Fairnilee, beside the modern mansion back in the jaws of the great defile, is part of the sixteenth-century tower wherein Alison

Rutherford, Mrs. Patrick Cockburn, wrote her famous rendering of the ancient ballad of Flodden Field, "The Flowers of the Forest".

From Walkerburn to Peebles, another 10 miles, the valley widens again. But now the flanking hills are high, with heather crowning them, and it has become definitely an upland strath. Walkerburn and Innerleithen are tweed-milling communities, the latter based on an ancient kirkton whose former holy well, given prominence and romance by Walter Scott, blossomed into a famous spa as St. Ronan's Well. There is just no getting away from the man, in Tweeddale. But Innerleithen owes much also to a less prominent native, one Alexander Brodie, an enterprising Traquair blacksmith, who went to London and made a large fortune, came home and started the first woollen mill here in 1790. Between them, these two turned the tiny hamlet at the mouth of the Leithen Water, subservient to Traquair estate, into a thriving burgh.

Traquair lies south of the town in a re-entrant valley of the Quair Water, about a mile, a secluded place with a great reputation. Here stands the most attractive and venerable mansion of the Stuart family, now Maxwell-Stuart, once the seat of its own earldom—even though the Earls of Traquair were in the main a less than heroic bunch, one of the feebler branches of a mighty tree. They sprang from that spectacular if savage progenitor, the Wolf of Badenoch, son of Bruce's grandson Robert II, and Earl of Buchan. An illegitimate descendant bought Traquair from the physician Rogers, one of James III's low-born minions on whom it had been bestowed—and he got it for a paltry sum, perhaps under threat. His descendant was created Earl of Traquair in 1633, and served King Charles but doubtfully, as Lord High Treasurer of Scotland. Perhaps he was too honest. Most such managed to feather their nests quite adequately, but this one died in abject poverty in Edinburgh, trusted of none. The second Earl was not of the stuff of heroes either, though supposedly the King's man, shutting his door here in the face of the great Montrose after the defeat of Philiphaugh—having already sent Leslie, the Covenanting general, news of Montrose's dispositions prior to the battle. The seventh Earl entertained Prince Charles Edward at Traquair, but otherwise confined his support to closing the gates behind the

Prince and swearing that they would never be opened again until a Stewart monarch sat crowned in London. That is Scott's story, at least, although there is another version making the "steekit yetts" to be kept locked after the funeral of the Countess until another as good lady should seek entry. Be that as it may, the great wrought-iron heraldic gates remain closed to this day. Seen beyond them, the ancient whitewashed mansion, grown out of the usual free-standing Border tower, is highly picturesque. It is open to the public, and a treasure-house of fascinating relics, so much having happened herein—for these Stewarts were by no means all feeble, and took their sizeable part in Scotland's story. Mary Queen of Scots lodged here, with Darnley and their baby, in 1566, and the little King James VI's cradle is still in the bedroom. One unusual feature of the house is that the lairds used to be able to fish for salmon out of certain of their windows, the Tweed then flowing sufficiently close for this convenience. However, one of the earls took it upon himself to change the course of the river, in the interests of dryness and freedom from flood.

Peebles lies a few miles to the west, and is somehow as different from the other Border towns as is Kelso. If just a little less handsome than the latter, it is nevertheless a most pleasing place, open, sunny, friendly, with little of the close-knit, slightly wary and tough atmosphere of a frontier town which for centuries had to keep eyes open and ears pricked for the gleam of invaders' steel or the beat of rievers' hooves. If Hawick is Queen o' a' the Borders, according to her own anthem—although that has never struck me as very apt description of so essentially masculine and thrusting a place—Peebles might be described as the comfortable, sonsy and still good-looking matron of the Borderland. And that is certainly intended as a compliment. Yet Peebles is no quiet backwater, and never was, however far from the actual Border-line, and received its share of ravage, burning and siege. It was savaged in 1545 during Hertford's invasion, when that bloodthirsty minion of Henry VIII burned five towns and no fewer than 240 villages and hamlets in his efforts to make Scotland accept his master's overlordship and marry the infant Mary Queen of Scots to Henry's son. There was another such onslaught two years later, so that it is scarcely to be wondered at that even peaceable Peebles decided to erect a town wall—even though not a notably strong one—for her defence. Traces of it may still be discerned near the former railway station, and the street-names such as Northgate, Eastgate and Port-brae are reminders. Significantly, however, this walling was erected round the *New* Town; for even at that period the Old Town of Peebles was hoary with age, set further to the west on the right bank of the Eddleston Water, in a less defensible position. Legend has it that the famed St. Mungo, founder of Glasgow, visited Peebles in the sixth century, and his well still marks the occasion. On firmer ground, we know that David I (1124–1153) was much attached to the place and built a royal castle here, which became a favourite residence of succeeding monarchs. David II, Bruce's son, gave Peebles its charter as a royal burgh in 1367. The hunting in the surrounding hills, the northern part of Ettrick Forest, probably accounted largely for this popularity; apprecia-tion extending to the English invaders likewise, for Edward I, in his typically large way, conferred Peebles as a gift on his Warden for Scotland, Aymer de Valence, Earl of Pembroke. Bannockburn changed all that, however, and de Valence found himself having to sell his *English* estates in order to pay his ransom as a captive thereafter.

It was the Church, however, rather than kings and invaders, which had the greatest influence on Peebles; for even though there was no great abbey here, it boasted so many religious establish-ments that it was like a smaller St. Andrews. The Church of the Holy Cross was the most ancient, a conventual foundation the square tower of which, somewhat restored, still stands. The Col-legiate Church of St. Andrew was burned by the English, but the Cross Church was spared, to become, after the Reformation, the parish church. The Chapel of the Virgin stood across the head of the High Street; and a Hospitium of St. Leonard, for the poor and aged, was nearby. Ever since St. Mungo's time Peebles had been linked, more or less closely, with the See of Glasgow, and the connection is enshrined by the little lane known as the Dean's Gutter. All this ecclesiastical influence did not imply any stuffily pious atmosphere, however; far from it, if we are to believe the author of "The Tales of the Thrie Priestis of Peebles", a cheerfully scurrilous satirical poem which vividly emphasizes the backslid-ings, failings and licence of the pre-Reformation clergy. Whether or no this blast was intended as a service to Church and nation, a still earlier churchman, Ingelram, Rector of Peebles in the twelfth century, did render Scotland great service when he went to Rome to contest the claims of the Archbishops of York to spiritual over-lordship of Scotland—and won his case with the Pope. Typically, it was a Borderer who achieved this. He was promoted Bishop of Glasgow for his services.

It is almost inconceivable that Peebles should be mentioned without at least reference to the famous lines:

> Was never in Scotland hard nor sene,
> Sic dancing nor deray;
> Nouther at Falkland on the Grene
> Nor Pebilles at the Play.

It is usual to credit this to the poet King James I; although others suggest another royal versifier, his great-great-grandson James V, who was much more interested both in 'the Play'—and that can be interpreted in the widest sense!—and in Falkland, a place with grievous associations for James I.

At any rate, Peebles had a reputation for the gayer side of life; and it has managed to retain something of this lightsome atmo-sphere to the present day. It is one of the most popular inland holi-day resorts of southern Scotland, and deservedly so.

To include the Tweed valley west of Peebles in the Borders is really stretching things—although some devotees and residents of, say, Stobo, the Manor Valley and Drummelzier may upbraid me for suggesting it. But we can safely halt at Neidpath, that massive castle standing stark and proud on a crag above the winding river, defending the narrow gorge one mile west of the town. Nothing could be more authentically Border-like, at least. Though the foundations are older, much of the present work dates from the early fifteenth century, with seventeenth-century alterations. A strength of the Frasers, before they were Highlanders, and then of the Hays and Douglases, it stood out longer against Cromwell and his artillery than any other fortalice south of the Forth.

Let us leave Peebles, and the Tweed, suitably, with a prayer of intent. The ancient Church of St. Andrew had a special endow-ment for a chaplain to say mass perpetually "for the hele of the body and the sawl of Jamys, Kyng of Scottis, for the balyeis, ye burges and ye communite of ye burgh of Peebles, and for the hele

of their awn sawlis, their fadyris sawlis, their modyris sawlis, their
kynnis sawlis and al Chrystyn sawlis."

Could any say fairer or kinder than that?

7

The Scots Middle March—Teviotdale

TEVIOT, although a lesser stream than Tweed, is a major river, with its own very distinct character, only 37 miles long against the other's 97, but bringing down a great volume of water neverthe-less, with many large tributaries with names resounding in the Border story such as Jed, Kale, Ale, Rule, Slitrig and Borthwick Waters. Nowhere itself forming the Border-line, Teviot neverthe-less keeps closer to that line for longer than does any other river. The similarity of its name to Cheviot is unlikely to be accidental, and it hugs the foothills of that great range throughout its course.

Teviotdale is wilder and less broad than Tweeddale, but it is still sylvan and very fair. After Roxburgh it is quite soon joined by Kale Water, flowing down from the Cheviots in its own attractive vale in which lie the villages of Eckford and Morebattle. The wide flatness of the area between these places, so unusual in the Borders, is accounted for by the fact that this was once a large, if shallow loch. Indeed, that is what Morebattle is a corruption of—the vil-lage on the mere. No trace of the lake now remains, save in such names as Lake Brae and Lake Burn; but it was a very prominent feature of the landscape once, 4 miles long. It is suggested that it was formed by the overflowing of the Kale Water, which for-merly found its way northwards into the Bowmont Water's course at Yetholm, and so to the Till and eventually the Tweed, far to the north-east. But a small tributary of the Teviot cut its way back and back, near Eckford, until it eventually tapped the wide shallow basin of this loch, and so drained all its water west-wards, forming the lower Kale's new course.

All this would have quite a lot to do with the site of Cessford Castle, the massive ruins of which now stand in an open and not notably defensive site in this wide vale midway between the vil-lages. When this loch was there, this must have been a very strong situation, guarded by water and marshland. It was, of course, the

seat of the turbulent Kers, whose chief is now the Duke of Roxburghe and living at the palatial eighteenth-century seat of Floors
Castle, Kelso, 7 miles to the north. The Ker clan was divided into
two warring main stems, Cessford and Ferniehirst, the latter
usually preferring to spell the name Kerr. They were in constant
dispute over seniority, and many are the tales that could be told of
this prolonged wrangle and rivalry—including the competition in
collecting honours and peerages. Ferniehirst Castle lies only 6
miles away as the crow flies, near Jedburgh; so that the two pro-
tagonists were much too close for comfort. There were innumerable and lesser Ker strengths all around, of course, so that, apart
from more normal Border hazards, the area never lacked for
excitements. The popular TV series, *The Borderers*, made some use
of this material. The Kers were traditionally a left-handed race,
and the term kerry or carry-pawed is still used in Scotland to de-
note left-handedness. Indeed it is probable that the name itself
derives from this condition, for the Gaelic for left or awkward is
cearr. The Highland name of Keir is of the same origin. There is a
theory that the turnpike stairs of the Ker castles turned anti-
clockwise where others turned clockwise—in other words, with
the central newel on the left instead of the right—allegedly in
order to allow the left-handed defenders better scope for their
swords. Personally I know of no verification of this; nor do I see
any great advantage—for the thing would cut both ways. The
left-handed defenders might be partly protected by the newel; but
the right-handed attackers would have the much greater range
and freedom of movement.

Be all that as it may, Cessford has been a fine and powerful
castle, with walls 12 feet in thickness. It fell to the Earl of Surrey
in 1545, but would have been inviolable against all local-type
assailants. Nearby is a large and artificial cavern for use as refuge,
and known as Hobbie Ker's Cave—Hobbie being Sir Robert Ker
of Cessford, Warden of the March, raised to the peerage in 1600
as Lord Roxburghe and sixteen years later as first Earl thereof.
The Kerrs of Ferniehirst tended to scoff at their rivals because they
were so unproductive of sons. This first Earl's only son died, and
the earldom had to go to his daughter's son, who was really a
Drummond. And his dead son had produced only a daughter.
Later for lack of closer heirs, the earldom passed to the Bellendens,

Ferniehirst Castle

who then died out also. After a long period in abeyance the earldom, now upgraded to a dukedom, was terminated in favour of
descendants in the female line of the name of Innes. They all took
the name of Ker, of course—and Innes-Ker they still remain.
Female blood is as good as male, any scientist will assure you; but
the Ferniehirst Kerrs, with son succeeding son in cheerful regularity, felt entitled to claim undoubted seniority, and to cock a
major snook. Especially as they had in the process collected the
Lordships of Kerr and Jedburgh, the earldoms of Ancram,
Lothian and Somerset in England, and finally the Marquisate of
Lothian. But not a dukedom!

There is another ancient and powerful family with its roots here,
which strangely enough has sunk almost without trace—and a
place-name transferred 100 miles away. You will find no trace of
Halyburton on any modern map. But it was very much present
once, and its lords great men when the Kers were mere reiving
lairdlings. Like Roxburgh itself, nearby, it has vanished. It stood
at the mouth of the Kale—possibly before it *was* the Kale, and only
the minor stream which stole the loch-waters. It was a burgh-of-
barony, called simply the Burgh-toun. One of its barons granted
land to the Abbey of Kelso, and it managed to acquire the distinction of being called the Holy Burgh-toun, or Halyburton. The
Halyburton family waxed great, and became Lords Halyburton,
one even being Lord High Treasurer of Scotland. But they took
the wrong side in the Reformation, and the up-and-coming and
very Protestant Kers got the lands. The Halyburtons had acquired
the great East Lothian castle of Dirleton by marriage, but this too
they lost soon after, in the murky Gowrie Conspiracy of 1600,
they by then being connected with the Ruthvens. However, a
junior branch of the family had married the heiress of Pitcur, in
Angus, behind Dundee, in 1432, and that line prospered in a
modest way. In time they outgrew the old castle of Pitcur and
built a fine new mansion nearby, calling it Hallyburton—giving
it an extra *l* in the by-going. The gazetteers and maps today know
only this estate as representing this ancient name; yet the true site
was a little town where Kale meets Teviot.

Before leaving the Kale I must mention Yetholm and Kirk
Yetholm, that remotely set community in the lap of the Cheviots
4 miles north-east of Morebattle and 7 south-east of Kelso,

crouching under abrupt Staerough Hill and famous as the capital of the Scots gipsies, the home of the once great Romany family of Faa. They were a picturesque and noted feature of the Border scene for long, and, from their wandering habits, could be highly useful to more settled folk, carrying news and messages—and other more debatable goods. For they were notable smugglers, and sundry commodities landing of a night on the Northumbrian coast found their way into Scotland via Yetholm as often as not:

> There's canny Wull Faa o' Kirk Yetholm,
> He lives i' the sign o' the Queen:
> He got a great slash i' the hand,
> When comin' frae Boulmer wi' gin.

The coronation of the Gipsy King was an exciting event which drew large crowds, 10,000 people descending on Kirk Yetholm as recently as 1898 for the crowning of Charles Faa Blyth—even though his 'palace' was no more than a but-and-ben cottage.

A comparatively little known but highly attractive road follows the Kale Water southwards from Morebattle, swinging gradually westwards through the green hills, by lonely Hownam and the Roman Camp at Pennymuir, then crossing the watershed amongst heather moors and turning down the Oxnam Water eventually to Jedburgh by the 'back-door'. The Roman road of Dere Street crosses this, at the Camp, and runs very near to the Border-line here. More ought to be made of such gems of scene and archaeological interest.

Jedburgh, at least, is well known if insufficiently appreciated. Here, nestling deep in the narrow side-valley of the Jed, just off the main Teviotdale, is the age-old royal burgh and county town of Roxburghshire, a small community of only 4,000 souls steeped, all but drowned, in a history as blood-curdling and colourful as any in the land, and proud of it—but not by any means a sleepy hollow dreaming of the past. It is as much a fighting community as ever it was; for, although grievously hit by the harsh economics of centralization, its main mills closed down, its railway link arbitrarily closed, it has hit back valiantly and taken its destiny in its own hands, so far as it can. After seeking in vain to entice industry to come here to employ the folk left idle by the mills, its former provost went personally right to the United States—and in due course came back triumphantly with the promise of an American precision tools factory for Jedburgh. Now, across from the noble ruins of the great abbey, pillaged so often as first stop for English invaders, rise the ultra-modern premises of the most advanced technological progress. It is perhaps as typical as it is amusing that the large transatlantic firm thus brought to the rescue —and apparently finding the process very much to its taste— should be called Starrett. For these very valleys were at one time set in a stir by a Borderer named Starrett, or Starhead who was outlawed for the assassination of the Scots Warden of the Marches just before Flodden, in 1512. That Warden was named Ker, Sir Robert—and thereafter his son, Dand, or Andrew, eventually tracked down Starrett, slew him in cold blood in his own home, and sent the man's head to Henry VII, as indication of what happened to Englishmen who meddled with the Scots Borderers. As ever, the crowding past remains just round the corner in the Borderland.

Despite all its sackings, Jedburgh Abbey remains the most entire of all the Border monastic houses, a very lovely and stately cruciform building which has been called "the most perfect and beautiful example of the Saxon and Early Gothic in Scotland". Its three tiers of arches, of nave arcading, triforium and clerestory, are a notable feature, and greatly admired; while its massive transept tower, 86 feet high, remains complete and splendid. David I founded a priory here in 1118; and this was raised to the status of abbey in 1147. Oddly enough, Malcolm IV endowed it with the churches and manors of Brandon and Grendon in Northamptonshire—an indication of the mutual amity of the two kingdoms before Edward I conceived his disastrous ambition to be overlord of Scotland, and all the misery and warfare which stemmed therefrom. Alexander III was married herein. But during the Wars of Independence which followed his untimely death, the place was so savaged that the monks had to remove elsewhere. However, by 1360 the canons were back, and actually exporting into England wool which had come from English sheep. Surrey burned it again in 1523 and Hertford in 1545. In the transept were buried the Kerrs of Ferniehirst.

Ferniehirst Castle was for some time a youth hostel but is now open to the public. It still belongs to the Marquis of Lothian, who has a large estate at Monteviot on the Jed Water, 2 miles south of Jedburgh. At Monteviot there is an interesting Woodland Centre with many recreational facilities. Ferniehirst is a handsome L-planned structure, mainly of the late sixteenth century with seventeenth-century additions, but on the site of an earlier forta-lice. It shows the French influence of its period, with conical angle-turrets, circular stair-turret, shot-holes and heraldic de-coration. A notable feature is the massive projecting chimney-stack to house the hall fireplace flue. This great hall, on the first floor of the main block, is a magnificent apartment. The prede-cessor of this castle was taken, after a valiant defence by Sir Andrew, or Dand, Kerr, in 1523, when the English under Lord Dacre over-ran the Middle March—which happened regularly for years after the *débâcle* of Flodden left Scotland largely defence-less. Dand's son, Sir John, retook it, with French aid, in 1549. And *his* son, Sir Thomas, swept over the Border in 1570 in a raid designed to blackmail Queen Elizabeth into releasing the captive Mary Queen of Scots. For this sally, Sussex was sent up to demolish the original castle; and it was not rebuilt, as now, until 1598. This laird's two sons, favourites of James VI and I, were created respectively Lord Jedburgh and Earl of Somerset—the latter the murderer of Sir Thomas Overbury. It is from the former that the Lothian line descends.

A notable later occasion, at Ferniehirst, was the joint visit here, in September 1803, of Walter Scott and William Wordsworth, with the latter's sister.

A cadet branch of Ferniehirst were the Kerrs of Ancram, or Ancrum; and these obtained their own earldom of that name in due course, and eventually succeeded the Lords Jedburgh as chief of their line. The present Marquis of Lothian's son and heir is Earl of Ancram. The picturesque village of Ancrum lies 3 miles north of Jedburgh, near where the Ale Water comes in to join Teviot. The dispute about the spelling of the name is of old standing; but in fact both are wrong. It should be neither cram nor crum but crom! Better still, it should be Alecrom. Or even better, Alne-crom. For the Ale Water used to be called the Alne—one of the many corruptions of the Gaelic word *abhainn*, a stream, pro-nounced a'an. Scotland—and to some extent England also, for most of it was a Celtic country once, though few Englishmen realize it—is littered with rivers called Avon, Afton, Almond, Alne, Devon, Deveron, and so on. This was one more. And the Gaelic word *crom* means a crook or bend, like the head of a shepherd's stick—the cromach we sing about in *The Road to the Isles*. This charming village on the south-facing hillside is set above a typical crook of the Ale or Alne Water, with its village green and thirteenth-century cross, said to have come from a Preceptory of the Knights of Malta, the site of which is known as Maltan Wells. Just north of the Ancrum estate is Lilliard's Edge, on the road to St. Boswells, where Lord Lothian has established a particularly ambitious caravan-site and tourist centre. Here was fought a battle, in 1545, when an English army of some 5,000, under Sir Ralph Evers, was ambushed by a lesser force under the Red Douglas Earl of Angus, and Scott of Buccleuch, and roundly defeated. A Teviotdale girl named Lilliard, to avenge the death of her lover, slain by Evers earlier, took part in the fight until she fell, with many wounds. Not only has she given her name to the battle and the plateau on which it was fought, but the following doggerel rhyme grimly enshrines her memory:

> Fair Maiden Lilliard lies under this stane,
> Little was her stature but great was her fame;
> Upon the English loons she laid many thumps,
> And when her legs were cuttit off, she fought upon her stumps.

Teviotdale between Ancrum and Hawick, 10 miles, is exceedingly fair, a smiling valley dominated by the thrusting cone of Ruberslaw to the south and the Minto Hills to the north. It is full of names which sing aloud the Border story—Timpendean, Lanton, Barnhills, Fatlips, Minto, Spittal on Rule, Bedrule, Denholm-on-the-Green, Hornshole, Cavers. Brief mention can only be made of one or two. Lanton, because it lies half a mile south of the main A698 road, on a side-road to nowhere in particular, is little known, but a pleasing sequestered village overlooking the dale, with a small, ancient tower-house, still occupied. It dates from the sixteenth century, plain and reroofed, but with wide splayed gun-loops and vaulted basement. It was harried by the English times without number. With its lairdship went the office of Crowner or Coroner of Roxburgh. Formerly belonging to the Lords

Cranstoun, it came to the Douglases of nearby Cavers in the seventeenth century.

Rule Water flows in from the south 2 miles further west, in a delightful narrow glen; and a mile or so up this is the hamlet of Bedrule, with its extraordinarily placed parish church perched high at the tip of a spur of ridge jutting into the glen. A more romantic site for a place of worship would be hard to find—and its ministers at least must have had stout lungs, for their former manse lies steeply below. The interior of the little church is interesting, with a colourful heraldic ceiling. This was the 'capital' of the vigorous Border clan of Turnbull, and nearby is the site of their one-time castle, where, in 1494, 200 of them were paraded before James IV, for their sins, with naked swords in their hands but halters round their necks. From here came William Turnbull, Bishop of Glasgow from 1448 to 1454, founder of Glasgow University and builder of much of the cathedral there.

Opposite the junction of Rule and Teviot rise woody, rocky Minto Crags, crowned by Fatlips or Minto Tower, a conspicuous local landmark, the restored fortalice of Turnbulls and Elliots. Just below is a ledge of the cliff known as Barnhill's Bed:

> On Minto Crags the moonbeams glint,
> Where Barnhill hewed his bed of flint . . .

as we read in *The Lay of the Last Minstrel*. Turnbull of Barnhill was a noted Border reiver, and his little castle lay in the low ground just below, where the farm of Barnhill still remains. Why he should bed on a ledge up here is best left to the imagination.

Denholm is a major village set around quite the largest green I know in Scotland, under the shapely pinnacle of Ruberslaw where Peden once preached to the Covenanters. It is a place of character, charm and exciting history—being, of course, plumb in the way of all raiders proceeding up or down Teviotdale. It was burned by Hertford in 1545, like so much else; but more renowned is its fate at the hands of the party of raiders of Dacre's army, led by the Prior of Hexham's steward, in 1514, the year after Flodden, when the pillage of Denholm was probably responsible for the deep and no doubt drunken sleep of the raiders at Hornshole, 2 miles further up Teviot, where they encamped for the night. And where they were set upon in the darkness and massacred almost to a man by the youths of Hawick, sons of the men who had marched off to Flodden the year before and never came marching back— the triumphant theme of Hawick's annual Common Riding celebrations.[1]

At Denholm was born in 1775 that prodigy of vigour and learning, John Leyden, in a humble thatched cottage still preserved. This extraordinary character, scholar, poet, orientalist, preacher, medico and much more besides, made a great impression on Scotland and far beyond. Before he was 20 he had acquired the French, Spanish, Italian, German, ancient Icelandic, Arabic and Persian languages. The education started by the Denholm dominie was continued at Edinburgh University, where, as well as these languages, he studied theology. But failing to obtain the presentation to a parish, he turned his avid mind to medicine. Not content with this he wrote and published poetry, and was one of Scott's collaborators in collecting material for *The Minstrelsy of the Scottish Border*, much of which he is reputed to have heard at his mother's knee. At 24 he published three volumes of *The History of African Discoveries*. Two years later he brought out *The Complaynt of Scotland*. And meanwhile he was editor of *The Scots Magazine*— which, I am glad to say, is still going strong. To prevent him from actually setting off to explore darkest Africa, his friends obtained for him the appointment of assistant-surgeon to the Madras establishment. That the post required a degree in surgery, young Leyden took in his stride, within six months. In India, where another Teviotdale man, the Earl of Minto, was Governor-General, Leyden was soon a professor at Bengal, and then a judge at Calcutta. Whilst so engaged, to prevent himself wearying, he learned numerous Indian languages and became an expert in oriental literature. Nothing, seemingly, was beyond this Denholm lad. He accompanied Lord Minto on an expedition to Java in 1811, and died of a fever there at the age of 36.

"The manners of Leyden, when he first entered the higher ranks of society, were very peculiar," declared a precious contemporary source. Comment is superfluous.

Leyden's father and grandfather were servants of the Douglases of Cavers. Cavers House, now a roofless though impressive and massive ruin, lies amongst small green hillocks 2 miles south-west of Denholm. The original tower was built by Sir Archibald

Douglas, younger of the illegitimate sons of that same Earl of Douglas who died so dramatically at Otterburn; and the banner borne by Douglas on that fatal day is still a cherished relic. The story of this branch of the Douglases, Hereditary Sheriffs of Teviotdale, would fill volumes. Often they were Wardens of this Middle March. With the twentieth of them, the male line became extinct. But the lands passed down the female line, and the Palmer-Douglases still have connections with the neighbourhood.

Hawick was also a Douglas possession, belonging to another branch, that of Drumlanrig; and their original tower is still incorporated in the Tower Hotel at the far end of the High Street, the town's most noted hostelry, unfortunately now suffering from a fire and neglect and awaiting new development. Hawick is a very special place, of course. Considerably the largest of the Border burghs—five times the size of Jedburgh, for instance—amongst its many attributes is that it may claim probably more foreign exchange for the economy than any other town of its size in the United Kingdom. In every corner of the world where top quality knitwear is esteemed—and where is it not?—Hawick and the names of its famous firms are household words. Here the finest jumpers, sweaters, cardigans, twin-sets and the like are produced, imitated all over but never rivalled in quality, style or design. In this highly competitive modern industry, the Scottish Borders lead the way—and Hawick is not backward in crying who is Queen o' a' the Borders.

Not a queen in beauty, perhaps, however typically attractive the setting in a hub of green valleys, with the Teviot threading the centre of the town, and joined therein by the rushing Slitrig which even has mills built over it on bridges. Not to be compared with Selkirk's more open and scenic prospect, nor with Kelso's mellow urbanity, Hawick is nevertheless a place of sterling and obvious character, bustling, busy, virile, a bastion of vivid individuality and independence of mind. This spirit of independence, so endemic in all the Borders, is something which the rest of Scotland, indeed the rest of Britain, should recognize more gratefully. Spirit is hardly the word, perhaps—say rather a rage, a fury of independence. I have not the least doubt that if, as sometimes seems to be on the cards, this blessed, sceptred isle of ours, even its more thrawn northern half, becomes swallowed up in the European Economic Community, or as the fifty-somethingth state of America, then the Border burghs will all somehow manage to opt out of the business. Not as a group, of course—that would demand some sort of slavish unanimity—but individually and separately.

Which is something that makes the present-day craze for take-overs of firms and centralization of big business a highly dangerous manifestation. For if the control of the Border knitwear, tweed and woollen industries passes from the Borderers, as there is a distinct tendency for it to do, then not only is there the possibility of disaster ahead, in the said industries as in the Borderland itself, but a most grievous blow will have been struck to something that is very important and precious to the nation as a whole.

Apart from the Tower Hotel, Hawick can boast no abbey or castle or other notable marks of antiquity to challenge the other Border towns. Its age is undoubted, but it was only a village of 110 houses in Mary Queen of Scots's time, when she confirmed a baronial charter. But it has one feature which is much revered locally as of great age and importance—the Moat. Prehistoric and semi-legendary significance is often attributed to this large earthen mound, 30 feet high and 312 feet in circumference, which stands on a terraced site on high ground, in a small park at the western end of the town overlooking the Teviot valley. The fact that it is clearly artificial has led to it being looked upon as a relic of the mysterious Dark Ages. But in fact such mounds or mottes were of highly frequent erection in the twelfth, thirteenth and fourteenth centuries, and on top of them were built the motte-and-bailey castles of the barons, before stone castles were the order of the day. These consisted of a palisade of timber, and within it a wooden castle, plastered over with clay to prevent it being set on fire by blazing arrows. By far the majority of Scottish castles were of this variety prior to the late fourteenth and later centuries; and Hawick's Moat is very typical. No doubt here, as elsewhere, when a new stone fortalice was erected to supersede it—the Drumlanrig Tower, or more properly, since Drumlanrig itself is in North Dumfriesshire, the Black Tower of the Drumlanrig Douglases—open-air courts of the barony would continue to be held on it, as the site of the original baronial authority. Such moot-hills as they are called are to be found all over Scotland. So that the name of

Moat could derive either from moot or motte; and moat itself was a now obsolete word for a mound which came to be *surrounded* by a moat. Here, at Hawick, is held one of the most dramatic and moving of the annual common riding ceremonies, when the Cornet and followers, magistrates and a great crowd, greet the dawn here—most of them having been up all night, after the dinners, dancing and festivities of the previous day.

Since the Border common and march riding phenomena are one of the most outstanding manifestations of local spirit, tradition and patriotism to be seen in these islands—or anywhere else, I imagine—today, and because I know the Hawick one best, perhaps this is the place to say a little more about it all. Although each of the burghs has its own distinctive aspects and details, all the festivals conform to a roughly similar pattern. They all typify and pay tribute to freedom, liberties and deliverances bought at great cost of blood and courage by our forefathers, commemorating famous battles and raids and rides of the old days when the Border was the Border indeed. There is no animosity towards England in these celebrations today, no harping on past wrongs, no churlish parochialism. Only a fine and healthy appreciation of privileges hard-earned, a lively sense of rivalry with neighbouring (Scots) communities, and a feeling for colour, verve and tradition.

The activities start as much as up to a month before the climactic week, with a series of ride-outs of an evening by the Cornet, Callant or burgh's elected standard-bearer and his host of mounted supporters—for this is all very much in the old Border mounted tradition. These ride-outs are to outlying points of the area, towers, landed seats, landmarks, cross-country gallops that test the horsemanship and staying powers of all concerned. They culminate in the actual festival week, in the second half of which the whole town usually goes on holiday, mills, shops and offices close, and the Cornet, Braw Lad, Kelso Laddie, Duns Reiver, or whatever he may be called in the various burghs, becomes the uncrowned king, a brave, youthful hard-riding and unmarried king, selected to carry the flag, wear the town's colours, and uphold its honour. In some cases a young woman helps him bear both his triumph and his burden; but not in all. There are strong and mixed feelings on this subject.

Then the real fun starts. There are official breakfasts of a dewy morn—and speeches at 8 a.m. require all the Borderers' virility to stand—processions, song-singing, ceremonies with the flag, races, orations, junketings—literally so at Hawick, where junket, or curds-and-cream, is served to all the company, laced with something stronger, usually—pageantry, civic dinners and much hilarity. A certain basic solemnity too, however, for though a vigorous and physique-taxing business, it is all done with an essential purpose and discipline, within a carefully maintained time-schedule. And the whole town takes part—that is the most significant aspect of it all, everywhere. These are no shows, spectacles, laid on for the populace to stare at and applaud, by benevolent municipalities. They are the authentic expression of the people's emotion. Everyone joins in wholeheartedly, from the councillors down to the young boys and girls let out of school for the occasion. Indeed, the youngsters, the laddies and young callants, probably provide the most gratifying and encouraging picture of all, for those with eyes to see. For they represent so vitally and so naturally the living tradition. First of all, sporting rosettes of the town's colours, they flock to points where it is known the riders will dismount for this ceremony or that. There they struggle for the opportunity to hold the horses, even to lead them up and down while the ceremony goes on. The next stage is actually to be allowed to mount the coveted steeds, to walk or exercise them while their riders are otherwise engaged. Over the years saving has been going on, and one day there is enough in the box actually to hire a pony. Thereafter the pattern is set. From one common riding to the next, the savers save, each year managing to hire a slightly better animal. The schoolboy becomes the message-boy, the apprentice, the student and is now a follower, one of the moss-trooping swaggering band that supports the standard-bearer, breeched, booted and gallant. It is the ambition, by hook or by crook, one day to actually own a horse, unlikely as that may sound outside the Borderland. Next to the inspiring hope of being Cornet himself—that is the summit of aspiration—with the badge that proclaims the most gruelling of ride-outs well and truly ridden.

There is the pattern. Intense local patriotism, love of the town and countryside, its history—and tradition; the corporate spirit; the long memory of moss-trooping and reiving forebears; healthy rivalry; and worthy ambition to be foremost in the fray. Is it all just xenophobia, as my English friend declared, at the Redeswyre Ride-out? Or was that perhaps not, rather, sour grapes? What other municipality in these islands would not give its mace, its chain-of-office and half its charters, to see such a spirit in its towns-folk—great and splendid municipalities no less than small and dull ones?

Why not the English communities, just across the Border, shar-ing the same history, the same blood-stained past, the same blood indeed? This I, for one, just cannot understand.

Everyone with a feeling for lively and enduring tradition, for sheer colour and vitality, ought to make a point of visiting the Scots Borderland during the common riding season, from June to August. They will be entirely welcome, quite bowled-over, and almost certainly worn out. But they will come back and back, of that I have no doubt.

After Hawick there are no more towns or even villages further up Teviotdale, with the hills shouldering close. Goldielands Tower, Branxholme Castle and Harden House lie here, Scott for-talices of great renown. One of the Goldielands lairds, descended from a bastard of the famous Sir Walter Scott of Buccleuch, was at the Raid of the Redeswyre; and there is a tradition that the last of the line was hanged from his own gateway for cattle-reiving—in which case he must have fallen out with his nearby chiefly Scott neighbours, who would otherwise never have let such a thing happen. Branxholme was, of course, principal setting for *The Lay of the Last Minstrel*, and for long the chief seat of the Scotts of Buccleuch, chief of that name. Originally it was much larger than today—even though it was unlikely ever to have been able to hold the "nine and twenty knights of fame" and the "nine and twenty yeomen tall" the Bard of Abbotsford suggested. It was burned by the Earl of Northumberland in 1532, and rebuilt on a smaller scale. It is still the property of the Duke of Buccleuch, although the family no longer lives there.

The Scotts of Harden, however, still occupy Harden House, in the person of Lord Polwarth. It is set romantically above a deep ravine of a tributary of the Borthwick Water 3 miles to the north. The present long, plain crowstepped-gabled house of the seven-teenth century replaced an earlier stronghold destroyed about 1590, the Scotts gaining the place from the Lord Home in 1501.

Of this line was Auld Wat of Harden, the famous freebooter, who married the Flower of Yarrow in the ballad. It was in his turbulent time that the first tower was destroyed. The cattle that he lifted were concealed in the deep and precipitous glen below; and when the supply of beef was dwindling, his flowerlike wife used to set a covered dish on the table before him, which when opened revealed only a pair of spurs—sign that it was time to be riding again. The spurs still survive. Once, when Auld Wat was driving home 'a bow of kye' he passed a very large haystack, and is reputed to have declared ruefully, "By my conscience, had ye but four feet ye shouldna stand long there!" It was his son, Young Wat, who made the decision to wed Muckle Mou'ed Meg Murray of Elibank, rather than hang. Although members of the Scott of Harden family declare the Muckle Mou'ed Meg story allegorical rather than factual. The lady was in fact called *Agnes*, and her husband *William* Scott.

Beyond these places Teviot dwindles rapidly; and at Teviot-head, 9 miles above Hawick, we come to the watershed, with the very different lands of the west-flowing rivers and the West March ahead. Here, at Caerlanrig, took place the famous hanging of Johnnie Armstrong of Gilnockie, another noted Border free-booter, by the young James V, in 1530, with forty of his clan—but that is another story, and belongs to the West March anyway.

Chipchase Castle, Wark

Westerkirk in the Esk Valley—birthplace of Thomas Telford in 1757

Lanercost Abbey, Cumberland

St Andrew's Church, Corbridge with its eleventh-century tower

The Coquet Valley near Alwinton

The late fourteenth–century keep at Warkworth Castle,
Northumberland

Haaf–netting on the Rivęr Nith Estuary as it used to be done

The west front of Jedburgh Abbey

River Ettrick near Ettrickbridgend

8

The Scots Middle March—Ettrick and Yarrow

AT FIRST glance, it may perhaps seem strange that Ettrick and Yarrow should be so essentially an important part of the Scottish Borders. It is itself a large and somewhat vaguely defined area; but no part of it lies much less than 20 miles from the actual Border-line. Yet this great territory, which includes most of Selkirkshire, much of Peeblesshire, even some of Midlothian, and quite a lot of Dumfriesshire, and covering perhaps some 350 square miles, has always been a recognizable and famous entity, and always and indubitably Borderland. And for good reason.

Its old name was Ettrick Forest, or just The Forest; if anyone in old Scotland used the latter phrase without further identification, all knew that it was this area that was being referred to, however many other and great forests there were. It comprised the drainage basin—although basin gives a wholly wrong impression of such an essentially upland area—of the Rivers Ettrick and Yarrow, and in fact includes most of the central roof of Lowland Scotland. It was always a lonely, remote and exciting terrain, devoid of any large villages or communities—although the towns of Selkirk, Peebles and Moffat lay on its fringes, Selkirk rather more so. And though today it is still empty green hills, grass and heather, it was heavily forested once, true if scattered open forest, a late-lasting part of the original great Caledonian Forest which covered the land. Here it was only partially Scots pine, with oak even more prevalent, and birch and hazel. It was, of course, the royal hunting forest of Scotland above all others, with Newark Castle, near Selkirk, its main seat. But more important in history, it was an enormous and secure sanctuary, not only for the deer, boar and wild cattle with which it abounded, but for men—outlaws always, fugitives, guerilla fighters, patriots on the run. As such it played a major and never-to-be-forgotten part in the country's story. And because it was only a score of miles from the Border-line, with in most

places only further empty hills between, it formed an extension of that Debateable Land; more than that, an integral part of the whole Border community, in peace—if that is ever a word to apply to the Borderland—and in war.

In a way, Ettrick Forest frequently formed the essential citadel of Scotland. For here was an area which large armies—or small ones, for that matter—could not penetrate, roadless, abounding in ambush-places, with no means of support for numbers of men. Nor could cavalry patrols move therein; and any lightly armed men, on foot, were at the mercy of any already there and who knew the wild terrain better. Even Edward I never made any major venture into The Forest—as he must fiercely have desired to do, for here of course was where Wallace and Bruce, in the early days of the Wars of Independence, hid, and from here they raided and slew to mighty effect. In typical arrogant fashion, Edward appointed his Earl of Gloucester—whom he did not love —to be Keeper of Ettrick Forest; but that was a gesture, and a rod for Gloucester's back. It is probably true to say that this desperate struggle for Scotland's soul could not have been won without The Forest—for often it was the only part of the kingdom south of the remote and uninterested Highlands which was not in English hands and under the mailed heel. The area is full of memories of Wallace especially, and it was here, at Selkirk, that he chose to hold the great assembly, almost a parliament, which appointed him Guardian of Scotland, in 1298, after Stirling Bridge.

In later days, The Forest remained as useful to harried men— even when they were harried by their own king and government. Many are the ballads that sing of this territory, telling of the Outlaw Murray, the Flower of Yarrow, Auld and Young Wat Scott, the Dowie Dens, Jamie Telfer of the fair Dodheid, and the Flowers of the Forest themselves.

Although it was a royal demesne, the great family of Douglas got at least nominal control of it, as hereditary keepers; and wherever that mighty house was concerned, sparks flew. The renowned Douglas Tragedy took place here, at Blackhouse Tower, where the seven Douglas brothers fell. When the Black Douglas power was eventually brought low—by the Crown and the Red Douglases in conjunction—the Scotts of Buccleuch were amongst those who rose on the ruins. The Scotts gained a large foothold in

Grey Mare's Tail

Ettrick Forest, and still hold it. Buccleuch itself, of course, is situated here, a lonely and small place to give title to a dukedom —although it was its own parish once, if scarcely a large one and mainly heather. The Duke of Buccleuch's favourite seat, indeed his permanent home, is at Bowhill, in Yarrow, 4 miles south-west of Selkirk, with ancient Newark Castle nearby.

If it is wondered at why Ettrick was tree-covered once, and is so no more, James V seems to be the answer. He is recorded as enjoying a great hunting here in 1528. It makes a stirring account, politics and sport mixed:

> . . . to all lords, barons, gentlemen, landward-men and freeholders, that they should compear at Edinburgh, with a month's victuals, to pass with the King where he pleased, to danton the thieves of Tiviotdale, Annandale, Liddisdale, and other parts of that country; and also warn all gentlemen that had good dogs to bring them, that he might hunt in the said country as he pleased; the whilk the Earl of Argyll, the Earl of Huntly, the Earl of Athole and so all the rest of the gentlemen of the Highland did, and brought their hounds with them . . . The second day of June the King past out of Edinburgh to the hunting . . . to the number of twelve thousand men; and then past to Meggitland and hounded and hawked all the country and bounds . . . he slew in these bounds, eighteen score of harts.

Stirring prelude to the taking and execution of Johnnie Armstrong, Scott of Tushielaw and other Border freebooters, and the imprisonment of greater men—the Earl of Bothwell, then Lord of Teviotdale; the Lords Home and Maxwell, and the barons of Ferniehirst, Buccleuch, Polwarth and Johnston. This, of course, was the real object of the exercise. But after this salutary tidying up of the Border situation, James seems to have turned Ettrick Forest into a vast sheep-run, something new for Scotland, however normal it was to become in later times. He turned 10,000 sheep to graze in The Forest; and, as is the way with sheep, these very quickly destroyed the young trees and prevented natural regeneration. Possibly this was part of the royal policy, the widespread wilderness being considered less of a sanctuary, for the broken men, lacking its trees.

A glance at the map shows the two rivers, Ettrick and Yarrow, joining 2 miles west of Selkirk, and the conjoint stream, keeping the name of Ettrick, reaching the Tweed less than 5 miles on, not far from Abbotsford. Roads now follow both Ettrick and Yarrow up their respective long valleys through the formerly trackless wilderness—a very lovely wilderness; and there is another transverse road which strikes south from Traquair, near Innerleithen, climbing regularly to 1,100 feet, crossing both lateral roads and eventually descending to Eskdale near Langholm, in the West March, a magnificent scenic route of 44 mountainous miles. This was partly the way the Romans threaded the wilderness, and remains of their camps and forts lie amongst the sheep-strewn hills.

Selkirk lies at the north-eastern tip of Ettrick, a very ancient and notable royal burgh, possibly the proudest of all the Borderland. With a population of 5,400 it has just 300 more than Peebles, and thus is third in size in the Middle March. It is also a tweed-milling and dyeing centre, of course; but somehow it manages to maintain the impression that here is no commercial town but a county seat of ancient lineage and no small dignity. It keeps its mills well down on the low ground of the Ettrick haugh, while the main town is terraced high above, eyes averted, to the south and east. Some of the council housing down there at the riverside is certainly something of an affront to a lovely setting, sadly uninspired. But by and large Selkirk is a quite handsome town in a modest way—and its vistas are notably fine, with the hills here drawing a little way back on all sides, and prospects wide and fair.

As has been indicated, David I founded an abbey here in 1113, which after thirteen years was removed to Kelso—a very odd circumstance. But the king did not thereby withdraw his favour from the place, for Selkirk—really Shiel-kirk, the church beside the shiels or summer dwellings of the royal foresters of Ettrick—claims that he created it a royal burgh. Some grudging folk have expressed doubts as to this, for before Berwick and Roxburgh fell into English hands, these were accepted as two of the four royal burghs of Scotland—the others being Edinburgh and Stirling. And when the first two were lost by invasion, Lanark and Linlithgow took their places. Since both these towns also claim to be royal burghs of David I's creation, and were not included in the original four, it seems that while there were a number of early royal burghs, a special four of them were always constituted a *Curia Quatuor Burgorum*, a semi-judicial body which eventually grew into the Convention of Royal Burghs. So who shall say that

Selkirk's claim is false? At any rate, the town's proud antiquity is unassailable; and for so modestly-sized a place, great is the role it has played on the Scottish scene. Because of its out-of-the-way position, it was burned less frequently by the English than the other Border burghs; but it by no means escaped entirely, for it went up in flames in the grim period after Flodden. However, thanks to the town's claims that it had played a notable part at that disastrous battle, the town clerk allegedly coming home, one of the few survivors, with an English flag captured, King James V (or his advisers, for he was but a child) granted Selkirk 1,000 acres of the royal forest as common, and permitted sufficient royal wood to be cut to rebuild the town. The Flodden flag is preserved in the museum.

Needless to say, all this is commemorated in Selkirk's common riding celebrations—which even its rival burghs concede to be a very fine affair and carried out with an air. The stirring ceremony when the burgh standard-bearer 'casts the colours' in the market place, represents the return of that renowned town clerk, Walter Brydon, alone of Selkirk's eighty volunteers. When he reached this spot he cast down the flag there in silent intimation that he was the only survivor.

Local tradition would connect the well-known Selkirk song with this same Flodden episode:

> Up wi' the souters o' Selkirk
> And down wi' the Earl o' Home!
> And up wi' a' the braw lads
> That sew the single-soled shoon!

Selkirk used to be famous as a shoe-making town, before the tweed mills came, and souters was the name they received. Natives of Selkirk are still known as souters, and proud to be—though there has been no shoe-making for long. The song is held to refer to the Selkirk contingent's gallantry at Flodden, and the alleged poor conduct of Lord Home and his men—for Home was the only man of note to come out of that *débâcle* with his life. But the facts are otherwise. There was no Earl of Home at Flodden; the earldom was not created until 1604. And the Lord Home thereat was no poltroon, but acquitted himself most effectively, winning his flank of the battle but unfortunately pursuing his beaten enemy so far from the field that he was of no use to aid his sore-pressed monarch. So he did not die with James, like the rest of Scotland's aristocracy, and a great part of her lesser men, and for this he was never forgiven. It seems clear that the song actually refers to an early football match held between a local team and one of the Earl of Home's. Never mind—the song goes with a brave lilt.

Selkirk is a great place for statues. Taking pride of place is one to Sir Walter Scott, who was for long Sheriff of Selkirkshire, and much beloved. Many relics of 'The Shirra', as he was called, are preserved in the town hall and the court house. Nearby is another monument, to Mungo Park, the explorer, who was born not far away at Foulshiels, and died on the Niger. A third statue is the Flodden Memorial, by the same sculptor who made the Galashiels Reiver, Thomas Clapperton, this time of a man-at-arms on foot, with halberd and standard. There are also memorials to J. B. Selkirk the poet, Tom Scott the artist, and others.

Two miles west of the town is Philiphaugh, where was fought that grim battle when Montrose and the royalist army suffered crushing defeat at the hands of David Leslie, major-general of the Covenant forces, in 1645, one of the decisive struggles of United Kingdom history—for it ensured the final defeat of Charles I's cause. It was an unequal contest from the first, even though Montrose had just completed a series of victories over the length and breadth of Scotland unequalled before or since by any commander. Weary, reduced in numbers to only 600 fighting-men, his little army not only here faced a fresh and professional host ten times as numerous, under Leslie, but had been betrayed by the Earl of Traquair, who had sent Leslie details of Montrose's whereabouts, dispositions and weaknesses. Although no large numbers were involved, compared with some battles, it was one of the blackest days in Scotland's story. Not so much for the battle itself, but for what happened afterwards. For thereafter took place one of the most shocking massacres of the prisoners, the wounded and the many camp-followers, ever to stain a nation's name. All who could be caught, men, women and children, were slain without exception and without pity—and all in the name of religion. For it was all done to the glory of God, the excesses urged on by blood-crazed zealot Covenanting ministers of the Kirk. That many of Montrose's men were Irish and Catholic—although by no means all, for it was the Lowland Scots habit in those days to call all Gaelic-speaking Highlanders and Islesmen Erse or Irish—was adequate excuse. The long series of Covenant defeats by the royalists had to be wiped out in blood. After the battle, 300 woman and children—Gaelic armies always were notable for their camp-followings—were butchered on the spot. Then were massacred 200 cooks, grooms and other non-combatants. A remnant of the Irish fighters had surrendered on terms, under Montrose's adjutant Stewart. Now the ministers protested against these being spared, declaring that the terms could only apply to Stewart himself—to which Leslie weakly gave in; and all were slaughtered. All over the Borderland fugitives were hunted and cut down like animals; and even those who managed to escape northwards heading for the Highlands, were rounded up, taken to Leslie's camp at Lin-lithgow and there flung wholesale over the bridge into the Avon and either drowned at once or stabbed to death by the pikes of the soldiers who lined the river-banks. This insensate lust for blood was one of the strangest and ghastliest manifestations of the religious wars of the seventeenth century—and the Covenanters were to feel the fierce backlash of it twenty years later when the tide had turned, episcopalianism was triumphant and Claverhouse, Dalziel and Grierson of Lag wrought their grim campaigns in Southern Scotland. When we talk of violence and savagery in Northern Ireland today, in sectarian strife, let us not forget Philiphaugh—or for that matter, many of the inhumanities perpetrated by Cromwell's godly Ironsides.

For Philiphaugh, David Leslie was rewarded with a payment of 50,000 merks (about £33,000) plus a gold chain, and was later created Lord Newark. Not always realized is that this able soldier, but man of weak principles, was the grandson of Robert Stewart, Earl of Orkney, Mary Queen of Scots's half-brother, and therefore a great-grandson of James V who keeps coming into the story of Ettrick Forest.

Yarrow and Ettrick fork a mile above Philiphaugh, and the main A708 road follows Yarrow westwards, eventually proceeding by St. Mary's Loch and Tibbie Shiels Inn and through the passes 34 miles to Moffat. The B709 follows Ettrick, to the south, 44 miles to Lockerbie or Langholm by the site of the former

Ettrick village. Both roads are scenic delights. Two miles up Yarrow, passing Bowhill, the Buccleuch estate and opposite Foulshiels, Mungo Park's birthplace, is the impressive and romantically-sited castle of Newark on its green mound above the rushing river. Despite its proximity to Philiphaugh, the name has nothing to do with David Leslie's title; he was a Fifer, and named his peerage from his castle there between Elie and St. Monans. There are innumerable Newarks in both Scotland and England. This one had an Auld Wark on the site or nearby, which was the royal hunting-seat of so many Scots kings. The present tall and imposing tower, although looking sufficiently old, was only built about 1423 by Archibald, Earl of Douglas, as Keeper; and it has caphouse watch-chambers at parapet-level of a century later. It is a picturesque strength, its 10-feet-thick walls honeycombed with mural chambers, and an enormous kitchen-fireplace screened off at the end of the Great Hall. Above first-floor level on the west wall is a weatherbeaten panel bearing the royal arms of Scotland. Even after its royal days, Newark retained its links with the royal Stewarts, for here was the home of the unfortunate Anna Scott, widow of Charles II's son by Lucy Walters, the ill-fated Duke of Monmouth, who was executed after Sedgemoor for claiming the throne. She was the heiress of the Scotts, Countess of Buccleuch in her own right. It was at Newark that Sir Walter made his Last Minstrel sing his lay to the sorrowing Duchess:

> He pass'd where Newark's stately tower
> Looks out from Yarrow's birchen bower;
> The Minstrel gazed with wishful eye—
> No humbler resting-place was nigh. . . .

For a hunting-seat this castle was involved in much discord and political trouble. It was besieged and taken by the English under Lord Grey in 1548; in its courtyard were shot over 100 of the Philiphaugh prisoners; and five years later it was occupied by Cromwell's troops after the Battle of Dunbar.

Blackhouse Tower may seem a strangely remote spot to have been the seat and centre of quite an important barony. Its ruins lie 2 miles up the side glen of the Douglas Burn from Craig of Douglas, 10 miles further up the Yarrow road from Newark and just over a mile short of the foot of St. Mary's Loch. Yet this was the most populous area of The Forest once, almost at its centre; and the towers of Dryhope, Deuchar, Henderland, Cramalt, Eldinhope and many another lie within a few miles. Even so, Blackhouse is the furthest back from the road. It has its own named range of hills surrounding, reaching heights of 2,300 feet. Here were seated the Douglases long before there were Stewarts to make them Keepers of the royal forest. Indeed, at Malcolm Canmore's parliament held at Forfar in 1057, Godscroft tells us that Sir John Douglas, eldest son of William, first Lord of Douglas, sat as baron of this Douglasburn. The present ruins date from long after that early period, of course, and represent a successor to the original castle. Here took place the grim story enshrined in the ballad of the "Douglas Tragedy". The elder daughter of the house had fallen in love with a young neighbouring laird, referred to as Lord William. Who he was is not clear, though it is evident from the ballad that his home was no great distance to the west, via St. Mary's Loch. So he may have been a Scott, or perhaps a Cockburn of Henderland. At any rate, one day Margaret Douglas and he eloped from Blackhouse Tower, and were pursued by the lady's father and seven tall brothers. William must have been a paladin indeed, for he took on the entire contingent, and slew each and all of the Douglases—presumably they fought chivalrously, one at a time. And the seven stones on the hillsides are alleged to mark their several falling-places. The old father doesn't seem to have rated a stone—though he is the only one the ballad makes the young woman to have shed a tear over. But the doughty William had not got off scot-free, whatever his name—althought he apparently did not reveal his damaged state until they reached St. Mary's Loch; where, by the light of the moon, they halted to quench their thirst. It was the spreading dark stain on the water which revealed to the Lady Margaret her lover's plight.

> "Hold up, hold up, Lord William" she says,
>   "For I fear that you are slain!"
> " 'Tis naething but the shadows of my scarlet cloak,
>   That shines on the water sae plain."

They rode on until they came to his tower, and the wounded man had the civility to request his mother to make their bed, for he had brought his chosen lady home:

"Oh mak my bed, lady mother," he says,
　"Oh mak it braid and deep;
And lay Lady Marg'ret close at my back,
　And the sounder I will sleep. . . ."

Lord William was dead lang ere midnight,
　Lady Marg'ret lang ere day;
And all true lovers that go thegither,
　May they have mair luck than they.

Lord William was buried in St. Marie's Kirk,
　Lady Marg'ret in Marie's Quire:
Out o' the lady's grave grew a bonny red rose,
　And out o' the knight's a brier.

This ballad is typical of many handed down in the Borderland, and very similar in some details to others—the bit about the rose and the brier being a favourite ending. But this one is unusually circumstantial as to topography; and the burial at St. Mary's Chapel has an authentic ring about it.

The chapel, which gives the great loch its name, is famous for more than this, of course. This is the home area of James Hogg, the Ettrick Shepherd, who "taught the wandering winds to sing". His cottage of Altrieve was nearby; and much he wrote about this lovely water and its chapel.

For though in feudal strife a foe
Hath laid our Lady's chapel low,
Yet stil beneath the hallowed soil
The peasant rests him from his toil:
And, dying, bids his bones be laid
Where erst his simple fathers prayed.

Here took place the principal incident of another ballad, "Mary Scott", when the daughter of Scott of Tushielaw, being brought for burial, awoke from her strange sleep; and here she was in due course married to Pringle of Torwoodlee. Both Scott and Wordsworth also wrote vividly about this place and its surroundings. The former introduces the second canto of *Marmion* with a description of it.

Large lakes are rare in the Borderland, and that alone makes the 4-miles-long St. Mary's Loch notable. But its inherent beauty is renowned, its setting amongst the green hills, which it mirrors so clearly, lovely indeed. The smaller Loch o' the Lowes at its head was originally all part of the whole, but became separated by deposits from the incoming Oxcleuch and Crosscleuch Burns.

Beyond the lochs a mere 3 miles, the road reaches the watershed, at 1,100 feet, near the famed Grey Mare's Tail waterfall and the Dumfriesshire border.

The Ettrick Water's valley, although it contains no loch, is just as romantic, and of course considerably longer. Unnumbered are the ancient towers and former lairdships which dot its fair flanks and sing the songs of the Border—Oakwood, Kirkhope, Hyndhope, Gilmanscleuch, Deloraine, Tushielaw, Thirlstane, Gamescleuch, Buccleuch and so on. Their names star the pages of the *Minstrelsy of the Scottish Border*. Oakwood, still entire, 3 miles up from the junction with Yarrow, is said to have been a house of Sir Michael Scott the Wizard. Certainly it was for long owned by the Scotts of Harden, in whose family it remained until recent years. There is doubt about whether the hero of "The Dowie Dens of Yarrow" ballad was the Baron of Oakwood, as once claimed. This was John Scott, sixth son of Harden, murdered by his kinsmen the Scotts of nearby Gilmanscleuch. Oakwood is an attractive, sturdy, tall building, now surrounded by the farm-steading. It has the distinctly unusual square angle-turret caphouses, at opposite ends of the roofline, similar to those at Newark and Kirkhope and Neidpath. These seem to be a Border speciality.

Kirkhope is a much more roughly built fortalice, though similar in style, set most remotely on a bare hillside far from any road, about a mile north-west of the village of Ettrickbridgend, 3 miles on. It was the stronghold of the eldest sons of the Scotts of Harden—who presumably must have found it convenient to keep their offspring at a distance. It was to Kirkhope, therefore, that Auld Wat, when he was less than that, would bring as bride the celebrated beauty, Mary Scott of Dryhope, the Flower of Yarrow. Allegedly also here came Young Wat, their son, with Muckle Mou'ed Meg Murray.

Ettrickbridgend is quite a community to find deep in the wilderness, and actually growing, with the discerning coming to recognize that here is somewhere truly 'away from it all' yet only a quarter of an hour's run from Selkirk. Indeed the present Member of Parliament for this area and Leader of the Liberal Party has come to live here. The former and original Ettrick village is sited 13 miles further on and not even on the main B709 road.

It is near the latter that James Hogg was born in 1770, in a cottage now gone; and he is buried in the graveyard of the parish kirk close by, his self-chosen title of the Ettrick Shepherd accurate indeed. He was an extraordinary man, by any standards, son of a line of shepherds and foresters who had a long tradition of witchcraft and feyness. One was alleged to have out-wizarded Michael Scott himself, having changed that redoubtable character into a hare with his own wand. James's own grandfather was reckoned the last man in the district who had actually conversed with the fairies. Be all that as it may, the grandson was a born poet, although it was as Jamie the Poeter he was known locally—there may be a subtle distinction there. Self-educated, he was something of a rough diamond always; and though Walter Scott greatly assisted him, introducing him to publishers and into Edinburgh society, the Ettrick Shepherd never sought to be anything else. He had a hot temper and his own ways of doing things. Once he started a letter to Sir Walter "Damned Sir". Lockhart, Scott's biographer, recounts Hogg's first visit to Scott's Edinburgh house. Mrs. Scott being at the time in delicate health, the Ettrick Shepherd, finding his hostess reclining on a sofa, took possession of another sofa opposite hers, and stretched himself upon it full length, muddy boots and sheep-scented clothing notwithstanding. He explained afterwards that he thought that in such society he could not do better than imitate his hostess. Unlike Robert Burns, whom he so greatly admired and somewhat resembled, he could never adapt himself to polite society—nor did he try very hard. He was soon calling Scott Wattie, to the horror of many—but not of Scott himself, who remained his friend.

Hogg's work was uneven, inevitably, and much of it not as good as he believed it to be. But some of it was superlative. For a man who could barely write, it was extraordinary indeed. Even the *literati* of Edinburgh in its Golden Age acknowledged it—whatever they said about his manners—and it was Christopher North himself who prophesied his enduring fame. His "Kilmeny" is something of which any poet anywhere might be proud. And his novel, *The Confessions of a Justified Sinner,* is so advanced in outlook as to out-Poe Poe, with André Gide, reviewing a modern edition, declaring that he read it with a stupefaction and admiration which increased with every page. There are not many writers of his century whom modern experts will say such things about. Nor many writers, of any period, who could make £300—a great sum in those days—out of a prose "Essay on Sheep". Nor indeed who could sell 10,000 copies of one of their volumes of poetry in the United States, as did Hogg. An extraordinary man—but a true Borderer. Truer than Walter Scott, perhaps. For when Scott, after actually obtaining a much-coveted ticket for him to attend the Coronation of George IV in Westminster Abbey, tried to persuade the Ettrick Shepherd to make the journey, Hogg said he was sorry, he would like to have gone—but it clashed with St. Boswell's Fair, from which of course he could not absent himself!

Let us leave James Hogg, and the Middle March of Scotland too, with these lines from "Kilmeny" in *The Queen's Wake*:

When many a day had come and fled,
When grief grew calm and hope was dead,
When Mass for Kilmeny's soul had been sung,
When the bedesman had prayed, and the dead bell rung;
Late, late in a gloaming when all was still,
When the fringe was red on the westlin hill,
The wood was sere, the moon i' the wane,
The reek o' the cot hung over the plain,
Like a little wee cloud in the world its lane,
When the ingle glowed with an eiry leme,
Late, late in the gloaming Kilmeny came hame.

If a man never wrote anything other than these lines, he deserves well of his fellows.

9

The English Middle March

THE striking differences between the English and Scottish Middle Marches are readily explained by even the briefest glance at the map. The Border-line runs all the way through the high Cheviots, on this March; but on the Scots side these quickly dwindle away to wide and fertile vales, while on the English side the hills and moors extend on and on southwards, save at the extreme east. In consequence, the English March is empty, by comparison—or by any standards. That is, until some score of miles, on an average, the valleys of the Tyne and Rede and Coquet begin to open out. So here are no thriving burghs or even large villages, for an area of perhaps 500 square miles, only a vast upland territory coloured mainly brown on the map and little populated inevitably. It is difficult, therefore, to see the English Middle March as an entity, apart from this lofty wilderness. Such population as there is, is a long way from the Border-line, and wide-scattered at that.

The Rede and the North Tyne valleys are the two conduits through this mighty watershed, from the Border-line to the more settled parts, with that of the Coquet, to the east, to a lesser degree. These of course were the inevitable routes of the raiders of old, going and coming, as they are of the traveller of today, the Rede giving access, by Otterburn and Catcleuch, to Carter Bar, the Redeswyre and Jedburgh; the North Tyne by Bellingham and Keilder and Deadwater to Liddesdale and the Note o' the Gate pass to Hawick. There is no through-route from the head of Coquetdale into Scotland—however expert were the reivers in threading the intervening welter of hills with their lifted cattle herds.

The upper reaches of these long shallow valleys are unlike anything on the Scots side, with miles meaning little, houses a rarity, and the call of the curlews and the baaing of sheep the prevailing sounds. That, and the unending rush and tinkle of water. Yet most evidently it was not always so, for these uplands are full of the relics of very early and prehistoric times. Camps, forts, enclosures,

earthworks, tumuli and cairns litter these Cheviot hillsides and moors; and Roman remains are prominent indeed. The great Hadrian's Wall, of course, built against the Picts and Caledonians, as the Scots were then called, runs across the land just south of this area, and the Roman road of Dere Street marches northwards straight over moor and fell into Scotland—we have already come across it spanning the Kale Water valley near Jedburgh. But while the Roman relics remain in disciplined proximity to their great highways, and are reasonably well known, the early native sites and works are widespread and legion, littering the countryside in a fashion which indicates how populous were these south Cheviot slopes in ancient times. For instance, within a 5-mile radius of Bellingham alone there are over twenty such sites, excluding the Roman ones. And if you take the circle round Kirkwhelpington, to the east, there are half as many again. And Otterburn can do even better. This is an aspect of Northumberland which is insufficiently appreciated, its great prehistoric and protohistoric interest, and its very large early population in areas now largely deserted. Such things hardly come within my scope here, since these remains date from a period long before there was any Borderland as such; although obviously the Romans saw the area as a borderland also, even though their line was distinctly south of the present one. But neglected riches are always worth mentioning.

Bellingham—pronounced Bellin-jam—is an interesting little town in many ways, the nearest sizeable community to Scotland, in the Middle March; though not so very sizeable, in fact, with a population of only some 1,300 for the parish. Yet it is an important market centre for the North Tynedale area, and supports a large annual agricultural show and notable stock-sales, sheep and lambs naturally most important. Actually it has a distinctly Scots air about it—and this is hardly to be wondered at, as will be explained hereafter. Its church is particularly Scottish in appearance; there is only one other in England like it, at Boltons in Cumberland—but innumerable in Scotland. It has a stone-slabbed roof supported on a rib-vaulted ceiling, thick walls, small windows and massive buttresses—all looking very much as though it was built for defence, as no doubt it was. Of original thirteenth-century erection, it was rebuilt in the fifteenth century.

Three miles to the north-west are the remains of Tarset Castle,

Morpeth Clock Tower

where the Tarset Burn comes down to join Tyne. This was a property of the great Scots Comyn family, Earls of Buchan and Lords
of Badenoch and Lochaber in the thirteenth and fourteenth centuries. The Red Comyn, Sir John (Lord of Badenoch and nephew
of King John Baliol, Edward I's puppet)—the same who was slain
at the altar at Dumfries by Robert the Bruce—owned this strength;
which must have ensured the discomfort of the neighbourhood
during the Wars of Independence, since not only was it on one of
the main invasion routes, coming or going, but it suffered from
internal Scottish animosities as well as the normal Scots–English
ones. Moreover this whole area had a reputation for lawlessness
unsurpassed on the English side of the March, the men of Tarset
and Tarret being notorious reivers, trouble-makers and most
independently-minded. They caused their own Wardens almost
as much trouble as they caused their neighbours—Charltons,
Robsons, Milburns and Dodds. The Charltons of Charlton—their
property lying midway between Bellingham and Tarset, and the
family still represented in the vicinity—were the leaders, and behaved quite as autocratically as any of their opposite numbers to
the north, such as the Scotts of Harden. Indeed, curiously enough,
the Charltons had exactly the same tradition of presenting a spur
in a covered dish to their chief when fresh beef ran out as did the
Scotts—although here it appears to have been one spur rather than
a pair. They were powerful enough to tackle even their Warden
and his forces in the execution of his duty, and in the early sixteenth century attacked and drove out Sir Ralph Fenwick and his
men from Tarset Castle, thereafter setting the castle on fire.

The Northumberland National Park is superlative by any
standards. It is an enormous area covering the open countryside
south of the Cheviot Hills right down to Hadrian's Wall and
including the Simonside Hills at Rothbury. Considerable parts of
it are forested, and it includes the Ministry of Defence gunnery
practice and training areas around Otterburn, famous for its
ancient Battle of Chevy Chase, and Redesdale. Adjacent to the
west is the vast Keilder Forest and Water development, open to
the public. This is both the largest man-made forest and the
largest man-made lake in Europe, set in fine scenery, covering
120 square miles of the uplands, the artificial Keilder Water reservoir having a surface area of no less than 2,684 acres, with many

bays, creeks and inlets. Here, there are excellent recreational facilities and information centres for the outdoor enthusiast. The Forestry Commission headquarters are at Keilder Castle, the former hunting-seat of the Percy family. Other large state forests lie nearby, at Wark and Redesdale and over the border at Wauchope.

The Keilder Stone, a huge boulder marking the actual Borderline 3 miles north-east of Deadwater, is too highly-placed, at 1,500 feet, to be lost amongst the new trees. This great sandstone block is very much the central point round which revolves another famous Border ballad, "The Cout of Keilder". The Cout, or Colt, was the nickname given to the young laird or squire of Keilder, probably a Charlton or a Robson, alluding to his vigour and great stature both. He came to grief at the hands of one of the most hated men on either side of the Border, of any age—Sir William de Soulis, Lord of Liddesdale, whom legend picturesquely declares to have eventually been boiled alive by his own vassals on Nine Stane Rig nearby, but who in fact died a prisoner in Dumbarton Castle as a result of a failed conspiracy to assassinate the great Bruce and put himself on the Scots throne (he was, in fact, a grandson of one of the original competitors for the throne).

This is one of the ballads collected and contributed by John Leyden, of Denholm:

> The eiry bloodhound howl'd by night,
>   The streamers flaunted red,
> Till broken streaks of flaky light
>   O'er Keilder's mountains spread.
>
> The lady sighed as Keilder rose,
>   "Come tell me, dear love mine,
> Go you to hunt where Keilder flows
>   Or on the banks of Tyne."
>
> "The heath-bell blows where Keilder flows,
>   By Tyne the primrose pale;
> But now we ride on the Scottish side,
>   To hunt in Liddesdale."
>
> "Gin you will ride on the Scottish side,
>   Sore must thy Margaret mourn;
> For Soulis abhorr'd is Liddel's lord,
>   And I fear you'll ne'er return."

But young Keilder was rash as he was strong, and deliberately flaunted and challenged fate, as he crossed into Scotland by riding widdershins—that is, anti-clockwise—around the Keilder Stone, something discreet men just did not do, with the little Brown Folk of the hills likely to be involved. These Brownies were an influence not to be discounted in the Borderland, even if you were the Lord of Keilder's son.

> Around, around, young Keilder wound,
>   And called in scornful tone:
> With him to pass the barrier ground,
>   The Spirit of the Stone.

Despite this unsuitable start, Keilder and his friends made good hunting amongst the Scots hills—and energetic and widespread hunting too, for he started at the Redeswyre and ended up at Hermitage in Liddesdale, 15 long heather miles even as the crow flies. And there their bold good fortune held, for the dreaded lord of Hermitage Castle, Sir William de Soulis himself, invited them into his hall to sup and dine with him. It was only after the eating, while the wine flowed and the minstrels played to them, that suddenly the Northumbrians realized that the melody being played for their entertainment was none other than "The Black, Black Bull of Noroway"—and like a frozen hand descending upon their hearts they knew that they had supped with the Devil indeed. Other men might be inhibited from harming guests who had eaten their salt—but not William de Soulis, the King of Scots' Hereditary Butler. For that Black Bull reference was ominous. It foretold assassination, there at table. Men had died at that dread sign, for centuries—and for centuries more would continue to do so, since it somehow seemed to absolve the host from the otherwise strict laws of hospitality, to place a black bull's head on the table before guests. The notorious Black Dinner which took place in 1440, 120 years later, before young King James II, will come to mind, when the sixth Earl of Douglas and his brother were decoyed to a banquet at Edinburgh Castle, and despatched before all the guests by their host, the Chancellor Crichton.

Young Keilder was no wilting craven, and jumped to his feet and somehow managed to cut his way out through the press of his treacherous host's minions—whatever happened to his companions. But at Hermitage Water he was cornered, forced into the river by lances, until he stumbled and fell, and thereafter was held down by the said lances until all was over:

> Swift was the Cout o' Keilder's course,
>   Along the lily lee;
> But home came never hound nor horse,
>   And never home came he.

> And the hunters bold of Keilder's train,
>   Within yon castle's wall,
> In a deadly sleep must aye remain,
>   Till the ruined towers down fall.

The little Brown Man who had guided him to the water, presumably went back to the Keilder Stone, satisfied.

It is perhaps interesting and apt here to consider another and more meaningful incident in which both this Sir William de Soulis and this territory of the North Tyne valley were involved, in 1314. At least, almost certainly de Soulis would be involved, since he was Royal Butler. For, only a month or two after the great victory of Bannockburn, Robert the Bruce led a quite extraordinary expedition over the Border at Deadwater and down Tynedale. This was not one more of the innumerable raids made deep into England for years before and after, in an attempt to force Edward II into signing a peace treaty such as Scotland so desperately needed, and to come to terms after his great defeat—something that weak but stubborn monarch just would not do because he considered Bruce to be a rebel, all the Scots rebels, and he would not sit down at any table with such. This expedition of the autumn of 1314 was no raid, even though its main objective probably was the same, to bring pressure to bear on Edward. It was a royal progress. Bruce rode southwards attended by his Court and ladies—including his wife, daughter and sisters, newly released after eight years of English bondage. And though he did burn a few farms and hamlets in North Tyne, this was only to warn the rest of the land not to get uppish. In fact, the hero-king came in peace, indeed demanding fealties from the landholders, and to "resume the Lordship and Liberty of Tynedale".

This peculiar proceeding greatly intrigued me when I was writing a trilogy of novels on Robert Bruce; and I could find no historical source to enlighten me as to its meaning and significance. It seemed a very odd thing for the embattled King of Scots to be doing immediately after his tremendous victory, but when his own country lay practically prostrate after eighteen years of dire war, and a thousand important items were urgently demanding his attention. Why go traipsing into Northumberland with his Court, like some idle sight-seeing princeling on tour? It took me a lot of research and probing, but at length I did discover the reason and circumstances—and a fascinating story and eye-opener it proved to be. At least, to me.

It seemed that Bruce went actually claiming that North Tyne-dale was a legal and integral part of the Kingdom of Scotland; and his progress and taking of allegiances and fealties was to establish the fact afresh, without any doubts. In other words, the Border-line hereabouts was *not* at Deadwater, where the North Tyne rises, near the Keilder Stone, but far to the south, in the Hexham area, a great salient into England, which included the large, impor-tant and rich Lordship and Honour and Liberty of Tynedale. That Lordship did not include the rich ecclesiastical jewel of Hexham itself, with its great priory and lands. But Bruce certainly demanded his dues therefrom. The point of the exercise, of course, apart from the chance of obtaining much-needed gold to help in the rehabilitation of war-ravaged Scotland, was so to worry Edward that he would be persuaded that it was wiser and cheaper to come to terms and proclaim peace between the two kingdoms. Unfor-tunately Edward still sulked in the south, and would not play—and the state of war went on for another thirteen years.

The suggestion that this Tynedale was actually and legally part of Scotland intrigued me not a little. At first I assumed that it was all just a colossal try-on, a piece of bluff on Bruce's part—though it was obvious that he, at least, took it very seriously. But, digging and delving uncovered this much; that the weak King Stephen had ceded the *whole* of Northumberland to Scotland in 1139; and that though this was regained by Henry II in 1157, North Tyne-dale was by a special arrangement granted back to William the Lion of Scotland two years later. It continued in Scottish posses-sion until the puppet-king John Baliol's forfeiture by Edward in 1295. This was highly interesting; but it seemed inconclusive. The assumption was that this was Scottish *property* in England, not that it was an integral part of the Scottish realm—a very different matter. There were many properties in England owned by Scots —Bruce himself had great estates in the South. But clearly he at least looked on Tynedale differently. I still sought to find out why.

It was quite a long and difficult search, but eventually I did run something conclusive to earth. In an Irish book, Olive Armstrong's *Edward Bruce's Invasion of Ireland*, I came at last upon the clue I needed. There was a reference to Bruce's claim to Tynedale, and a footnote to see the Northumberland Assize Rolls of 1278.

I sent to the Public Records Office in Chancery Lane, London, where after much seeking, I was told all such legal records were deposited; and asked for a photostat copy of any references to the Lordship of Tynedale in 1278. After a long delay two such excerpts reached me. One was not very relevant or conclusive; but the other, apparently sent along more or less as an afterthought and make-weight, was a catch indeed.

It was the official record of a jury trial of the period, in the Northumberland Assize Court, dull lawyers' stuff—but with an explosive delayed-action ending. It referred to the case of one Beatrix of Quytfeld, or Whitefield, in Tynedale, who accused certain named persons of robbing her house to the value of 100 merks—but at trial was unable to substantiate her charges before the sheriff. In consequence she was gaoled for false charges. But then comes the bombshell. "The jury attest that the trespass alleged was done in Tynedale, in the Kingdom of Scotland, out of the Kingdom of England, and the truth cannot be enquired into here."

So there we have it, plain and factual, in Northumberland's own court-of-law, the admission that Tynedale was in fact not just property owned by Scots, or the King of Scots, but part of Scotland and not part of England. Now we know what Bruce was up to in 1314. It would make an interesting exercise to discover when, if ever, that legal position was specifically altered. Bruce's plans in Tynedale, it is thought, included the possibility of an exchange for Berwick-on-Tweed, its almost impregnable fortress still then in English hands. Come to think of it, it might still be a good exchange!

The main seat of the Tynedale Lordship was at Wark Castle— not to be confused with that other Wark, on Tweed—and here Bruce took up residence, and here the Tyneside gentry came to swear allegiance to him as monarch, reluctantly or otherwise. Most of them, of course, saw little profit in adhering to far-away, uninterested and incompetent Edward, and were only too anxious for peace, having been in the front line, as it were, for long years. But obviously the Scots influence was strong here anyway, and many may have found it no trial to accept Scottish sovereignty. Wark village lies about 5 miles south of Bellingham, where the Wark Burn joins Tyne. In medieval times Wark would be a large and important place, seat of the Court of the Liberty of Tynedale. The Mote-hill still rises, a green mound on which the early motte-and-bailey castle formerly stood, and where justice was dispensed even after the stone castle was erected nearby. This is wide, open country, with low green hills, and Wark's planted forest stretches hugely to the west. Nearby are the highly interesting and attractive ancient estates of Chipchase, Haughton and Swinburn, whose families have played a resounding part in Border history. The Herons of Chipchase were the Hereditary Keepers of Tynedale, and continually in trouble, not unnaturally, with allegiances generally so uncertain. One of them, Sir George, was slain at the Raid of the Redeswyre. Here belongs the story that after that affray, the Scots presented certain live falcons to their ransomed English prisoners before sending them home "in exchange for dead herons"!

Chipchase Castle, on the site of the original fourteenth-century tower, has been described as the finest example of Jacobean architecture in Northumberland.

Haughton Castle, 3 miles further down Tyne, is a finely restored rectangular and towered baronial pile, dating from the fourteenth century onwards, a stronghold of the Swinburne family and then of the Widdringtons, and still an occupied house. It is said to have been haunted by the ghost of one Archie Armstrong, a Scots free-booter from Liddesdale, who starved to death in the dungeon here when his jailer, Sir Thomas Swinburne, happened to forget his existence and rode off to London. Sir Thomas must have been a softer-hearted man than most, in those days, for when he got as far as York, and remembered his prisoner, he immediately turned back—or so it is averred. Why he could not just have sent a messenger is not explained. At any rate, when he got back to Haughton, it was to find the unfortunate Armstrong dead, with much of the flesh of his forearm gnawed away prior to succumbing. The wails of this poor reiver continued to disturb the neighbourhood of a night until comparatively modern times, when the Rector of nearby Simonburgh had to be brought in to exorcize the tortured spirit. There is a similar story at Spedlins, in Dumfriesshire.

Here we are at the Roman Wall country, a subject well outside the scope of this admittedly very limited and selective survey. But it is fair comment to mention that *this* was the Border-line once, even before the Tynedale salient. Immediately north of this the Pights' Wall, the Ottadini were considered by the Romans just as much dangerous Celts and Picts, as were the Votadini and other Southern Picts farther north.

Hexham-on-Tyne deserves a whole volume, much less a chapter, to itself even in its purely Borderland connection—and alas space forbids more than a mere mention here. So its magnificent priory—larger than some cathedrals—its splendid position and gallant air, its ancient gates and streets, like its lively history, must be read elsewhere, and only one or two items touched upon, typical of its Border links. Like Coldingham, in the Scots East March, this great priory was proud and rich and had its own 'shire'. The Lordship and Liberty of Tynedale did not actually include Hexhamshire, however much Bruce would have liked it to; it was an independent and ecclesiastical jurisdiction under the Archbishops of York.

In the priory, amongst the other time-worn flags and standards, hangs a rather fresher blue banner with a gold saltire, and the date 1514. This though modern, is a flag with a story too. It is only a replica, but a dramatic one. It was in 1514 that the Prior of Hexham sent, as contribution to the army of Lord Dacre, a contingent of his servants and tenants, under the command of the Priory Steward. Scotland, that year after Flodden, lay wide open to invaders, with most of its able-bodied men slain at that *débâcle*—some say as many as 80,000 died around their king. Raids on great or small scale, at any rate, were easy and profitable, and Hexham's prior was not averse to gain. This was the party that went sacking and burning up Teviotdale, ravaged Denholm, and then camped for the night at Hornshole, preparatory to dealing with the town of Hawick the next day. And were, of course, surprised and massacred by the youths of the burgh. The Hexham banner, just like this one though lacking the 1514 date, was captured, and carried triumphantly in the Hawick Common Riding celebrations ever after—until, in due course, it wore out and a replica was made. Centuries of common ridings have required further replacements. And some years ago the good folk of Hawick thought that it would be a nice gesture to present one of the replicas to Hexham —just to show that there was no ill feeling. So there it hangs. I wonder if any of the excellent worshippers whose eyes rest on it at sermon-time ever are stirred by errant thoughts to consider taking up the challenge implicit in that banner? For I am pretty sure that the Teries—the Hawick townsfolk, whose strange slogan is "Teribus ye Teriodin"—had more than just genial neighbour-liness in mind when they sent it, being Borderers. I think they were to some extent 'trailing their coats', hoping that Hexham might trip just a little; or to mix my metaphors somewhat, rise to the bait and initiate some sort of common riding activity of their own which would throw down the gauntlet again, seek to wipe out the stain of that 450-year-old humiliation, and generally add a measure of spice to the whole situation. So far, no. But, who knows . . .?

It is rather amusing that the patron saint of this great priory church is Scotland's own Saint Andrew—hence the saltire on blue. The church, now locally known as The Abbey, had a magnificent new organ installed in 1974.

With a population of 9,000, it is strange that Hexham is not a borough, but governed only by a district council—something that until recently did not happen over the Border. Possibly the reason for this is that its ecclesiastical lords were jealous of their rule, and wanted no interference from citizens, as from other authorities. Though admittedly there has been plenty of time since the Reformation for borough-status to be sought! The special position of Hexham was a very unusual and significant one—and undoubtedly was made use of by the Scots, in policy as well as in the mere gathering of loot in Border raids. The Scots leaders perceived a chink in the Auld Enemy's defences here, so conveniently close to their own salient of Tynedale. For until the said Reformation, Hexham, though in Northumberland and within the palatinate see of Durham, was the property of the Archbishops of York; and their seneschals, later chief governors of the town, possessed all the powers of sheriffs and coroners, so that not even the officers of the king could interfere with their jurisdiction—much less the rival prince-bishops of Durham. Hexham was, in fact, a small county palatine of its own. The jealousy and friction was unending, not unnaturally—and exploited by the Scots. Until 1832, Northumberland returned only two Knights of the Shire as members of parliament—and one of these represented Hexham.

The Moot-hall, a handsome tower-like building, massive, dominant, through which a narrow pend permits the public street to squeeze, was the palace of the Bishops of Hexham and the seat of jurisdiction. It was of Norman construction, completed about 1100, but largely rebuilt in the fourteenth century. The court-hall on the first floor and the dining-hall above, have been the settings for tremendous scenes, with kings, archbishops, great lords and Wardens acting out their parts on its stage. Lesser folk too, made their entrances—and more difficult exits—for in later times this was the debtors' courts, large and small, such debtors being confined on the upper floor. At least they were allowed to walk on the flat, platform roof for air and exercise, an improvement on the more usual deepest-dungeon treatment. Now the Moot-hall houses the County Library—in which one may perhaps detect a moral? The fourteenth-century Manor Office, behind, was used as a prison when the other was a palace. This fourteenth-century building now houses the most admirable Middle March Centre, an imaginative museum displaying graphically the life and times of the Border reivers. It is also a local information centre. All is not ancient in Hexham however. The pedestrian shopping precinct is an asset and in the adjacent Industrial Estate is a large chip-board factory processing timber from the nearby forestry developments.

Corbridge, which lies 3 miles downstream of Hexham, was the site of the Roman Corstopitum. It is an attractively positioned riverside village of climbing gardens, which had the distinction of being burned seriatim by Wallace, Bruce and Bruce's son David II. Three of its four early churches are gone; but the fourth is something very special, being possibly the oldest surviving ecclesiastical building in all the Borders, having been built allegedly between A.D. 600 and 800, largely out of stones from the Roman remains—indeed with an entire Roman arch incorporated. It also is dedicated to St. Andrew. Oddly enough, in the churchyard rises a peel-tower, formerly a fortified vicarage. No doubt its vicar found it useful. The fine bridge over the river here, built in 1674, was the only one to remain standing after the disastrous floods of 1771. At Hunday nearby is the National Tractor and Farm Museum, opened in 1979, close to Hadrian's Wall, showing Europe's most comprehensive collection of agricultural machinery, old and new. A narrow-gauge railway offers a panoramic view of the Tyne Valley.

The Wansbeck rises only a few miles north of Hexham amongst the sandstone crags of low moorland hills known as The Wannies, around the 700-foot contour, to flow fairly consistently eastwards. This was another favourite route of the raiding Scots—or, for that matter, the northwards raiding English—as the name of Scots Gap, 3 miles north-east of Kirkwhelpington, indicates. Ten miles downstream from the Scots Gap and Wallington area—the latter great demesne, incidentally, the largest National Trust property in England, at 13,000 acres—nestles the ancient borough of Morpeth. And while this places it a long way from the actual Border-line, I would be the last to assert, as some do, that Morpeth is not a Border town. The Lords Dacre, who owned Morpeth Castle, were not infrequently Wardens of the Marches.

Morpeth, sited in a great loop of the Wansbeck, crowded by low green hills, is a most attractive market-town of some 14,500 population, its narrow streets formerly threaded by the too-busy A1 highway, but happily now by-passed. It is rich in natural features, which fortunately have been made the most of, its gardens, parklands and riverside walks a great asset, the river and its windings, meadows and quacking ducks an ever-present delight. Although unable to show anything like the walls and gates of Alnwick, much that is ancient and characterful remains. Of the once-great castle up on the hill overlooking the town, in Carlisle Park to the south-west, only the gatehouse-tower survives, to make a delightful house. For this mighty stronghold of the de Merleys, Greystokes, Dacres and Howards inevitably took repeated battering, and indeed was one of the last places to withstand full-scale siege warfare in these islands, when the great Montrose invested and took it, for King Charles, in 1644.

The fifteenth-century clock tower of the former tolbooth

stands in the centre of Oldgate, near its junction with the main Bridge Street shopping area, splendidly contemptuous of traffic, as most tolbooths were. It is a lofty square tower of five storeys, somewhat heightened from the original, with a clock said to have been brought from nearby Bothal Castle. Since Norman days a curfew has been rung from here at 8 p.m. each evening, an excellent traditional custom—however little attention may be paid to its summons today.

The Scots presence never seems to be very far away, at Morpeth, and the links are varied. One of these, and with the reigning royal houses of both Scotland and England, is not always appreciated. Margaret Tudor, Henry VIII's sister and the not-very-popular wife of James IV, seems to have been a highly-sexed piece, however lacking in physical beauty—in this resembling her brother, no doubt. She was wed, at an early age to James, as a matter of state policy, a union which brought no inordinate delight to either. After the King's death at Flodden, the Queen wasted no time in marrying the young Earl of Angus, head of the Red Douglases, who, according to Lord Dacre, was "young, childish and attended by no wise councillors". This hasty match, so soon after the *débâcle* of Flodden and the demise of the beloved King James, was highly unpopular in Scotland, and indeed seriously endangered the country, for the Douglases were too strong already, and the custody of the infant King James V, in his mother's care as Regent, was just too much. What amounted to civil war broke out—much to Henry VIII's glee. He declared that his beloved sister was in bodily danger from rebels, and urged that she flee to his care in England, bringing her sons with her—thus giving him what he had sought for so long, hegemony over Scotland by having control of its king. However this move was thwarted; but Dacre, Warden of the March and Henry's very able minister, did the next best thing, and in concert with his opposite number, the Lord Home—who was of the Queen Mother's party—got her and Angus out of Scotland, though they had to leave the little king behind under a new Regent, Albany. Dacre brought the valuable fugitives—or hostages—first to Harbottle, which Queen Margaret felt was too harsh and remote a place, and then to Morpeth. At Harbottle was born to Margaret her child by Angus, and this girl in due course became the Countess of Lennox, mother in turn of the Lord Darnley who was to marry Mary Queen of Scots and be the father of James VI and I. Margaret Tudor remained a considerable time at Morpeth, indeed she fell dangerously ill here—whereupon her arrogant pup of a husband deserted her, not only in person but politically, and returned with Home to Scotland, to get a grip on his stepson, the king. Margaret never forgave him this, and when at length she was able to return to Scotland, became enamoured of Henry Stewart, a son of Lord Avondale, and raised him to power as Treasurer. But that is another story.

Perhaps the most striking of the Scots presences at Morpeth, however, was the aforementioned siege by the Marquis of Montrose in 1644. For both the attackers and defenders on this occasion were Scots, strangely enough, and the two leaders actually friends. It so happened that the Scottish Covenanting army under General Sandy Leslie, Earl of Leven, in its campaign in the North of England to aid the English Parliamentarians, and heading south this way, had left a garrison of 800 men in Morpeth Castle, under the Master of Somerville, a former associate of Montrose—who himself had been a Covenant supporter when the Covenant was purely religious and not political. In due course Montrose arrived from Carlisle, with a small army, to make a diversion which might take some of the pressure off his master, King Charles, in the South, by menacing Leslie's lines of communication with Scotland. So James Graham, with the Earl of Crawford, Viscount Aboyne, the Lord Ogilvy and other Scots, besieged Sandy Somerville, John MacCulloch and 800 of their compatriots, and so knocked about Morpeth Castle, with cannon brilliantly filched from under the noses of more of Leslie's lieutenants at Newcastle, that it was never the same place again. And on the evening that Somerville surrendered, Montrose entertained him and his men to a great banquet in the town, in typically courteous fashion—although no doubt the burghers of Morpeth had to provide the wherewithal, and would curse the Scots, both sides of them, in equally typical and traditional fashion. The trenches which Montrose dug for this siege are still to be distinguished on the west side of the castle.

A more modern but still venerable link with Scotland is Morpeth's famous bridge, successor of the medieval bridge, which gives the main street its name. This handsome three-arched structure was built in 1831 by the celebrated Scots engineer, Thomas

Telford. He was a Borderer himself, born in 1755 on the West March, in Eskdale, son of a humble stonemason. Oddly enough, he wanted to be a poet; indeed he addressed the following lines to Robert Burns himself:

Nor pass the tentie curious lad, who o'er the ingle hangs his head,
    And begs of neighbours books to read; for hence arise
Thy country's sons, who far are spread,
    Baith bold and wise.

Telford discovered a more profitable trade than versifying, however, and, emigrating to London, got himself employed by Sir William Chambers the most successful architect of the reign of George III, in the building of Somerset House. Thereafter he never looked back, designing the famous Menai Bridge, the Caledonian Canal, the St. Katherine's Docks, and a host of other structures. He who used to cut the lettering of gravestones in the kirkyard of Westerkirk in Eskdale, lies buried in Westminster Abbey.

Not far from his bridge, in Morpeth, is the three-gabled Queen's Head Hotel, where another Scot, though born in Newcastle, distinguished himself in 1772—though he ought to have known better. This was John Scott, later Earl of Eldon, Lord Chief Justice of England and Lord Chancellor, who contracted a runaway and irregular marriage with one Bessie Surtees. They eloped over the Border to be wed at Fala, just beyond Soutra Hill, after the Gretna Green fashion, and then returned to this hotel, where the Bessie Surtees Room is still pointed out.

One final note about Morpeth and Scotland. A mile west of the town lies the scanty and grievously neglected ruins of Newminster Abbey, in a lovely setting by the riverside. This was once a rich and powerful establishment, founded in 1138. It was here that Edward I so clearly and eloquently expressed his attitude to Scotland and the Scots, which was to be the cause of so much misery and bloodshed for both kingdoms, when in September 1296 he appointed John de Warenne, Earl of Surrey, to be Governor of the Scotland he intended to impose his will upon. He threw the Earl the Seal of Scotland, with these words: "A man does good business when he rids himself of a turd!" It was a turd which was to stain his name for ever.

I have left myself space sufficient merely to mention one other

highly significant and attractive area of the English Middle March
—Coquetdale and Rothbury the 'capital' thereof. The Coquet is
one of the finest rivers of the English North, beloved of anglers,
and pursuing an almost uniformly picturesque course from its
source below the heathery slopes of Thirlmoor, only a mile or so
from the Border-line 7 miles east of Carter Bar, eastwards by
south some 40 miles to the sea at Warkworth, only a short distance
south of the mouth of the Aln, the two rivers' courses being
roughly parallel. The Coquet therefore traverses both the Middle
and East March areas; and Rothbury, rather nearer the sea than
the source, might conceivably be claimed by the east rather than
the middle. At this distance from the actual division line—about
15 miles as the crow flies—clear distinctions are difficult. But the
entire upland character of the district, its traditions and the lines of
its communications, are with the Middle March.

The little town of Rothbury is a pleasant quiet place crouching
under the bold but not high Simonside Hills, with its four-arched
medieval bridge linking the streets and the woodlands. There is a
triangular green with market cross, and nearby a rebuilt church,
square-towered, with thirteenth-century nucleus. A deservedly
popular haunt of holidaymakers in search of the quiet and peace of
pleasant countryside, it has nevertheless a name for having been
otherwise once, for its folk were stigmatized as "amongst the
wildest and most uncivilized in the county. For fighting, gaming
and drinking they had a worse reputation than the inhabitants of
Tynedale and Redesdale."

A mile below the town is the narrow rocky gorge of the Thrum,
where there is an old mill of the same name amongst
the woods. All this area was forested once—indeed the name
Rothbury is said to mean a clearing in the forest—and trees are
still very much in evidence. The great Armstrong estate of Cragside with country park of 900 acres is heavily wooded, its
pine-forest, like its rock-gardens, artificial lakes and rho-
dodendrons, famous—however architecturally unlovely the
large mansion house of 1870 itself. The estate is open to the
public, during the season.

On an outlier of the Simonside Hills, Dove Crag, to the south,
is the great Celtic encampment of Lordenshaws, reminder of the
days when both countries were peopled by that race, and there

was no Border other than that of the Roman invaders. There are many Celtic relics and remains in this area; although for some reason, most Englishmen seem to shut their eyes to their Celtic ancestry and prefer to associate themselves with the infinitely more barbarian Saxon invaders—who, of course, were comparatively few in numbers and had a merely superficial effect on the country hereabouts, as the Normans were to do later. The font in Rothbury Church is famous, and its shaft esteemed as one of the oldest surviving examples of Saxon Christian carving in Britain. The spectacular decoration is pure Celtic.

Probing towards the Border-line, the Coquet makes a great bend where the Grasslees Burn comes in from the south, and near here is the ruined tower of Hepple, seat of a former barony, thought to have been burned by Bruce himself. Further upstream is Holystone, which was the most unlikely site of a nunnery, some say Benedictine, some Augustinian. What made the founder, one of the Umfravilles of Harbottle nearby, set up such an establishment here takes some fathoming, for as well as being on a prime invasion route and in a notoriously lawless countryside, at Holystone one is deep into the remote and difficult Cheviot uplands. It was the only such establishment on the Border; and I cannot imagine that it was a haunt of gentle peace. The ladies must have been tough. Almost as curious was the position of the Umfravilles themselves—for though they were good Northumbrian Normans, Robert de Umfraville having been granted Redesdale and Coquetdale by William the Conqueror himself, nevertheless they were also great Scots nobles, Earls of Angus, no less, one of their number having married the heiress of the ancient Celtic dynasts of Angus. Gilbert de Umfraville was earl at the time of Edward I's campaigns, and seems to have been a somewhat shadowy figure. Not so his cousin, Sir Ingram de Umfraville, who actually became Joint-Guardian of Scotland, succeeding Bruce himself, then Earl of Carrick, in that thankless office, in 1300. Despite his English blood, he fought on the Scots side at Bannockburn. Nothing could more clearly indicate the strangely equivocal position of this Borderland.

An interesting sidelight on this Coquetdale family is that they are the probable ancestors of the great and widespread Scots ducal house of Hamilton—little as most Hamiltons would thank you for the information! The first of the line was Sir Walter fitz Gilbert de Hameldon, or Homildon, near Wooler, from his arms and name almost certainly of this Harbottle family. He held lands in Renfrewshire by 1294, and was governor of Bothwell Castle for the English just before Bannockburn—but had the foresight to surrender it to Edward Bruce in time, and so survived to become the ancestor of the Hamiltons.

The Umfraville castle of Harbottle lies a couple of miles up Coquet from Holystone, now only some fangs of masonry crowning a green mote-hill above the very pleasing tree-girt village. It was long reckoned to be the 'capital' of the Middle March, on the English side. It was besieged and captured by the Scots King William the Lion. Its main function was to try to "distress the thieves of Redisdale" and keep them in hand—a hopeless task, however full its dungeons were apt to be. It was here that Dacre brought Margaret Tudor and the Earl of Angus, and where two days later her daughter by Angus was born, the Lady Margaret Douglas who was to be Darnley's mother. By one of those coincidences of genealogy, the present Duke of Hamilton, Douglas-Hamilton by name, is also Earl of Angus, in direct descent from Margaret Tudor's second husband. So Harbottle is very much mixed up with his ancestry. Since his mother was a sister of the Percy Duke of Northumberland, the link is even closer.

We shall leave the Middle March with one final item. On high ground between Harbottle and Holystone is a spot known as Rob Roy's Cave—an intriguing name. Was the famous Highland free-booter even indeed in this area? In much research into his activities —I have written about him at some length—I have found no evidence that he was. But our old friend Sir Walter Scott does introduce him, in his novel *Rob Roy*, into this very district, very near the beginning of the book. Indeed he makes Biddlestone Hall nearby the original of Osbaldistone Hall therein, and Scott is known to have stayed some time at the Rose and Thistle Inn—apt name—at Harbottle, while collecting local material for the novel. So is this cave one more example of Scott's genius for making other people improve upon both history and geography? Much stranger things have happened than that eager enthusiasts should discover and identify a refuge for this hero hundreds of miles from his normal stamping-grounds on the verge of the Highlands.

10

The Scottish West March

THE East and Middle Marches are very different in character, admittedly. But their difference is minor compared with that of the whole atmosphere and ethos of the West March. Just why this should be is hard to fathom, for topographically and historically the areas are not dissimilar, though in reverse situation, mountainous to the east, with the plain of Solway to the west not unlike that of the Tweed and the Merse at the other side of the country, the raiding and invasion just as prevalent. Instead of the dales of Teviot, Tweed, Lauder, Ettrick and Yarrow, there are Liddesdale, Eskdale, Annandale and Nithsdale, formerly inhabited by equally warlike clans. Yet overall, something is different, difficult as it is to pinpoint.

The bounds and marches are simple enough, at any rate. From the Kershope Burn's junction with Liddel Water, where the Middle March ends, the Border-line follows that river down Liddesdale for about 10 miles to below the confluence of Liddel and Esk. Thereafter it leaves the clear river-line and strikes due west, overland, by the artificial boundary known as the Scots Dyke, to the little River Sark; and down this modest stream it continues the remainder of the way, another 7 miles or so, to salt water at Gretna. It is all a much less complicated line than on the other two Marches—but a much less easily defended one, for these rivers are readily forded compared with great Tweed, and the hill passes are not on the line itself but some considerable way northwards in the north-south-running dales. Not to be wondered at, therefore, that this easterly portion of the West March was known as The Debateable Land, the adherence of its independent and troublesome people claimed by both nations and rendered to neither.

The area west of Gretna is still Borderland, of course, with here the wide Solway estuary as March. But just how far the essential 'feeling' of the Borders extends is an open question. In theory, the

West March reaches as far as Kirkcudbright, so that much of the Stewartry is included; but in fact few in this area think of themselves as Borderers today, whatever may have been the case in the past; and by the time that Dumfries is passed, the authentic Border atmosphere is dissipated, save for one or two determined enthusiasts perhaps. Indeed the entire stretch of 24 miles from Gretna to Dumfries, along the north shore of Solway, with its hinterland of the foothills and the dale country, becomes progressively less redolent of the frontier as one moves westwards. Which is strange; for though the wide salt-water barrier does tend to dispel the sense of clash, nevertheless this was almost as popular and effective an invasion route, north and south, as any to the east. Indeed, in the earlier days, especially during the Wars of Independence, this was the more lively frontier by far. And great Caerlaverock Castle, the seat of the Maxwell Wardens of the West March, stands guard in the Solway marshes at the mouth of the Nith, just south of Dumfries itself. Moreover, the ballads sing of the West March just as consistently as elsewhere—as witness such as "Young Lochinvar", "Kinmont Willie", "Johnnie Armstrong", "Fair Helen of Kirkconnel", and so on.

Liddesdale itself, needless to say, could not be more authentically Borderland, the territory of the most picturesque and untameable of the mosstroopers and freebooters—or, alternatively, 'thieves and limmars'—of all the troubled frontier. Rising in the lofty mosses of the Deadwater heights, very near to where the North Tyne has its genesis, the Liddel Water flows in the opposite direction, south by west, by Sauchtree, Riccarton, Larriston, Dinlabyre, Castleton and Newcastleton, to Kershopefoot and the Borderline, the majority of it, 15 miles, therefore in the Middle March; thereafter it stretches 12 miles before joining the Esk near Canonbie. Not a long course, but a resounding one in consistently romantic, attractive and under-populated country, with Newcastleton, a village of about 1,000 souls, the only sizeable community in 27 miles. Yet it was full enough of life—and death—once, to be sure, for there were no fewer than between thirty and forty peel-towers of the Elliots alone in Upper Liddesdale and Hermitage Water; while the Armstrongs had more than that, in the more fertile lower dale. Of these, practically all are gone almost without trace, dinged doun in the local and national strife which was endemic to

Hermitage Castle

the area—even though their names often remain in the sheep-farms which dot the dale and echo the ballads of long ago.

Newcastleton is a strange place to come across in this wilderness, so obviously a planned and 'synthetic' entity, with its neat criss-cross streets and three squares. It was in fact built in 1793, by the third Duke of Buccleuch, as a weaving community. It was dealt a most severe blow by the arbitrary closing of the Edinburgh–Hawick–Carlisle railway-line, which was its main link with the rest of the country as well as a source of employment, the infrequent bus service being quite inadequate. Twenty miles from Hawick and 25 from Carlisle, it is one of the most isolated sizeable villages in the south of Scotland. Led by its minister, it put up a stout fight for its rights, but to little effect on far-away and uncaring authority. Depopulation on a still larger scale will be the inevitable result.

Transport has always been something of a problem hereabouts, since the days when all a man needed was a sturdy, short-legged, sure-footed garron. It is recounted that when Sir Walter Scott came to Newcastleton, in his search for ballad material, he created a great sensation by arriving in a gig, the first wheeled-vehicle seen in Upper Liddesdale in the memory of man. Today, probably, the most significant vehicle for the area is the caterpillar-tractor, for enormous Forestry Commission plantings are tending to transform much of Upper Liddesdale, an extension of the Keilder and Wauchope Forests, which together make up the great Border Forest Park. These vast empty uplands are probably better growing trees than merely heather and reeds and moss; but the regimented pine-forests do so greatly alter the whole character of a storied land.

Hermitage Castle still stands, proud, remote, inviolate, at a bend in its side-glen 5 miles north of Newcastleton, safe in the care of the Department of the Environment, a roofless ruin but complete to the wall-heads—though there has been some renewal at that level. It makes a splendid picture in its massive strength. Originally a late thirteenth-century hold, the present work consists of a fourteenth-century central main block, with large square towers projecting at the four angles, the wing to the south-west being much larger as well as later than the others. The east and west sides of the main block are notable for tall archways which link the towers.

There has been a *bretache,* or timber gallery, projecting round the building at third-floor level, below the parapet, for defensive purposes. Sir Nicholas de Soulis, Lord of Liddesdale, built the original fortalice, before the Wars of Independence. A descendant, Sir John, was one of the Guardians of Scotland, after Wallace and Bruce and Umfraville, a thankless position. And Sir William, already mentioned, for conspiracy against Bruce in 1320, was forfeited and died in prison. Bruce gave Hermitage to an illegitimate son of his own; but the English took it during the Edward Baliol wars which succeeded Bruce's death. It was Sir William Douglas, the celebrated Knight of Liddesdale and Flower of Chivalry, so-called, who retook it—and managed to hang on to it thereafter. He rather blotted his chivalric copybook however by starving to death in Hermitage dungeon Sir Alexander Ramsay. The castle remained with the Black Douglas line until the collapse of that great house, when the Red Douglases, who helped engineer the said collapse, got it, and much else. The Earls of Angus, aforementioned, were the Red Douglases. James IV, misliking his posthumous successor as husband of Margaret Tudor, gave Hermitage to Patrick Hepburn, Earl of Bothwell; and it was here that his descendant lay ill when Mary Queen of Scots made her extraordinary and famous ride across the watershed of Scotland—and back the same night, a fantastic feat for a woman—from Jedburgh. Her subsequent illness it was that was one day to wring from her lips the wish, "Would that I had died at Jedworth!"

Thereafter the strongly burgeoning house of Scott of Buccleuch gained Hermitage, and have managed to retain it ever since. The castle was very frequently the western headquarters of the Warden of the Middle March, and as such saw violent ongoings innumerable. Today it is a mecca for discerning visitors, with will to take a little time and trouble—and deservedly so.

Between Newcastleton and Kershopefoot is Mangerton, where once was the castle of the chiefs of the Armstrongs. Although Johnnie Armstrong of Gilnockie is often looked upon as chief of that unruly clan, in James V's day, he was in fact only younger brother to the chief, Mangerton—who was presumably a less drastic character. Reference will be made to Johnnie hereafter. The extraordinary position of The Debateable Land, and its inhabitants, is well illustrated in the Armstrong clan, the most powerful of a wild area. So well entrenched were they, so difficult to bring to book, so well able to look after themselves, that they were in effect written off by both nations as without the pale, and no concern of theirs. Nationality just did not apply to them—except when useful. For instance in 1550, one Sandy Armstrong on the English side of the Border threatened "to become a Scottishman" unless his interests were better protected, from the depredations of the Maxwell's, by his English Warden. In 1598 Sir Robert Carey, the then Warden, complained to the King of Scots of a great raid by Liddesdale Armstrongs on Haltwhistle, in South Tynedale. To which James VI replied that the offenders were no subjects of his, and Carey might take his own revenge—if he could! The English then set about the ravaging of Liddesdale, with a large force, said to include some of the King of Scots's forces—which of course resulted only in further and worse raids on Haltwhistle. And so on. The story is told of this Carey's Raid, as it was known in Liddesdale thereafter, how, while he was engaged in besieging some of the offenders in the wastes of Tarras Moss, a notorious sanctuary in a side-valley between Liddel and Esk, the Armstrongs mounted a secret and rather special reprisal. They sent a strong party swiftly south to the Warden's own lands, which soon returned safely to their own fastnesses with most of Carey's cattle. With the Englishmen not getting on very well at Tarras Moss, Carey was thereafter sent one of his own cows with the message that the Armstrongs, fearing that he might well run short of provisions in these barren solitudes, hoped he would accept a present of some prime English beef.

A sequel to all this, with the same players on the stage, is perhaps of interest. Five years later, in 1603, Queen Elizabeth died at last, after long delay in her heir's opinion. Sir Robert Carey, waiting in London, had arranged with his sister, the Lady Scrope and one of the Queen's women, to get him the first news of the death. She detached a ring, a gift from King James, from the dead finger, almost at moment of expiry, and flung it out of the royal window to her brother waiting below. This was at three in the morning of the Thursday. Thereafter Carey, who must have been a bonny horseman as well as a most ambitious character, made one of the greatest rides in history, galloping non-stop northwards, with relays of horses, so as to be the first to present the magnificent news to King Jamie in Edinburgh that he was now the first monarch of the United Kingdom—which he did at Holyroodhouse on the Saturday night just after the King had gone to bed, a fantastic accomplishment, 400 miles in three and a half days. Jamie, after grumbling about being disturbed, was delighted—not sufficiently so to bestow the peerage and honours on Carey which that individual sought. He had, in fact, to wait years for his reward, prodigal as James was in his scattering of honours hereafter.

Curiously enough, the Armstrongs too celebrated this uniting of the kingdoms in their own fashion, by staging an especially ambitious and large-scale raid which went as far south as Penrith, with between 200 and 300 riders. James was at Berwick on his triumphal if fear-fraught journey south, when he heard about this shocking breach of the new amity; and promptly despatched Sir William Selby, Governor of Berwick, with all forces at his command, to teach the unruly mosstroopers that the day for this sort of thing was now past. It was, in fact, the last major raid in Border history; and Selby, anxious to impress his new master, took his orders so seriously that thereafter most of the Liddesdale castles and peel-towers were blown up, pulled down, or burnt. It was the end of an old story.

Before we leave Liddesdale and the Armstrongs, something of Johnnie Armstrong must be recounted; for he was certainly one of the most renowned, colourful and successful characters ever to set the Borders by the ears—which is saying something. Gilnockie, his castle, often called Hollows Tower, stands a little above the confluence of Esk and Liddel, north of Canonbie. It has lovingly been restored from ruin by an Armstrong descendant. A site a little way to the south is often erroneously pointed out as Gilnockie. Johnnie, although only a second son, was a born leader, completely unscrupulous, energetic and with a sense of humour—a potent admixture in The Debateable Land. Soon he, not his brother, was leading the fierce and unruly Armstrong clan, with ever-mounting audacity and brilliance. He seems to have preceded Rob Roy MacGregor in bringing to fine art the protection racket—although he also claimed a Robin Hood-like gallantry towards the ladies. Or at least, the Scots ladies:

> . . . never a Scots wyfe could have said,
> That e'er I skaithed her a puir flee.

A man's house, cattle and goods were safe, in his day, from molestation by any soever, so long as he paid the necessary black-mail; but once let him slip up on his premium-payments, be he farmer, parson, squire or great lord, and he quickly discovered his economic unwisdom, for Johnnie was insurance-agent, protector and hazard in one. Here is no place to recount his career; but by the premature end of it he was reputed to have behaved like a king in the Borderland, to boast that he controlled all between Teviot-head and Newcastle, and to declare that he never rode abroad with a tail of less than thirty-six gentlemen of his own name. So serious did his activities become—and so violent the protests of Henry VIII to King James V—that that young Scottish King, aged only 17 at the time, decided that something must be done. Cunningly he set out as for only a great hunting in Ettrick Forest; but there he assembled a large force in case of need—for the Armstrongs at a pinch could field their thousands. Then he sent a fair invitation to Gilnockie for Johnnie to meet him at Caerlanrig Chapel, at Teviothead, a "luving letter" as the ballad says. Johnnie chose to obey his liege lord's request—and he might not have done; but perhaps unwisely he elected to ride to Caerlanrig with no fewer than his thirty-six gentlemen in train, all clad in their best, more richly turned out than the monarch's court. "What lacks this knave that a king should have?" the young James Stewart de-manded hotly, at the sight; and beat about the bush no longer commanding that Johnnie and his thirty-six should be strung up from convenient trees there and then. The Armstrong did not plead for his life, but he did bargain. His offerings, however, were such as only to make matters worse, like terms for a treaty be-tween princes. He offered to provide the King with forty armoured and horsed gentlemen to attend him at all times, at his own expense —apart from the squadrons of mosstroopers he could always raise. He offered him twenty-four milk-white horses, and as much good English gold as four of them could carry. He offered him the pro-duce of twenty-four meal-mills annually. He offered to bring to the King of Scots any Englishman he liked to name, be he duke, earl or baron, quick or dead, by any given day. And finally he offered a rent on every property between where they stood and Newcastleton.

When all this, not unnaturally, only made young James the

more anxious to dispose of him, Johnnie Armstrong made the famous valedictory speech: "It is folly to seek grace at Your Grace's graceless face; but had I known it I should have lived long upon the Borders in despite of King Harry and you both; for I know that King Harry would downweigh my best horse with gold to hear that I were condemned to die this day."

And so the Armstrongs were hanged. And the Borderers declare that the trees which bore them withered away thereafter, at the manifest injustice of the deed; at any rate, there are none there now. And even the renowned Sir David Lindsay of the Mount wrote thereafter, putting the words into the mouth of a pardoner, dealer in relics:

> The cordis, baith grit and lang,
> Quhilk hangit Johnie Armstrang,
> Of gude hemp, soft and sound.
> Gude haly pepil, I stand ford,
> Wha'evir beis hangid in this cord,
> Neidis never to be drowned!

Eskdale strikes north-west where Liddel strikes north-east, and is divided into two very distinct districts. The lower dale is accepted to include the more level lands of Canonbie and Half Morton, and is fairly fertile and reasonably populous. Then, after the burgh of Langholm, where Ewesdale comes in from the north and Wauchopedale from the south-west, the hills draw close and become higher, barer, and it is a different land. Eskdale goes on thus for another 20 miles, through lofty and little populated uplands reaching towards the Ettrick Forest, with 790 people occupying the huge conjoined parish of Eskdalemuir and Westerkirk, 71,000 acres, a green land of sheep-farms, heather and rushing waters. Yet out of this remote territory has come more than wool, mutton and wild Armstrongs and Johnstones. At Westerkirk, a third of the way up, was born in 1757 Thomas Telford, the celebrated bridge-builder, architect and engineer of the Caledonian and Ellesmere Canals. Laughing Tam he was called locally; and he did not forget his calf-country when he grew famous, leaving money to provide his native parish with a library such as, until recent times, few other rural areas in Britain could rival, with 6,000 volumes no less. From here also came the forebears of Lord

Thomson of Fleet, the newspaper magnate. And, oddly enough in these permissive days, Eskdale was once famous for a practical experiment in trial-marriage, the annual Handfasting Fair being a notable occasion at which young unmarrieds elected to take each other, before the gathering, for a year's trial of living together; whereafter they either married conventionally or parted—if the latter, any offspring being allotted to the unsatisfied party, a curious provision. Robert III was claimed to be a handfast child; but such were accepted as legitimate under Scots law. This pre-occupation with the problems of wedlock in this corner of South-west Scotland is rather strange—for Gretna Green is not far away.

Langholm is not really typical of the West March, and might easily have strayed somehow across the hills from Teviotdale or Tweeddale, a true Border burgh in a narrow valley, with mills and common riding. Not very large, with a population of only 2,300, it is a go-ahead little town in its own way, with plenty of character. It is the only town I know of to boast a picture-gallery in the canteen of a working mill; and one of its firms proudly advertises the most expensive twist suitings cloths in the world. Even its common riding has the stamp of its own sturdy character, for at it are traditionally carried strange emblems—the Barley Bannock with a salted herring pinned on by a long 'twal'-penny nail'; the Spade; the Thistle; and the Floral Crown. The precise significance of these features is obscure, lost in the mists of time—although the herring may have had something to do with the baron's rights of fishing in the Esk, whatever the probability of his catching herrings therein. Probably the nail through it has more significance. The Spade, of course, represents the turf-cutting which annually renewed the exact boundaries of the burgh's jealously-guarded common lands; and the Thistle may well have been no more than a warning to lairds and others not to meddle with the privileges of the townsfolk, or get jagged. As contrast to these traditional symbols, and indication that Langholm folk are far from insular, old-fashioned and backward-looking, they have the extraordinary custom of using as the necessary colours, for Cornet, committee and supporters' rosettes, ribbons and favours —always an important and lively aspect of any march-riding ceremony—the colours of the winning owner of that year's

Derby. How this odd arrangement came about is not now known; but it has been done since the 1880s. So that while all the other Border burghs have their own permanent colours, Langholm changes theirs each year—which makes the Epsom classic result of more than academic interest in this remote upland valley.

The Muckle Toon o' Langholm consists actually of two, the Old and New Towns, on opposite banks of the Esk, the old a burgh of barony under the Dukes of Buccleuch from 1643, the new, or Meikleholm, dating from 1778, built in most regular pattern. It is a great place for bridges, necessarily—three rivers joining here. When one of them was built, an apprentice working on one was called Thomas Telford. A well-known landmark rises above Langholm, a 100-foot obelisk on the summit of Whita Hill (1,162 feet) prominent enough to be seen from across the Border-line 8 miles away. This commemorates General Sir John Malcolm, Governor of Bombay, another Eskdale loon from Westerkirk, who is buried in Westminster Abbey. And just to indicate that this was no flash-in-the-pan, his three brothers were all knighted likewise. One was an admiral—his statue is down beside the town hall. They were members of a family of seventeen children, which perhaps may have had something to do with it. In modern times Christopher Murray Grieve, the poet who wrote as Hugh MacDiarmid, was born in Langholm, despite his Highland-sounding pseudonym.

An interesting point about this area, not always realized, is that when Anne, Countess of Buccleuch in her own right, heiress of the Scotts, married King Charles II's son by Lucy Walters, James, they were jointly created Duke and Duchess of Buccleuch and Monmouth, Earl and Countess of Dalkeith, and Baron and Baroness Whitchester and Eskdaill, the Duke taking the name of Scott—a highly unusual proceeding, indicative of the power and prestige of the Scott family. Eskdale, spelt 'daill', remains the courtesy title of the Duke of Buccleuch's heir's heir. The Duchess's sister had married a Scott kinsman at the age of 14, and they were created Earl and Countess of Tarras—but these did not have any issue, and died young. The Tarras Water joins the Esk just south of Langholm.

Annandale is the next major valley westwards, although the amusingly-named narrow dale of the Water of Milk intervenes.

Annan, however, is really nowhere an upland valley until the Moffat area is reached 25 miles north of the Solway, but a wide green and fertile strath, rich, fair and peaceful-seeming. Which is as misleading as most of the rest of Borderland impressions. For Annandale has quite as bloody a reputation as anywhere else, and worse than most. This was partly on account of invasion and Border reiving, and partly because of the internecine warring pro-clivities of the clans of Johnstone and Maxwell, continually at deadly feud, and ambitious to slaughter each other in the biggest way possible. Here indeed was fought the greatest clan battle in all Scotland's history—not in the Highlands, as might be assumed—when, at Dryfe Sands, in 1593, the Maxwells were defeated by the Johnstones with a loss of no fewer than 700 men, their leader, the Lord Maxwell, cut down with the rest. Johnstone casualties are not given. The Johnstones had a particularly unpleasant habit of slashing the faces of their victims; this was known as the Lockerbie Lick.

Altogether Annandale had not a very good reputation, however attractive it was to look at. The chronicler Bellenden is not flatter-ing: ". . . for nocht annerlie in Annandail bot in all the dalis afore rehersit ar mony strang and wekit theuis, inuading the cuntré with perpetuall thift, reif & slauchter, quhen thay se ony trublus tyme. Thir theuis (becaus thay haue Inglismen thair perpetuall ennymes lyand dry marche upon thair nixt bordour) inuades Ingland with continewal weres, or ellis with quiet thift; and leifes ay ane pure and miserabill lyfe. In tyme of peace thay ar so accustomit with thift that thay can nocht desist. . . ."

The Annandale folk had their excuse, for their valley was utterly open to invasion from England, with no protective natural barriers and little help apt to come from the rest of Scotland. A glance at the map shows the situation. And for centuries it was the property of the Bruce Lords of Annandale, whose attitudes were not such as to encourage peaceful co-existence. In the Wars of Independence the dale suffered terribly, since it was Bruce's own territory—and could not retire elsewhere, as did he! Indeed it suffered almost as much from his own scorched-earth policy as from his foes. And this continued for long afterwards. Edward Baliol descended upon it within three months of his coronation; and the Douglases struck back. So it went on right up to the Union of 1603—so that, by 1609, Annan townsfolk were too impoverished to build a church for themselves. Even Berwick-on-Tweed can hardly show a grimmer history. Annan, of course, lived under a curse. For that vigorous Irish reformer, St. Malachy O'Moore, stayed here in 1140, and, outraged by the then Bruce lord's secret hanging of a robber for whom he had pleaded, cursed the house of Bruce and the town of Annan comprehensively—who knows with what effect?

Is it to be wondered at if the Annandalesmen lived and fought rough?

Nowadays, Annan is a pleasant little red-stone town by the riverside—the name of which, ironically, is Gaelic for the quiet water—with a population of 5,600, and rather dominated by the huge cooling-towers and installations of the giant nuclear power-station at Chapelcross. At its venerable academy were educated those two heroes of the first half of the nineteenth century, Thomas Carlyle and Edward Irving, friends despite their differing points of view. Robert Burns did reluctant duty here as an exciseman—but got his own back by composing in Annan the smugglers' and drinkers' song, "The Deil's Awa wi the Excisemen". Annan mounts its annual march riding, like the rest—but took the business so seriously as to make a by-law, in 1682, that every inhabitant must wait upon the magistrates and town council, on their best horses and in their best apparel, for the Riding of the Town's Marches, under pain of forty pounds Scots.

Ecclefechan, the *eaglais* or church of St. Fechan, a sixth-century Celtic missionary—the same name really as St. Vigeans in Angus —lies some 5 miles up the dale from Annan, a modest village with a population of only 600, yet renowned. This because it was the birthplace of Carlyle. It is a strange thing this veneration for the places where the great men of yester-year grew up. It does not seem much to apply today. We still produce giants in this sphere or that, surely—but few know or greatly care where they were born. But in previous centuries it was very different. Unlike so many great ones, Carlyle was also buried where he began, here at Ecclefechan, with a simple granite slab to mark the spot in the village kirkyard. Actually most of the houses in the village seem to have been built by his father and uncle, masons to trade.

Nearby is the great sixteenth-century castle of Hoddam, now

restored in part as a visitor centre, caravan park and children's playground. It is unusual in design, L-planned but the main block, to 72 feet, and a circular caphouse for the stairway rising higher still. It is well supplied with machicolated projections, crenellations, gunloops and other defensive devices, plus a warning beacon on the watch-platform—precautions much needed here when it was built, for this was a Maxwell stronghold, uncomfortably close to the Johnstone lands. The Maxwells held the lower end of Annandale, after the Bruce period, with their enemies esconced in the central and upper reaches, and Hoddam must have witnessed some grim scenes. Its lairds were the Lords Herries, a turbulent lot. The present castle—there was an earlier one, built by the Bruces, nearer Ecclefechan—was partly erected out of the stones of a chapel which Herries demolished for the purpose; and, as an alleged result, was so preyed upon by his conscience that he was constrained to build Repentance Tower, which stands in a prominent position on the summit of Trailtrow Hill a little way to the south, to serve as a watch-tower and warning for the neighbourhood—a piece of altruistic public-spiritedness which, of course, benefited the Laird of Hoddam as much as anyone else. Despite the name he gave it, Repentance Tower was probably built as much to appease the powerful Archbishop of Glasgow, whose chapel had been demolished, as the Herries conscience. And the laird made a virtue out of a necessity, moreover seeming to require the King and Privy Council to keep it in repair; for he wrote to James VI in 1579 ". . . the wache toure upoun Trailtrow callit Repentance mon be mendit of the littil diffacing the Englishche army maid of it". It is obvious from the 'standing orders' he compiled for it, that the Tower was as much concerned with the Johnstones as the English, for the bell was to be rung ". . . whenever the Fray is, or that the Watchman seiing the Thieves disobedient come over the Water of Annand or thereabouts, and knowes them to be enemies; and whosoever bydes fra the Fray, or turns again so long as the Beaken burns or the Bell rings, shall be holden as Partakers to the enemies and used as Traitors".

Lockerbie, though only another 5 miles up the dale, where the Dryfe Water comes down out of the hills—where the name Drysdale comes from—is firmly in Johnstone territory. It is a pleasant little town, as red as the rest, in attractive hilly surroundings, happed in green braes. It can claim to have a longer history than most other communities of the area, for here, on the flat-topped Birrenswark Hill south-east of the town, was a large fortified Roman camp. The Romans under Agricola, found Annandale as convenient and easy a route into Scotland as did later invaders. But no doubt the Picts whom Fechan came to convert, were here before the Romans, and they certainly were still here when they left—a simple point worth remembering.

Despite its inevitable preoccupation with war, invasion and reiving, Lockerbie is famous for something much more worthwhile, useful and almost as stirring, the Lockerbie Trysts and Lamb Sales. These were established in the seventeenth century, and grew to be amongst the most renowned markets in the two kingdoms —for as many English buyers as Scots attended, and still do. As many as 70,000 lambs have changed hands here, of an August sale, and in consequence, Lockerbie's influence as a catalyst of friendly trading relations between the two countries is not to be overlooked. But it was a profitable intercourse, and in due course Lockerbie was able to buy the adjoining Lamb Hill for the town, out of the surplus of the £10,000 raised to build their town hall— a very different story from that of Annan.

The Water of Milk follows a roughly parallel course to that of Dryfe, to the south, before joining Annan; and this area was the territory of the small Border clan of Jardine, who tended to follow the Johnstones in their activities, geography rather dictating so. Castlemilk, not to be confused with the large castle and modern housing estate of that name in the suburbs of Glasgow, was their main seat, 3 miles south-east of Lockerbie, the present large mansion dating only from 1866, although the original castle was built by the Bruces. An equal distance north-west of the town is the estate now known as Jardine Hall, wherein rises the interesting restored Jardine fortalice of Spedlins, a strong fifteenth-century peel-tower heightened two centuries later by a double roof, gabled, with angle-turrets. In the thickness of the south-east angle, a small stairway rises; and at the foot of this is a trap-door, giving access to an unpleasant example of mural pit or prison, such as all these baronies were apt to possess. It is wholly within the thickness of the walling, without window or ventilation. Nearly 12 feet deep but only 2½ feet wide by 7½ long, it is a fearsome hole. The only way out, once a prisoner was dropped therein, was to be hauled up on a rope—if the victim had strength enough left to cling to one. Spedlins had a miller called Porteous who had the misfortune to offend the laird, the first Jardine baronet actually, sometime around 1670. By an oversight the new baronet, when called away to Edinburgh, went off with the key of the pit in his pocket, thinking no more of his prisoner. Porteous, after gnawing away at his hands and feet, eventually succumbed, forgotten. It is reported that the household thereafter was much vexed by his ghost—a notably similar case to that at Haughton Castle in Northumberland.

The royal burgh of Lochmaben ought to be a great deal better known and appreciated than it is. For although only another small red-stone town, little more than a village indeed with only 1,200 of population, it is nevertheless not only the true capital of Annandale but a highly important place in Scotland's story as well as a most attractive spot, delightfully situated at the junction of no fewer than four lochs—with three others in the vicinity. No sea-port is more water-dominated. It lies midway up Annandale 4 miles west of Lockerbie. Here was the main Bruce seat, in a highly defensible position—which Annan certainly was not—and around Lochmaben Castle, on a peninsula jutting into the Castle Loch, the tides of Scottish history tended to swirl; so that by the early thirteenth century it was probably more important than any other place in the South-west. In the Wars of Independence, naturally, it played a major part, now held by one side, now by the other, Bruce time and again recapturing his old home. It claims, incidentally, to be the hero-king's birthplace, although that honour usually goes to Turnberry Castle, near Ayr. This great stronghold covered no less than 16 acres, and was the strongest fortress in the Borderland. Robert I was in fact the seventh Robert Bruce of Annandale, and here the great Norman–Celtic family maintained princely sway. The castle had no fewer than four concentric moats, and much of the town has been built from its stones. James IV was fond of it, and spent years rebuilding; and Mary Queen of Scots came here in her brief wedded life with Darnley, in 1565. After the Union, the Keepership and lands passed, first to the Murrays, then to the Johnstones, whose chiefs had warstled up the brae to being Marquises of Annandale. This Keepership carried worth-while perquisites: £300 a year salary, a fat cow from every parish in Annandale, thirty-nine geese and specially-fed hens, as well as the fishing in the Castle Loch. Here swim the rare vendace, a unique delicacy. It is not quite true that this is the only place in Britain where these fish exist, for the powans of Lochs Lomond and Eck are near relatives. The Marquises, with their increasing demands on the townsfolk, grew increasingly unpopular in Lochmaben, and the burgesses were independent enough actually to rebel in 1730, taking their lord to law, where the Court of Session granted an injunction against him, forbidding his levies upon them. But it took more than a court-order to halt a Johnstone, and the fight was still on when, in 1747, the heritable jurisdictions were abolished by Parliament. The Marquis claimed £1,000 compensation, but was granted not a penny. The marquisate has died out, but the line is still represented by the Hope-Johnstone family, whose chief has recently established his claim to the more ancient earldom.

The little town has its ambitions, despite its village-size, with a wide and spacious High Street, and a town hall designed by David Bryce in 1878. The large parish church, although the present building dates only from 1820, has a bell declared to be a present from the Pope to Robert the Bruce. If this is so it must have been a very late and unexpected gift, for all his life the Bruce was at vigorous odds with the Vatican, and excommunicated for most of his reign for the murder of the Red Comyn at Dumfries. In the church's predecessor, the defeated Maxwells took refuge after the Battle of Dryfe Sands—but to no effect, for the Johnstones burned them out.

The Lochmaben folk never seem to have done things by half. Even when they went in for municipal extravagance, they did so in a big way, so that at one time the provost, bailie, Dean of Guild, treasurer and all five councillors, were declared bankrupt, having squandered the town's considerable resources, and the corporation revenues dropped to £10.

One last word anent Lochmaben, once again from chronicler Bellenden. "Ane loch namit Lochmaben fyue mylis of length and foure of breid, full of uncouth fische." He adds, as the character of the people: ". . . quhais cruelteis wes so gret that thay abhorrit nocht to eit the flesche of yolding prisoneris. The wyuis vsit to slay thair husbandis quhen thay were found cowartis or discomfist be thair ennymes, to give occasioun to utheris to be more bald & hardy. . . ."

Citizenship of this small royal burgh must have been something of an adventure.

If it was stretching things to include the Tweed valley west of Peebles in the Borders, it is probably more so to take in Moffat and upper Annandale; even though it is, as it were, level with Peebles, being between 25 and 30 miles from the Line, and with something of the 'feel' of the Borderland. Moreover, in 1448 the Earl of Douglas, Warden of the Marches, in ordering that bale-fires should be burned on all the Border hills, included the Gallows Hill at Moffat in that order. But I must now discipline myself, for reasons of space if nothing else, and leave this most delightful and intriguing little burgh and its interesting hinterland, for another occasion.

The last of the Scottish West March dales is that of Nith. But to be honest, the present writer cannot discover any atmosphere of the Borderland north of Dumfries, and not a very great deal there either—heresy as this will sound to some. I take my hat off to Dumfries, Queen of the South, the finest as well as the largest town south of Ayr, and full of character; but to me that character is not essentially, or even notably, of the Border. It has always been important commercially, politically and strategically; but its affinities seem to lie more with Galloway and the rich pastoral lands of Ayrshire and Carrick than with the tough, hard-riding, mosstrooping Borders. Admittedly the Merse, of the East March, is flatter and as green; but the ambience is different. The Merse is *preoccupied* with the Border-line. Dumfries is not.

Nevertheless, this sunny, vivid red-stone town and royal burgh is, and always has been, the metropolis of the West March, even though 20 miles from the Line, at Gretna. Nearer, 7 miles to the south, where the Nith reaches salt water, stands Caerlaverock Castle, which was apt to be the principal seat of the Wardens of the West March, in an immensely strong position between the swirling Solway tides and the Lochar Moss marshlands, a defensive site selected by the Romans, if not before. By 1220 it was in the possession of the Maxwells—who had actually come from the

Merse. In 1300, Edward I, with 3,000 men, took it after a two-day siege; and time and again it was wrested from the Maxwells by the English—or for that matter, the Scots kings—but always won back eventually. So that, as Earls of Nithsdale, the Lords Maxwell were still there when they suffered attainder for their share in the Jacobite Rising of 1715. Caerlaverock passed to the Herries line of the family, and so remained—though that line ended in an heiress, Gwendolen Constable-Maxwell, who in 1904 married the then Duke of Norfolk and carried the Herries barony and estates to that illustrious English house. It inevitably happened that often the position of Warden of the West March was held by the owners of Caerlaverock, so that the castle was frequently the seat of power therefor. But by no means always, for others, notably the Douglases, were not backward in claiming the position, and they had their own castles. Especially, of course, great Hermitage, which was really a more suitable centre for control of the wild Debateable Lands—or attempted control. Caerlaverock is unique amongst Scottish castles, being built in a style quite unlike any other, shield-shaped, with a great donjon gatehouse-keep with twin drum-towers and high curtain-walls, all islanded within a system of deep moats, which still remain, more Continental in appearance than our normal, but very fine, indeed beautiful in its mellow rose-red splendour today. The façade we see dates only from the early fifteenth century, although incorporating earlier work. And internally, within the central courtyard, is a surprising and highly decorative 'palace' block in Renaissance style, commodious and excellently planned. After being long a neglected ruin, the castle is now well cared for by the Department of the Environment and deservedly popular with visitors.

An earlier castle, possibly not on exactly the same site, recaptured from English Edward, was held for Bruce by Sir Eustace Maxwell; but though it was retained inviolate through many attacks, thereafter Bruce, in his policy of denying the invaders any strongpoints to hold in southern Scotland, requested Maxwell to demolish it—and paid him compensation for the loss. Another link with the hero-king was that here, in 1357, Sir Roger Kirkpatrick of Closeburn, who 'made siccar' when Bruce stabbed John Comyn, Lord of Badenoch at Dumfries, was himself assassinated by Sir James Lindsay, fifty-one years later. He must have been a very old man indeed by then—or a very young one when he performed the deed which made him famous and give the Siccar motto to his house. We tend to overlook the youthfulness of many of the colourful figures of our storied past, assuming them to be all mature men of the world. Bruce himself was only 23 when he took up the sword against Edward; and the famous Good Sir James, the Black Douglas, who struck such terror into English hearts, was only just of age when he did many of his stirring exploits. Kirkpatrick's fortalice of Closeburn, massive and plain and undoubtedly one of the most ancient inhabited houses in Scotland, stands a dozen miles up Nithsdale from Dumfries. It is interesting that it was a Lindsay who eventually slew Comyn, for it was Lindsay of Dunrod who aided Kirkpatrick in his making siccar. The Empress Eugénie, wife of Napoleon III, was of this Kirkpatrick family.

The western flanking-tower of Caerlaverock is called Murdoch's Tower, for herein was confined Murdoch, second Duke of Albany, in 1424, on a charge of high treason. He with his father, the Regent Albany, respectively cousin and uncle of James I, had misgoverned Scotland for eighteen long years while the young James was held prisoner in England, by their connivance. When James eventually got home, he had his revenge; and Murdoch's head was delivered to his widow at Tantallon, in Lothian, with the King's compliments, along with the heads of two of their sons —a barbarous act which, however, held its own rough justice, for the lady was by no means guiltless.

Dumfries deserves a book to itself. But as space runs out, and this volume is nominally concerned only with its Borders connection, we must be ruthless—or try to be. Dumfries had its own castle, on the site of what is still known as Castledykes. It does not seem to have been a very strong place, and changed hands with monotonous regularity. Here it was that, immediately after the murder of Comyn, Bruce, realizing that he had to act swiftly now, raised the royal standard and claimed the throne of Scotland for the first time, on 10th February 1306. He had his coronation rushed through within weeks, at Scone. This haste was essential— for he knew well that the murder of his rival, however justifiable as the execution of a traitor, would result in his own excommunication by the Pope, inevitably. And no excommunicate might lawfully be installed and annointed king by the bishops of Holy Church—as was required if he was to unite and rally Scotland to his banner. Time was of the essence—for it would take perhaps six weeks for the news to reach Rome and for the excommunication documents to be brought back to Scotland. Bishop Lamberton, the Primate, and the Abbot of Scone, knew well the situation; but they were patriots first, and did not hesitate to do their part to ensure that their country started on its long road to freedom. A memorial stone marks the site of the castle; and a bronze plaque the position, in Castle Street, where was the Greyfriars monastery before the altar of which Comyn fell. There was another memorial, once, to this highly significant day in our story, for the first man to pay homage to the new and self-proclaimed monarch was Sir Christopher Seton, Bruce's Yorkshireman brother-in-law. And here Edward, having captured Seton a few months later, executed him shockingly on the scene of his homage-giving; and in due course the Lady Christian Bruce, his widow, built a chapel in memory, now long gone.

The Mid Steeple, in the centre of the High Street, is still one of Dumfries's best-known landmarks, former town-house, jail and tron. And this also has an interesting link with those days when independence was being hammered out. For, although it dates only from 1707, the year of the Union, it retains an earlier indication—the distances therefrom of various Scots towns; but also that of far-away Huntingdon, deep in England, because this earldom used to be held by the Scots kings—and indeed it was through his descent from David, Earl of Huntingdon, brother of Malcolm IV and William the Lion, that Bruce claimed his kingship. The old Scots ell measure is also sculptured on this building, and pointed out with pride—but so it is elsewhere; whereas I know of nowhere else in Scotland where Huntingdon, or anything similar, is pointed to.

Dumfries has its common riding like all the other Border burghs, although this one has distinct differences, and goes by the rather difficult title of the Guid Nychburris Festival. The reference to good neighbours is derived from an old Dumfries custom whereby citizens at odds with one another were required to come before a magistrate and swear to maintain 'gude nychborhude'. Whether this laudable directive did in fact result in a general state of sweet reasonableness, unique certainly in the Borderland, is not actually proven; but at least it does provide an excellent traditional background for a colourful annual week of lively good-fellowship and vigorous celebration. The cry of "A Loreburn!" much resounds —just about as mystic of meaning as Hawick's one of "Teribus y Teriodin!" Just how this slogan arose is not clear—and the suggestion that invasion being apt to come via the lower parts of the town, along a burn on the line of the present Loreburn Street, so that the rallying cry used to be "All to the Lower Burn!" strikes me as having all the marks of much later and rather desperate invention. However, whatever its origins, the Loreburn cry seems to have proved effective enough down the centuries.

The staid and orderly business of banking is probably one which few would link with the Borderland. But Dumfries has a notable place in banking history, nevertheless. Here was set up the original of all savings banks, by the Reverend Dr. Henry Duncan, of Ruthwell parish, in 1810, a small acorn from which was to grow a mighty oak indeed. Duncan was a remarkable man, theologian, poet, novelist and soldier, as well as highly practical man of affairs —it is recounted that he actually donned Highland dress in his military ardour, at a time when this was considered almost indecent for any civilized Lowlander, indeed when the tartan was prescribed by law, and Scottish national sentiment at its lowest ebb. Also this extraordinary clergyman founded the *Dumfries & Galloway Courier*, in 1809, a pillar of local journalism.

But this is not the only banking connection for Dumfries. For nearby was born, in 1660, William Paterson, the man who was to set not only Scotland but much of Europe, and some of the New World by the ears, and to found the Bank of England, no less. And the originator also of the great but disastrous Darien Scheme for the development of a colony at Panama, a project deliberately wrecked by trade and colonial interests in London, and the collapse of which all but brought Scotland financially to its knees. It is rather extraordinary that Paterson should have continued to work for the Union of the Parliaments, of 1707, after this ominous indication of what was likely to happen to Scottish interests when they clashed with those of the South of England. Stranger even that it should have been a Borderer who worked so hard for what was going to do away with at least the political and governmental significance of the Border. He died at an advanced age, in very poor circumstances, a man of great integrity and boundless vision, of whom his generation was not worthy.

To leave even the most cursory consideration of Dumfries without at least a mention of Robert Burns is unthinkable—even though this aspect has been properly dealt with under *Portrait of the Burns Country* in this series. For the town meant much in the poet's life, and not merely in that he died here in 1796, and was buried in the kirkyard of St. Michael's Parish Church—though disinterred nineteen years later, and reburied in the Mausoleum built by public subscription, in the form of a Grecian temple—the Prince Regent contributing 50 guineas. Herein also were buried his widow and five sons. Before he came to live here, in 1791, Dumfries was important to Burns, for he often visited the town, and was made an Honorary Burgess in 1787. For once, one of these honorary bestowals proved of real as distinct from merely decorative value—he collected not a few—in that amongst its terms was the privilege that children of such honorary burgesses might be educated in Dumfries for 10 merks Scots annually, instead of £80 Scots, a benefit the poet was able to claim for his sons in 1793.

The house the Burns family occupied in Mill Brae or Vennel, now renamed Burns Street, is preserved as a museum for the poet, and was rented from Captain John Hamilton of Allershaw at £8 a year—a sum Burns was not always able to raise. It was as an exciseman, of course, that he had to come to Dumfries, when his health would no longer stand up to the rigours and dire physical demands of being a small tenant-farmer in those days. The exciseman's life was far from hard, by comparison; but Burns always disliked the task, and indeed despised himself for having had to take it. He himself described it as "... grinding the faces of the publican and sinner on the merciless wheels of the Excise ...". His last years, therefore, was scarcely his happiest—although while in Dumfries he wrote nearly a hundred of his most popular songs, including "Auld Lang Syne", "A Man's a Man for a' That", "Scots Wha Hae" or, more properly, "Bruce's Address to his Troops at Bannockburn". (There should be a law banning the title "Scots Wha Hae". It must make Burns turn in his grave, since it means merely 'Scots who have', and was never meant to be a title, only the first three words of a most splendid composition which has become practically the National Anthem of Scotland.) Robert Burns died at Dumfries, five years after he arrived, at the age of 37—and oddly enough was accorded a full military funeral, with shots fired over his grave by the Dumfries Volunteers.

One last brief reference, in this grievously inadequate and highly selective survey of the Scots West March. Between Ecclefechan and the Border-line, near where the busy A74 highway, and the railway main line, cross the Kirtle Water at Kirtlebridge, stand two sturdy Border peel-towers on the lip of a den or ravine, one called Bonshaw, the other Robgill. Both towers were Irvine or Irving holds, the first, and least altered, that of the chiefs of the name. Though never a large clan, the Irvines cut a wide swathe on the Border, and indeed in all Scots history, producing many more than their due share of notable characters modern as well as ancient. No space here to recount their doings; but it is perhaps interesting that the last of the line, Captain Sir Robert Irvine of Bonshaw, was the famous master of the great liner *Queen Mary*, when she regained the coveted Blue Riband of the Atlantic, in the days not so long ago, before air travel made such achievements out of date. He will be remembered, too, as the man who managed to dock his enormous vessel in New York harbour, unaided by tugs, during a dock strike there, a magnificent feat. He died in 1954. Another younger son of Bonshaw was Christopher Irvine, of the seventeenth century, who suffered for supporting King Charles, and became a medico hundreds of years before his time. He had some of the most extraordinary ideas as to transplants, which made him a mockery then but which makes today acknowledge him as a master. He was also an author of wide-ranging scope. His *Medecina Magnetica*, by C. de Iryngio, on the art of curing by sympathy—psychiatry in fact—was published in 1656. He seems to have been a true Scot; and a reviewer, presumably English, noticing his famous book, *The Nomenclature of Scottish History*, a dictionary of place-names, observes sourly that "he seems to have considered Scotland the centre of greatness, and all other transactions in the world as naturally merging into a connexion with it. Thus, in juxtaposition with Argyle we find 'Argiva, Argos and Arii.' And the Dee is discussed beside the Danube." A revealing reviewer! He might have benefited by a little geographical catholicity himself, for he declares that the author came from Bonshaw in *Lanarkshire*. It was another younger son of Bonshaw, William Irvine, who was the Bruce's faithful armour-bearer and esquire throughout much of the Wars of Independence, and was in due course rewarded by knighthood and the grant of that portion of the forfeited Comyn lands called Drum, on Deeside—where happily the Irvines of Drum are still connected. Robgill Tower, too, had its heroes, and was the home, for instance, of General Sir Aemilius Irving, a hero of the Napoleonic Wars. Stapleton Tower, not far away, was another of their strongholds; and although the mansion thereof has been fairly recently swept away, the old keep with its immensely thick walls has resisted the demolisher's hammer and still stands, a monument to the enduring past—like the Irvines themselves.

11

The English West March

I HAVE remarked before how very different, by and large, is the English side of the Border from the Scots, throughout most of its length. Not so in the Cheviots themselves, of course, one hillside being apt to look very like another. But along the lower ground, often with only a river separating the countries, it would be a somewhat insensitive and unobservant visitor who, as a general rule, could not sense the difference—although exactly wherein that difference lay might not be so easy to assert, in an amalgam of topography, man-made features and, more important, atmosphere. But this does not apply to that quite large stretch of the West March from Kershopefoot down to the Scots Dyke and the Sark. If this area is almost indistinguishable from its Scots neighbour, it is hardly to be wondered at. For it was indeed part of the Scots kingdom once. Such could be said, of course, of all the West March, for the Kingdom of Strathclyde stretched down almost to Lancaster until William Rufus managed to annex it, and built Carlisle as fortress to hold it. But the portion I refer to here was always very much part of The Debateable Land, with the northern part, the Larriston and Bewcastle Fells area, a hopeless no-man's-land; and the lower reaches detached from Scotland by the 1552 delineation. So that here was an area really English only in name and by law.

Typical of confused nationality are such places as Kirkandrews and Netherby. A more typically Scots peel-tower than Kirkandrews would be hard to find—and, strangely enough, the peels and lesser castles of Northumberland and Cumberland are *not* normally similar to the Scots variety, belonging to a totally different architectural tradition. But the sturdy red-stone keep of Kirkandrews, 3 miles south of Canonbie and on the *north* side of Esk, seems almost to peer across at Scotland wistfully, as though wondering how it got detached. Which is not strange, for Kirkandrews, as its name suggests, was wholly of Scots 'lineage', owned

Bewcastle Cross

by the great de Soulis family for long, then passing to the Douglases, and finally to the Grahams with whom it remained. The large Graham estate of Netherby lies immediately to the south. It would be difficult to find a more Scots name than Graham, however spelt. Yet these Grahams, by accident of political expediency, have been English since the sixteenth century—although they claimed descent from Malise, Earl of Strathearn. They were, inevitably, of a very 'debateable' turn of mind, and in 1600 the English Warden, Lord Scrope, complained that "the Graemes and their clans . . . were the chiefest actors in the spoil and decay of the country". And as early as 1553, one year after the new Line was established, the Bishop of Carlisle was accusing his new countrymen of lawless acts, indicting in the list the following: Ritchie Grame of Bailie, Will's Jock Grame, Fargue's Willie Grame, Muckle Willie Grame, Will Grame of Rosetrees, Ritchie Grame younger of Netherby, Wat Grame called Feughtail, Nimble Willie Grame and Mickle Willie Grame—presumably not to be confused with Muckle aforesaid. It must have been very confusing to have to deal with so many William Grahams, most of them apparently awkward. Scott tells of these in his introduction to the ballad of "Hughie the Graeme".

The Grahams seem to have been natural material for ballads. Everyone knows that of "Young Lochinvar":

> O Young Lochinvar is come out of the West,
> Through all the wide Border his steed was the best. . . .

> He staid not for brake and he stopped not for stone,
> He swam the Eske river where ford there was none;
> But ere he alighted at Netherby gate,
> The bride had consented, the gallant came late;
> For a laggard in love and a dastard in war,
> Was to wed the fair Ellen of brave Lochinvar.

> . . . one touch to her hand and one word in her ear,
> When they reached the hall-door, and the charger stood near;
> So light to the croupe the fair lady he swung,
> So light to the saddle before her he sprung.
> "She is won! We are gone, over bank, bush and scaur,
> They'll have fleet steeds that follow!" quoth Young Lochinvar.

There was mounting 'mong Grahams of the Netherby clan,
Forsters, Fenwicks and Musgraves, they rode and they ran;
There was racing and chasing on Canonbie Lea,
But the lost bride of Netherby ne'er did they see. . . .

Less renowned is the ballad of "Graeme and Bewick", a pathetic tale of the sons of the Lord Graeme and Sir Robert Bewick, who, though friends, slew each other in the cause of filial honour; and of Jellon Graeme, a grim story of the slaying of a pregnant girl by her lover, to save marrying her, and his ultimate death at the hands of the babe born when she fell. These Netherby Grahams sprang from the Grahams of Esk, one of whom was created a baronet in 1629. Richard Graham of Netherby accompanied Charles I, when Prince of Wales, on his journeyings through France and Spain; and on one occasion, when trying to capture a kid to supplement their Lenten diet, while the goat-herd was kept preoccupied by 'Steenie', then Marquis of Buckingham, Graham was chided by Charles, who called out, "Why, Richard, do you think you may practise here your old tricks upon the Borders?" The Netherby family themselves seem to have become respectable enough to be granted a baronetcy, too—but not until 1783, the second holder of the title occupying various high offices of state.

The peculiar position of the Grahams, and the Kirkandrews and Netherby area, is notably illustrated in the famous incident immortalized in the ballad of "Kinmont Willie". This is too well known to be recounted here; but it will be remembered that William Armstrong of Morton Tower, a most daring Border reiver, was captured on the *Scots* side of the Border by certain English enemies, and on a day of truce following the Wardens' meeting at Kershopefoot in March 1595, and thereupon held by the English Warden, the Lord Scrope, tried and condemned. Great was the fury amongst the Scottish Borderers—for Willie was popular as well as bold—and great the offence of Sir Walter Scott of Buccleuch, Keeper of Liddesdale, whose authority was thus flouted. He swore to take Kinmont Willie out of Carlisle Castle, Scrope or none—and the ballad described how he did so. Possibly he could not have done so had it not been for the help provided by the Grahams, English though they now legally were. Scrope, in his letter to London, indicts them thus: "The Graemes were privy and acted with Buclugh in the enterprise of the castell

. . . also the sonne of one of them brought Buclugh's ringe to Kinmonte before his losinge for a token for his deliverance, and one of them known to be in the castell corte with Buclugh." This is confirmed by Buccleuch himself in a letter to Edinburgh: "Whereas your lordship desires by your letter to know of mee what borderers of Ingland were my greatest friends for the re-coverie of Kinmonth . . . I assure you that I would nought have done that matter without great friendship of the Grames of Esk and specially my gude friend Francis of Canabie . . . and of Walter Grame of Netherbie—who were the chief leaders of that clann. . . ."

The 'lifting' of a notable prisoner out of one of her greatest fortresses made Queen Elizabeth very angry, and vehement were the repercussions. The Carlisle folk themselves, however, seem to have been rather amused, once the initial alarm wore off—for they disapproved of London's habit of sending up Southron lords to be Wardens of the Marches. Unlike Berwick, Carlisle had remained consistently English since William Rufus annexed it in 1092, restoring it to be England's main fortress on the Western Border. It had been a Roman strength holding the gap where the hills came down to the Solway, and where Hadrian's Wall reached salt water. Incidentally, there was a scheme put before Elizabeth, in 1587, to renew or rebuild the Pightes' Wall—an interesting name then apparently in use for Hadrian's Wall, indicating that the North Country English retained the Roman name for the inhabi-tants of Scotland long after the Scots themselves had abandoned it. Hadrian's Wall, built between 122 and 128 AD, deserves fuller treatment than can be offered here. Fascinating discoveries are being constantly unearthed. One of especial importance is Vin-dolanda, near Bardon Mill and the oddly-named Once Brewed. It was a fourth-century fort and barracks for 500 Roman soldiers. A wealth of Roman objects has been uncovered here and there is now a museum and audio-visual display. The Birdoswald fort area near Gilsland perhaps represents the Wall at its best.

Today's Carlisle, after long having been looked upon largely as one of the worst traffic bottlenecks in the United Kingdom, has again by means of a by-pass a chance to regain its well-deserved reputation as being one of the most interesting and colourful towns in the North of England. It is a place with many and varied attractions. Much of its ancient character has gone, but it strides ahead with vigour and determination—county town of Cumberland, with burgeoning and spreading industry, an airport, the headquarters of Border Television and a population of 71,500. If the essential atmosphere of the Borderland is not very easy to recapture amidst all this, it is there nevertheless. Even though its gates and walls have vanished, its English, Scotch and Irish Streets, once gaits, still remain. Its fine cathedral stands to the west, built between 1092 and 1419, its choir one of the finest in England; its castle to the north, suitably facing Scotland across the green levels of the River Eden's haughs, now parkland. There is no comparison, scenically, with Berwick, its partnering anchor-town at the other end of the Border-line; but then Berwick is only one fifth the size, and placed on a steeply-rising bank above Tweed, with the sea close by, a highly dramatic setting. Modern Carlisle claims to be the largest city, in actual area, in England. Carlisle's official boundaries now stretch from Burgh-on-Sands to Gilsland and north to the Scottish border. The M6 motorway puts it within two hours' driving of every major town between Birmingham and the Scottish Highlands. The removal of the through highway has enabled the city to provide welcome pedestrian areas such as The Lanes which is an extensive precinct skilfully and tastefully designed to follow the lines of the old city closes and lanes. Nearby is a bronze statue of a local fiddler and ballad-singer, one Jimmy Dyer, wart on his nose and all. Near the Cathedral is the fine Tullie House Museum and Art Gallery, in a handsome mansion of 1689, where there is much Roman and prehistoric archaeology. In the grounds is the city's only actual visible Roman structure.

The Scots threat was the place's constant preoccupation right up to the Union of Crowns—indeed well beyond it, for General David Leslie besieged it, on behalf of the Covenant in 1645—and grievously damaged the splendid nave of the cathedral in the process. And Prince Charles Edward and his army took over the city in 1745. Nevertheless, Carlisle did suffer a declension after the Union of 1603, the great castle being reduced to a care-and-maintenance garrison of only twenty men—a grievous comedown. An aspect of English policy had always made this West March more important than the others. This was the habit, already mentioned, of appointing southern lords and politicoes to be Warden. Probably the most illustrious Warden of all—if that is a description which could be applied—was Richard Crookback, Duke of Gloucester, later Richard III, appointed to this position in 1470 at the age of 18. He was given the great castle of the Nevilles at Penrith (the Nevilles having taken the wrong side in the Wars of the Roses). The Gloucester Arms Hotel there still commemorates the fact. Another reminder of his tenure of office is the stone panel built into the Tile Tower of Carlisle Castle, showing the carving of a boar, the Duke's suitable emblem—though most of this tower has been rebuilt since his time, he remained Warden right to his ascent of the throne in 1483—indeed he led 5,000 Cumbrian troops to march on London to make sure of his succession. It was as Warden that Richard led the notorious expedition into Scotland, though from Berwick, the previous year, when he blackmailed the Scots government into ceding Berwick finally to England. So pleased was the English parliament with this proceeding that they decreed that the Wardenship of the West March was to remain always with Richard's heirs male—a proclamation which, however, came to nothing.

Another odd appointment to the office, with the governorship of Carlisle, was that of Piers Gaveston, the playboy favourite of Edward II, whom he made Earl of Cornwall. This, needless to say, was a failure; and he, like his master, came to an unenviable end soon after.

His successor was a man of very different character, Sir Andrew Harcla, a notable soldier and successful general, who gallantly resisted the great Bruce's siege of Carlisle in 1315. This resulted in the granting of a new charter to the city, and Harcla's promotion to be Earl of Carlisle. However, he too fell, Edward having him put to death soon afterwards on a charge of plotting with the Bruce.

Carlisle's wary preoccupation with the Scots is markedly illustrated by the official regulations repromulgated as late as the sixteenth century, in Elizabeth's time. No Scot was to live within the city; nor to be seen walking therein after watchbell rang at night, save in the company of a freeman; no apprentices were to be admitted, coming from north of Blackford or the Irthing. Watchmen were to guard the walls day and night, gates to be shut before dark, and chains to be drawn tight between the city and the Eden bridges.

This was very much a frontier town.

It would be unsuitable to leave Carlisle without mention of the sad visit here of Mary Queen of Scots in 1568, when after the Battle of Langside she fled southwards, and in a tragic moment, decided to throw herself upon the mercies of her kinswoman Elizabeth. Ferrying by fishing-boat across Solway, from Dundrennan in Galloway, she reached Workington on the Cumberland coast—and was promptly whisked to Carlisle and held in custody by Sir Richard Lowther, the Deputy Warden, for Lord Scrope who was in London. At this stage, however, the Queen was not critical or suspicious of her treatment, writing to the Earl of Cassillis that she was "right well received and honourably accompanied and treated" and that she expected to be back in Scotland at the head of an army soon, indeed about 15th August. This was on 20th May. Her semi-captivity was hardly rigorous—we read that she attended football-matches on the green; but she was kept under the strict guard of 100 men, while Elizabeth in London made up her mind what to do with her. She remained at Carlisle over a month, and then was removed, amidst tears, to more rigorous confinement at Bolton Castle in Yorkshire. Mary's long-drawn journey to her doom had begun.

A happier if seldom mentioned event took place, with the marriage of that great Borderer Walter Scott to Miss Carpenter, in Carlisle Cathedral in 1797.

Apart from the Carlisle–Eden valley gap, the only obvious southern route, so well protected, the English West March, unlike the Scots side, offered no easy access deep into the heart of the land, such as Eskdale, Annandale and Nithsdale. The vales of Line and Irthing do probe eastwards, but fairly quickly lose themselves in the empty hill masses of the south-west Cheviots and the northern flanks of the great Pennine chain. The Irthing, which joins Eden 4 miles east of Carlisle, does allow however a sort of indirect penetration of the interior when, at Gilsland, a dozen miles up, a pass of about 4 miles long opens off south-eastwards, along the line of the Tipalt Burn, permitting access to the upper reaches of the South Tyne—which long river, it should be noted, rises much nearer the Atlantic than the North Sea, on Cross Fell, actually in Westmorland. This Gilsland gap is therefore one of the most strategically important points on all the English Border—as is witnessed to by the concentration of defensive structures and sites hereabouts. The Romans saw its advantages and dangers, and brought their Hadrian's Wall through part of it, littering the approaches with camps and forts. Later castles proliferated, on both sides of the gap, grouped close together—Thirlwall, Blenkinsopp, Bellister, Featherstone, Unthank, and the large Naworth Castle of the Howards, the last near the strategically-sited and picturesque little town of Brampton, with its ancient moot-hall. And in the midst of this defensive concentration rises the fine and renowned ruined priory of Lanercost, which played an important part indeed in the Border story.

Lanercost is probably best known, as a name, for the famous Lanercost Chronicle of 1201 to 1346, covering of course those most dramatic years of the Scottish Wars of Independence. But this was actually composed at Carlisle. It was edited in 1839, by Father Stevenson, for the Bannatyne and Maitland Clubs, and has provided a valuable, if necessarily distinctly biased, history of the Border area. This inevitable bias in the sources of early written history is something never to be forgotten. It is seldom indeed that the chroniclers sought to be objective or detached. They wrote for their times and their own people, probably few ever imagining that their accounts were going to be relied upon long centuries afterwards, and apt to be treated as gospel. Many were, in fact, little better than propagandists and entertainers. Yet lacking other source material, later historians have been all too apt to build upon them. Add to this the fact that it is almost a truism to say that the winners wrote the history, for the losers were dead—and their previous writings often deliberately destroyed. History, therefore, can seldom be the exact study which many assume it to be.

The once great and wealthy Lanercost Priory was founded as an Augustinian establishment in 1169, in the valley of the Irthing, 16 miles north-east of Carlisle. It has long been ruinous, but its nave and north aisle remained in use as a parish church. These are notable for the series of magnificent tombs—or at least the remains of them—of the Dacre and De Vaux families, some as early as the fourteenth century. One complete effigy remaining is a Dacre figure 6 feet 3 inches long, in tunic and close-fitting hose, the hair long and curled, seemingly of late fourteenth- or early fifteenth-century date. But by some ridiculous error of taste and judgement, it has been inscribed for a second burial for one John Crow, aged 25, who died in 1708, who allegedly broke his neck while climbing on the ruins of the church. One wonders at the mentality capable of this.

Lanercost, it is to be feared, grew wealthy largely at the expense of the Scottish religious houses not so far across the Border. For, in the century after its foundations, Edward I made much use of it for far from religious purposes, it indeed acting as his base for many of his assaults on Scotland. And was duly rewarded, with the spoilts. Here was planned the subjugation of the northern kingdom, and Bruce's downfall. Edward came back and back, always loading it with treasure, much of it stolen from Scots abbeys and monasteries. And here the Hammer of the Scots lay gravely ill in 1307, all but dying at the priory—but at the last moment had himself moved down to the Solway coast at Burgh-on-Sands, where he could see Scotland and curse it, and Bruce—rather oddly donating the litter on which he was carried before the high altar of Carlisle Cathedral. It was at Burgh-on-Sands, of course, that he gave the son whom he despised, about to become Edward II, the orders to take his body, immediately he was dead, and to boil it in water until all the flesh was off the bones, the latter to be carried by his son, with his army, never to leave his side or to be buried until the Scots were utterly subdued, and all who had supported Bruce to be either burned, or dragged at horses' tails and then hanged and disembowelled. His heart, however, to be sent to the Holy Land in the care of 100 knights—an extraordinary mixture of blinding, burning hate and piety, for a death-bed scene. Lanercost had received more than treasure; here were brought the heads of two of Bruce's supporters, Malcolm MacQuillan, Irish kinglet of Antrim, and the Lord of Kintyre—and live, Bruce's two young brothers, Alexander and Thomas. These two, with other captives, Edward hanged and then beheaded. Small wonder that King Robert, when he could, in 1312, invaded England and wreaked his wrath on Lanercost, before marching on to Haltwhistle and Hexham. Perhaps Lanercost was always fated to come to a bad end, despite its present beauty and air of sequestered peace. For local tradition gives it a bad start. It was founded by the Norman Robert de Vaux, Lord of Gilsland, given that barony by Henry II, ousting the Celtic Gil, son of Bueth, in the process. Presumably to obviate any possible come-back by the said Gil, de Vaux treacherously invited him to a banquet in his former home, and there had him assassinated—the founding of Lanercost Priory following as a sort of insurance against divine wrath hereafter. True or not, this is the tradition. The scene of the tragedy was not at Gilsland itself, where the Norman built, but at Bewcastle up in the hills near the Border-line—Bueth's Castle—where a stone is still pointed out as relating to the crime. Memories are long in these parts.

The famous Naworth Castle lies only a mile south of Lanercost, a magnificent pile, its keep, the Dacre Tower, dating from 1335 but most of the building belonging to the sixteenth century and later. Although originally a Dacre house, it passed by marriage to the Howards in 1577, in the person of the renowned Lord William, Belted Will, third son of the fourth Duke of Norfolk. Belted Will, of course, figures prominently in Scott's *The Lay of the Last Minstrel*. His ducal father, who was Lieutenant of the North, was executed in 1572 for being in sympathy and communication with the imprisoned Mary Queen of Scots; there was even a suggestion that he should marry her. At the Union of the Crowns in 1603, it was Belted Will Howard and the aforementioned Sir Walter Scott of Buccleuch who, in co-operation, conducted a vigorous campaign of pacification in the Borderland—which did not always tend to increase their popularity amongst their neighbours. Lord William's great-grandson was created Baron Dacre of Gillesland, Viscount Howard of Morpeth and Earl of Carlisle, in 1661. Oddly enough, he had previously, in 1658, been created Viscount of Morpeth by Oliver Cromwell, one of the dubious ennoblings of the Lord Protector. However, Charles II does not seem to have held it against him. Naworth has remained with the Earls of Carlisle—as that other Dacre property, Greystoke Castle, near Penrith, where Belted Will died, has remained with another branch of the Howard family.

Incongruous on this Borderland landscape, some 4 or 5 miles north of both Naworth and the Gilsland gap, tower the extraordinary modern constructions of the rocket-testing establishment of Spadeadam. This upland and now forested moorland area was once notable as a resort of reivers and broken men, an extension of The Debateable Land, traversed by the line of the Roman road striding northwards from the Wall. Perhaps a reminder of modern warfare and its horrors, in this haunt of ancient strife, is timely, however unlovely. Age puts a patina of respectability, even romance, over all. It may be good for us to remember that much of the colour and excitement of the Border story was at the cost of much sorrow, bloodshed and tears. Spadeadam's harsh reminder that warfare is essentially grim and unbeautiful, may well be salutary.

Spadeadam and its new-planted forest lies on the southern skirts of the Bewcastle Fells, at the extreme north-east of the English West March, one of its wildest corners, both in topography and history, the centre indeed of The Debateable Land, partnering the Larriston Fells on the Scots side. After Richard of Gloucester's period, Bewcastle's strategic importance was recognized, and it was taken into Crown protection, its castle put in the keeping of Captains. These Captains of Bewcastle, with their special status, seem to have become fairly independent powers in the land, and by no means always were properly amenable to the English Wardens of the March. Indeed, we read that in 1593 Lord Scrope, the Warden, complained to Cecil, in London, that the Captain of Bewcastle had aided and abetted two notorious Border thieves to escape from custody. And in the ballad of "Jamie Telfer of the Fair Dodhead", we see the Captain of Bewcastle actually the leader of a cattle-stealing foray over the Border into Teviotdale:

> The Captain of Bewcastle hath bound him to ryde,
> And he's ower to Tividale to drive a prey. . . .

On this occasion the Captain got the worst of it, and was wounded and captured:

> The Captain was run through the thick of the thigh,
> And broken was his right leg bane;
> If he had lived this hundred years,
> He had never been loved of woman again.

Sir Walter Scott suggested that this ballad might well relate to the entry listed by the Commissioners at Berwick in 1587: "October 1582. Thomas Musgrave, Deputy of Bewcastle, and the tenants, against Walter Scott, Laird of Buckluth, and his complices, for 230 kine and oxen, 300 gait and sheep."

These reiving raids, it is clear, were by no means apt to be small-scale pilferings. Another complaint of Lord Scrope refers to a raid in 1593 wherein "William Elliot of Larriston, the Laird of Mangerton, and William Armstrong called Kenmott [Kinmont Willie himself] with 1,000 horsemen of Liddesdale, Annandale and Ewesdale, run an open day foray in Tyvedale and drove off nine hundred, five score and five head of nolt, 1,000 sheep and goats, 24 horses and mares, burned an onset and mill and carried off £30 sterling of insight gear. . . ."

Incidentally, one stanza of the "Jamie Telfer" ballad is useful to correct a misapprehension that is widespread and of long standing. This is the appellation of peels or peles to typical Border towers. It is a mistake perpetuated in the Ordnance maps and other official publications, which should know better, peels being marked in great numbers all over the Borderland. In fact, of course, the peel or pele was merely the pale or paling, a wall surrounding the tower, corresponding to the curtain-walled enclosures, or bar-mekins, of larger castles. So that the buildings themselves were towers within a pale or courtyard—peel-towers, not peels. The ballad makes this entirely clear:

> And when they cam to the fair Dodhead,
> Right hastily they clam the peel.
> They loosed the kye out, ane and a',
> And ranshackled the house right well.

We cannot leave Bewcastle without referring to its relic of a much earlier period, when there was no Border nearby and this was all part of the Pictish land. This is the famous Bewcastle Cross, an early Christian monument probably of the late seventh century, 14 feet high, which stands in the churchyard. It is in the splendid Anglian tradition which followed upon the Christianization of the Anglian kingdom of Northumbria by the Celtic missionaries from Iona earlier in that century—which artistic excellence was, in turn, to have such great influence on the ecclesiastical sculpture of Pictland as a whole. The interlaced ornament of the Bewcastle Cross is most typically Celtic, and makes an interesting illustration of the close links, with the Celtic world of the North of England. The Ruthwell Cross, near Dumfries, is of course of the same tradition.

Haltwhistle, a dozen miles away on the other, eastern, side of the Gilsland gap, where the Tipalt Burn meets the South Tyne, is surely one of the most remotely-situated little towns in the North of England. It is a climbing place, in the lap of the hills, and of great antiquity. Its strange name is of uncertain origin—but undoubtedly unconnected with either halting or whistling. Hautwessel was the old spelling, and is still the local pronunciation, and the haut probably refers to height.

It has a strange history, too, very closely connected with Scotland—and in more than mere raiding. In fact it belonged to the Scots Abbey of Arbroath, and suffered less grievously in the Wars of Independence because of this connection. Even after Wallace's defeat and the fall of Stirling, when all was going Edward's way, that king restored Haltwhistle to Arbroath. And in 1329, only a few days before his death, Robert Bruce wrote to Edward III seeking restoration, once again, of Haltwhistle to Arbroath. The church itself, very attractive, dates back to the twelfth century. Its revenues must have been large, to account for all the royal interest. The "Fray of Hautwessel" is a well-known ballad in the English North, wherein one Alec Ridley distinguished himself against the "limmer theives o' Liddesdale". This is the heart of the Ridley country, a family which for long centuries cut a very wide swathe in the Borderland.

Allendale, West and East, is not far away, probing down into the Pennine mass, a fair and unspoiled if remote land, once part of the great Regality of Hexham. But space forbids further probing on our part. Besides, this area could be Middle March equally with West.

The English West March, then, may be very different from the others. But it lacks nothing in scene and story. It is an essential part of the whole—and the whole is the richer.

Postscript

As I knew that it would be, from the beginning, this has been a markedly deficient, hurried, not to say scrappy survey of what is really a quite indescribable area and entity, arbitrary, highly selective, inconsistent, with too much emphasis here, too little elsewhere. I am much more aware of what I have missed out than of what I have managed to set down; and still more aware of my inevitable failure, in the setting down, to convey any true picture of the land, the folk, the very conception of the Borderland, which I brashly undertook to try, to do any sort of justice to my theme. My only consolation is that this *is* a picture, a portrait, after all. And one should never stand too close to any portrait—this applying especially to the painter himself who has just finished daubing it. The thing is, indeed, only a great collection of brush-marks. The viewer must try to see the picture as a whole, not the laboured strokes; more important, to see behind the portrait, to the essential subject and inspiration of it all, however sketchily and lop-sidedly limned.

I have put much too much emphasis on the past, of course, on history; too little on the present, and almost nothing on the future. This was, I suppose unavoidable, my own failing and preference. Yet it is deliberate, too. For the past largely makes the present, and the future too; and if anything is the key and essence of the Borderland, it is tradition and story, vivid, challenging, colourful, enduring tradition. It is that tradition, therefore, which I have sought to present here, above all else. If the reader becomes aware of something of it, out of all my inadequate words, then he has at least a groundwork on which to build a true and fuller appreciation of a unique and lovely land.

It occurs to me, however, that despite all my groping, certain essential aspects of the Borders have not sufficiently emerged, if at all, even on the traditional scene. I think of salmon-fishing, for instance, which a great many people will associate with the area, and rightly, and which has been touched on briefly in connection with the Tweed netting and the drift-net controversy at sea. The salmon has always been important on the Border scene, and was frequently the subject of Border charters and writings—and disputes. The Tweed's fame as a salmon-river need not be stressed; but the Esk, the Dee, the Nith and other West March streams are almost equally rich in this respect. The Netherby fisheries, for instance, were notable, and many were the upheavals and broken heads on the subject of who was entitled to take the fish. One aspect of Border salmon-fishing, too, was the 'hunting' of the great fish on horseback, with spears, on the Solway sand-flats and tidal shallows. Scott mentions this extraordinary activity in *Redgauntlet*. And Camden, writing in 1586, says: "The land nourisheth a warlike kind of men who have been infamous for Robberies and Depredations; for they dwell upon the Solway Frith, a foordable Arm of the Sea at Low-waters, through which they make many times outrodes into England for to fetch Booties, and in which the Inhabitants thereabout on both sides with pleasant Pastime and delightful Sight on Horseback with Spears hunt Salmons whereof there is abundance."

Salmon is still fished for on the Solway sands, and distinctively, but now no longer with a curious kind of net called a haaf-net, stretched on a wooden frame and wielded each by a single man. I have not discovered the derivation of this word. It could merely mean half-net, of course, meaning smaller than normal drift-nets. *Haaf*, in Scotland, is not uncommon, being of Scandinavian origin, meaning deep sea. But this is the reverse of deep-sea netting.

Another picturesque feature of the Borderland which is apt to impress itself on the visitor is the large number of fine horses to be seen, grazing in the lower parts, riding horses, thoroughbreds, hunters, even race-horses. Always, and of necessity, the horse bulked large on the scene, of course; and this is a feature of the old days which, happily, has not died away in these more settled and mechanized times. The popularity of the common ridings, on the Scottish side, has ensured that there is always a huge demand for mounts for the cavalcades and ride-outs, with, as has been indicated, many people actually owning horses who would never be expected to do so elsewhere, irrespective of class or station. Incidentally, class and station are notably less important in the Borderland than in most other parts of our enlightened land—not the

least of its attractions. The large number of fox-hound packs and
hunts, too, on both sides of the Line, contribute to the continuing
popularity of the horse hereabouts. And the success story of
Kenneth Oliver's training establishment for racehorses at Hassen-
dean, in Teviotdale, helped to introduce a new element into the
picture.

Something should be said about the *Leges Marchiarum*, the
Border Laws peculiar to the area which, however lawless the
Borderers often seemed to the remainder of their respective
countrymen, were maintained most jealously and much respected
here. These were thrashed out in many ancient conferences, usually
out of vivid experience and harsh realities, and not infrequently
re-emphasized at official level. Today some of them may appear
not only strange but positively perverted; but they were, in fact,
very practical measures in the circumstances, and accepted in the
main by all directly concerned, and by the authorities on both
sides. If these were seemingly extraordinarily lax in some respects,
they were stern enough in others. A conviction for ordinary,
straightforward murder, for instance, was a very difficult matter
to win from a Border jury; but cattle- and sheep-stealing was a
different thing, and hanging was considered entirely acceptable for
anyone actually caught red-handed at the business. There were, in
fact, rules for this essential activity, and the thing had to be done
decently and in order. And before we condemn the reiving as a
shocking manifestation of criminal conduct, let us remember the
circumstances. In a land where invasion on a major or minor scale
was an almost daily occurrence, it was worth no man's while to
plant and grow crops on any large scale. So that cattle and sheep,
very movable commodities, were the obvious means of support.
But these could be driven off by raiders from over the Border at
any time, officially and otherwise. So that it became a matter not
so much of who *owned* stock as who could *hold* the animals. In this
connection, the beef-tubs scattered about the Borderland are a
notable feature. The vast one at Moffat is well known; but there
are innumerable others, all over the Cheviots especially, deep hidden hollows in the hills, into which cattle could be driven secretly,
and there penned until it was politic for them to emerge again,
where there was water and grazing and only one access, which
could be readily guarded. These were used both defensively and

aggressively; beasts could be hidden from raiders, and they could be assembled on large-scale incursions. The Border story would not be the same without the beef-tubs.

The famous hot-trod custom was enshrined in these Border Laws. By its provisions, anyone whose beasts had been stolen—or rather, *lifted*, for the term stolen was contra-indicated as unsuitable —had the right to pursue, while the trail was still 'hot', with burning peat at his lance-tip to proclaim his position, over the Border if need be, and use any means in his power to regain his property, if necessary to the effusion of blood, all within the law. This was much made use of, without the official Wardens ever being brought into the picture at all. There were inevitable disagreements as to what constituted a hot trail, of course. Some said that the trail was hot only until twelve hours after the cattle were taken; others that it was twenty-four hours. The latter seems to have been the more popular interpretation; more practical, too.

Many Border disputes were held to be most suitably settled by personal combat; and there are many illustrations of priests and prelates, especially, complaining that it was undignified and unsuitable that *they* should have to maintain their ownership thus, and to abide by the results so settled. And, since the Borderland oddly enough was always notably full of abbeys, priories and religious establishments, and these tended to become quite objectionably rich, the matter was far from academic.

These self-help laws applied not only to individuals but to whole clans and 'names'—and the clan system was just as fully developed, at least on the Scots side, in the Borders as in the Highlands. An attack on one even humble member of a clan, be he Scott, Kerr, Turnbull, Elliot, Armstrong or Maxwell, was accepted as involving all, from the chief downwards—and the Wardens had to allow for this; indeed, since they themselves were usually chiefs, they not infrequently *led* such unofficial raids, wearing as it were a different bonnet. This in distinction to the Warden Raids, which were official sallies instituted by the Wardens when they had failed to gain satisfaction by less drastic means. This was considered lawful and proper—with the very same people taking part, leaders and rank-and-file, legally, in exactly the same sort of activity in which they were apt to indulge privately and unlawfully. Small wonder, therefore, if there was considerable confusion as to right and wrong, meum and tuum, in the Borderland of old. When it is remembered that one of these clan raids would take vengeance not only upon the original culprit but upon his entire clan and kinsfolk, the dimensions and repercussions can be imagined.

Yet there was, in these seemingly almost anarchic conditions, a kind of order, good-faith and trust. A word given was accepted as binding; and a complainant, riding with a glove on the tip of his lance, proclaiming the perfidy of a word-breaker, was given safe passage and aid throughout the Borderland. It was no uncommon result, indeed, for a clan themselves to rise and slay one of their own number who had brought disgrace upon them by going back on his given word, even to an enemy. Parole, too, was sacred. If a man was captured during a raid, and a bargain struck for his ransom, he could thereafter safely be released, confident that he would indeed forward the agreed sum—usually cattle, in fact.

That the game of rugby is today so essential a part of the Border scene, like the Common Ridings, can be traced back directly to the living tradition. For the arranging of great games of football was the favourite means of gathering together large numbers of men for manning raids and forays. Indeed, so ominous were such sporting events, that the English Wardens used to maintain spies to inform them of any such being organized on the Scots side— and to make counter-preparations in consequence. Let those who attend the famed seven-a-sides at Melrose on occasion remember, and ponder. Likewise, horse-racing was inevitably a widespread sport, and the races, on the last day of the Hawick Common Riding, up on the moor, as elsewhere, have their origin in times when the quality of horseflesh was of life-and-death importance. Undoubtedly the motor-racing at Charterhall, and the outstanding success of Border enthusiasts, was only a modern development of the same theme.

But I must not go on. Enough has been said, surely, to make clear the whys and the wherefores of the Border tradition, and to emphasize that it was, and still is, a living thing, no mere superficial and romantic veneer, but part of the very land and people. If the Borderers are a people apart, they have reason to be. And to be proud of it. This Britain of ours would be a poorer and less colourful and vital place without them.

The present writer commiserates with all those who, like himself, cannot claim to be Borderers. But at least we can all visit, appreciate, enjoy, seek to understand and cherish the Borderland —to our own advantage and delight. If this portrait helps at all in that good cause, however feebly, it will have been worth the writing and the reading.

Index

Index